THE PEOPLE OF DERRY CITY
1930

Extracted from the
Derry Almanac and Directory

By
Brian Mitchell

CLEARFIELD

Copyright © 2019
by Brian Mitchell
All Rights Reserved

Printed for Clearfield Company by
Genealogical Publishing Company
Baltimore, Maryland
2019

ISBN 9780806358949

Introduction

Derry Almanac and Directory of 1930 names 9,084 heads of household and family businesses in Derry city.

As the 1926 census for Northern Ireland was used for waste paper in World War II the first census that survives for city and county of Londonderry, since 1911, is that of 1937 and this will be available for inspection in the year 2038 (unless the 100 year closure rule is waived before then). This means that each annual edition of *Derry Almanac* is the closest surviving census document for Derry city in the period from 1912 to 1936.

From 1868 right through to 1949 inclusive each annual edition of the *Derry Almanac and Directory* contained a 'Street Directory' where heads of households were identified against their street address in Derry city. The recording of house numbers, against each householder, first appeared in the *Almanac* of 1897.

This list of inhabitants, in alphabetical order by surname, in Derry City in 1930 contains 5 fields:

Surname of Head of Household
First Name of Head of Household
Street Address
House Number
Page Number of the listing in *Derry Almanac*

Historical Background

'During the two years following the end of the First World War [1918], Derry moved brusquely from a peak of unprecedented prosperity to an economic crisis of equally unprecedented proportions.' (Robert Gavin, *Atlantic Gateway: The port and city of Londonderry since 1700*, p. 179)

Rationalisation and restructuring within the UK economy and adoption of protectionism, with introduction of trade barriers, outside the UK, together with Derry's peripheral location on a contentious border, created by partition of 1921, spelt economic hardship for Derry and the North West for the remainder of the inter-war years.

Derry's manufacturing base really suffered. In 1922, the future of shipbuilding in Derry looked secure; the workforce stood at 2,600 and the yard had the third largest output in Ireland. Yet by 1924 the yard was closed, and it never re-opened.

The closures of Watt's Distillery in October 1921 and of the Foyle Shipyard in October 1924, two significant employers of men in the city, left a struggling clothing industry as by far the dominant industry in the city. The clothing industry also faced a crisis with collapse of shirt orders in 1920 and 1921; the workforce that had stood at around 8,000 in 1919, numbered only 4,500 in 1924. By 1924, however, the shirt industry had recovered and achieved a stability it was able to maintain through the rest of the inter-war years.

Partition, and the imposition of protective tariffs, resulted in the collapse of cross-border trade. Much of the cross-channel goods imported through Derry quay were destined for Donegal via the city's substantial retail and wholesale network. Shirt exports across the land border plummeted. In 1923, Derry's biscuit manufacturers were selling large volumes of biscuits throughout Ireland. In 1924, duties on biscuits were imposed and, by 1926, Derry's biscuit manufacturers were working at a third of their capacity.

From full employment in 1918, an unemployment rate of almost 30% was being experienced in the city by the mid-1920s.

Derry, however, still retained its maritime importance as both a gateway to North West Ireland (i.e. counties Derry, Donegal and Tyrone) and as a corridor across the Atlantic linking Western Europe with North America.

The city retained its position as a premier emigration port in Ireland. In *Derry Almanac* of 1930, the Anchor Line were promoting their 'Londonderry & Belfast to New York' service on their 'New Oil-Burning Liners "California," "Caledonia," "Cameronia," "Tuscania," "Transylvania," – all 16,700 Tons'; and the Anchor-Donaldson Line their 'Londonderry and Belfast to Canada' service which sailed 'in Summer to Quebec and Montreal; in Winter to Halifax and St. John, N.B., or Portland, Maine'.

Derry was also centre stage in two big trans-Atlantic news stories that captured the world's imagination. On Saturday 21 May 1932, Amelia Earhart, the first women to fly the Atlantic solo, landed her plane *Friendship* – a Lockheed Vega aircraft – at Robert Gallagher's farm at Springfield just to the north of Derry.

Amelia Earhart, the first female to fly the Atlantic solo, pictured in the doorway of Robert Gallagher's house, Springfield, near Derry, after her eventful flight, lasting almost 15 hours, on 21 May 1932.
(Courtesy of Bigger & McDonald Collection, Libraries NI at Derry Central Library)

On Sunday 2 July 1933, an Italian squadron of 24 seaplanes, led by General Italo Balbo, arrived at Derry, to a rousing reception from crowds of spectators lining the quays, on the second stage of their journey to cross the Atlantic to attend Chicago's World Fair.

The People of DERRY CITY, 1930:
Extracted from the *Derry Almanac and Directory*

Surname	First Name	Street	House Number	Page Number
Abraham	Samuel	Cuthbert Street	31	168
Acheson	George	Clarendon Street	15	127
Acheson	Joseph	Beechwood Avenue	68	121
Acheson	Mrs	Alexandra Terrace	52	150
Adair	George	Mountjoy Terrace	1	118
Adair	James R.	Duke Street	88	169
Adair	James R.	Simpson's Brae	1	174
Adair	John	Clarendon Street	6	127
Adair	Mrs	Florence Street	31	170
Adair	Robert	Culmore Road	Cosy Lodge	129
Adair	W. J.	Meadowbank Avenue	9	147
Adair	William	Spring Grove		137
Adair	William	Governor Road	32	138
Adair	William	Bond's Street	7	166
Adair	William & Son	Bishop Street	28	123
Adams	Albert J.	Marlborough Villas	5	146
Adams	Andrew	Florence Street	22	164
Adams	Archibald	Bishop Street	286	124
Adams	David	Gortfoyle Place	3	171
Adams	George	Iona Terrace	31	172
Adams	James	St. Columb's Wells	58	157
Adams	John	Lorne Terrace	49	118
Adams	John	Francis Street	45	137
Adams	John	Duke Street	34	169
Adams	John	Ebrington Street	11	170
Adams	Miss Jeannie	Chapel Road	41	167
Adams	Mrs	Ernest Street	2	163
Adams	Robert	Bellevue Avenue	17	121
Adams	Robert	Bellevue Avenue	24	121
Adams	T. B.	Bishop Street	The Courthouse	123
Adams	T. B.	Lawrence Hill	5	143
Adams	William	Fountain Place	3	135
Adcock	Fred	Creggan		131
Agnew	H. A.	Victoria Park		176
Agnew	H. A.	Foyle Street	35, Labour Exchange	135
Aickin	W. G.	The Rock	99	156
Aiken	Joseph	St. Columb's Terrace	101	143
Aiken	R. J.	Clarence Avenue	19	127
Aiken	R. J.	Shipquay Street	30	154
Alenay	Michael	Thomas Street	5	158
Alexander	A. F.	Shipquay Street	25	154
Alexander	A. F.	West-End Park	6	161
Alexander	Dr. John	Infirmary Road	Infirmary	142
Alexander	J.	Castle Street	9	126
Alexander	James	Barnewall Place	20	165

Surname	First Name	Street	House Number	Page Number
Alexander	Mrs	Hawkin Street	3	140
Alexander	Mrs	Deanfield	11	168
Alexander	Mrs	Dervock Place	2	168
Alexander	Samuel	Princes Street	14	152
Alexander	William	New Row	5	156
Alford	Thomas J.	Fountain Hill	100	171
Algeo	Mrs	Clarence Avenue	8	127
Algeo	William	Marlborough Road	1	147
Algoe	David	Creggan		131
Allen	Archibald	Carlisle Road	22	125
Allen	Archibald	Horace Street		141
Allen	Archibald	Violet Street Upper	2	176
Allen	Charles	Violet Street Upper	14	176
Allen	David	Meadowbank Avenue	15	147
Allen	David	Sir E. Reid's Market	3	154
Allen	David & Sons	Richmond Street	5	153
Allen	James	Kennedy Street	10	142
Allen	James	Victoria Street	17	159
Allen	James	Florence Street	30	170
Allen	James	Spencer Road	21	174
Allen	John	Glasgow Terrace	23	138
Allen	John	Victoria Street	10	159
Allen	John	Spencer Road	124	175
Allen	John J.	Strabane Old Road	40	175
Allen	Mrs	Princes Street	13	152
Allen	Mrs	Derry View Terrace	2	168
Allen	Mrs	Dungiven Road	21	169
Allen	Thomas	Hollywell Street	12	141
Allen	W. J.	West-End Terrace	1	161
Allen	William	George Street	11	138
Allen	William	Northland Avenue	8	150
Allen	William	Florence Street	36	170
Allison	Joseph	Argyle Street	55	119
Allison	Miss	Rosemount Avenue	27, Parkview	164
Allison	Robert	Marlborough Terrace	4	147
Anderson	Alexander	Limavady Road	3, Silverton	172
Anderson	Charles	Great James Street	2B	139
Anderson	Charles	Marlborough Villas	4	146
Anderson	Charles	Clooney Terrace	34E	168
Anderson	David	Charlotte Place	3	127
Anderson	David	Nassau Street Upper	16	149
Anderson	Elizabeth J.	Great James Street	23	139
Anderson	Frank	Ewing Street	1	132
Anderson	George	Ewing Street	25	132
Anderson	George	Clooney Terrace	3	167
Anderson	George J.	Edenmore Street	32	132
Anderson	James	Bennett Street Lower	34	122
Anderson	James	Great James Street	33	139
Anderson	James	Stewart's Terrace	20	155
Anderson	James	Aberfoyle Terrace	23	156

Surname	First Name	Street	House Number	Page Number
Anderson	John	Bennett Street Lower	49	122
Anderson	John	William Street	62	162
Anderson	John	Wesley Street	8	165
Anderson	Joseph	Barrack Street	12	120
Anderson	Miss J.	Mount Street	2	164
Anderson	Mrs J.	Asylum Road	13	120
Anderson	Patrick	Nelson Street	11	149
Anderson	R. N. & Co.	Abercorn Road		118
Anderson	Robert	Bennett Street Lower	20	122
Anderson	Robert	Foyle Road		137
Anderson	Robert	Miller Street	26	148
Anderson	Robert	Pitt Street	9	151
Anderson	Robert G.	Fountain Street	97	134
Anderson	Rt. Hon. Sir R. N.	Deanfield	Deanfield House	168
Anderson	Samuel	Nassau Street Upper	2	149
Anderson	Samuel A.	Cooke Street	8	128
Anderson	T.	Castle Street	8	126
Anderson	T. G.	Clooney Park West	7, Arranside	172
Anderson	William	Abercorn Place	5	118
Anderson	William	Messines Park	35	128
Anderson	William	Strand Road	34	156
Anderson	William J.	Duke Street	10	169
Andrews	Arthur	Kennedy Place	1	142
Andrews	Arthur W.	Clooney Terrace	27	167
Andrews	Herbert	Bond's Street	13	166
Andrews	James	Templemore Park	8	158
Andrews	Matthew	Hayesbank Terrace	49	167
Andrews	Mrs	Abercorn Place	1	118
Andrews	Mrs A.	William Street	77	161
Andrews	Robert H.	Kennedy Place	13	142
Andrews	Samuel	Charlotte Place	5	127
Anthony	John J.	Princes Terrace	5	152
Arbuckle	Alexander	Bridge Street	9	124
Arbuckle	David	Abercorn Road	32	118
Arbuckle	John	Ivy Terrace	7	142
Arbuckle	Richard	Northland Terrace	8	150
Arbuckle	Robert S.	Abercorn Place	14	118
Arbuckle	William	Ewing Street	32	133
Archibald	Alexander	York Street	24	176
Archibald	David	Fountain Place	1	135
Archibald	L. B.	Water Street	1	160
Archibald	Thomas	Brandywell Road	7	124
Ardrey	Constable D.	Cooke Street	9	128
Armour	James	Wapping Lane	15	159
Armour	John	Wapping Lane	17	159
Armour	Thomas	Windmill Terrace	3	162
Armstrong	F. W.	Marlborough Villas	2	146
Armstrong	G. E.	Clarence Avenue	18	127
Armstrong	George M.	MalvernTerrace	17	169

Surname	First Name	Street	House Number	Page Number
Armstrong	J.	Shipquay Street	32	154
Armstrong	James	Strand Road Lower	169	156
Armstrong	John	Clarence Place	1	127
Armstrong	John	De Burgh Terrace	9	130
Armstrong	John L.	Westland Avenue	5	160
Armstrong	Miss E.	Shipquay Street	30	154
Armstrong	Mrs	Academy Terrace	5	118
Armstrong	Mrs	Lecky Road	279	143
Armstrong	Mrs	King Street	58	172
Armstrong	Mrs	Spencer Road	152	175
Armstrong	Sydney	Shipquay Street	10	154
Armstrong	Thomas	Northland Villas	4	120
Armstrong	Thomas	Florence Street	39	170
Armstrong	William	De Burgh Square	11	130
Armstrong	William	Howard Street	16	141
Armstrong	William	Miller Street	38	148
Armstrong	William	Alfred Street	1	165
Arnold	Mrs S.	Dungiven Road	28	170
Arthur	Hugh	Marlborough Street	37	146
Arthur	John	Messines Park	10	128
Arthur	John	Edenmore Street	9	131
Arthur	Mrs	Long Tower	1, 3	145
Arthur	Mrs	Westland Avenue	37	160
Ashe	Mrs	Francis Street	7	137
Ashton	Howard	Wellington Street	5	160
Atcheson	George	Wesley Street	1	165
Atchinson	Edwin	Messines Park	8	128
Atchinson	Mrs	Bishop Street	27	122
Atkinson	Frederick	Foyle Road	37	136
Atkinson & Boyd		Strand Road	9	155
Austin	A. E. S.	Clarendon Street	17	127
Austin	Alwyn G.	Victoria Park	4, Ardkeen	176
Austin	Charles	Argyle Street	1	119
Austin	George	Culmore Road	Silver Dale	129
Austin	George	Victoria Park	5, Hillmount	176
Austin	Hugh	Hogg's Folly	4	141
Austin	James	Diamond		130
Austin	James	May Street	13	173
Austin	M.	Carlisle Road	13	125
Austin	Miss	Clarendon Street	47	127
Austin	Sarah	Alexandra Place	2	119
Austin	William	Derry View	5	168
Austin	William & co.	Foyle Street	21	135
Austin & Co.		Ferryquay Street	1, 3, 5	134
Austin's Medical Hall		Ferryquay Street	2	134
Ayres	William C.	Benvarden Avenue	34	166
Ayton	Hugh	Bond's Place	12	166
Ayton	Mary	Spencer Road	126	175

Surname	First Name	Street	House Number	Page Number
Babington	Mrs Hester	Deanfield	9, Thorncliffe	168
Bagnell	George	Spencer Road	86	175
Bailey	Catherine	Great James Street	47	139
Bailey	Mrs V.	Fairman Place	26	133
Bailey	Thomas	Messines Park	36	128
Bailey	Thomas	Barnewall Place	5	165
Bailey	William	Emerson Street	13	170
Bailey & Parke		Strand Road	8	156
Baird	Andrew	Glasgow Terrace	10	138
Baird	Henry	Governor Road	12	138
Baird	James	Glendermott Road	8B	171
Baird	John	Linenhall Street Upper	9	144
Baird	Matthew	Princes Street	31	152
Baird	Mrs	Brandywell Avenue	6	124
Baird	Thomas	Cuthbert Street	14	168
Baird	W. J.	Carlisle Road	14	125
Baird	W. J.	Fountain Street	9	134
Baker	Edward	Thomas Street	6	158
Baker	Miss	Bellevue Avenue	11	121
Baldrick	David	Creggan Road	139	162
Baldrick	George	Rossville Street	47	153
Baldrick	Margaret	Eglinton Terrace	13	132
Baldrick	Mrs	Glendermott Road	36	171
Baldrick	Thomas	Glenview Avenue	19	137
Baldrick	William	Corbett Street (Pilot's Row)	2	128
Baldrick & Co.		Cottage Row	2	164
Ball	Archibald	Howard Street	12	141
Ball	Sarah	Moore Street	11	148
Ballantine	J. & J. Ltd	Bluebellhill Terrace	yard	144
Ballantine	M & J	Mill Street	33, stores	173
Ballantine	M. & J.	Bond's Hill	stores	166
Ballantine	William	Castle Street	2	126
Ballantine	William	Marlborough Street	48	147
Ballantine	William A.	Glendermott Road	The Workhouse	171
Ballantyne	William R.	Ebrington Terrace	12	170
Ballard	Albert	Bond's Street	10	166
Ballintine	J. & J.	Quay Queen's	yard	152
Ballintine	J. & J. Ltd	Strand Road	36	156
Ballintine	J. & J. Ltd.	Strand Road	87A	157
Ballintine	J. & J. Ltd.	Strand Road	112	157
Ballintine	Jane	Stewart's Terrace	4	155
Ballintine	Mrs	Clarendon Terrace	2	127
Bannon	Patrick	Mount Street	9	164
Barber	Joseph	Sackville Street	5	154
Barbour	John	Howard Street	15	141
Barbour	Mrs	College Terrace	3	127
Barclay	H.	Northland Road	29, gate lodge	150

Surname	First Name	Street	House Number	Page Number
Barclay	Rev. R. J.	Alexandra Terrace	54	150
Barnes	Mrs	Clarence Place	6	127
Barnett	Aaron	Duke Street	32	169
Barnett	George	May Street	4	173
Barnett	Mrs	Blee's Lane		124
Barnett	Robert	Spencer Road	17	174
Barnett	Thomas	May Street	2	173
Barnett	W. & R. Ltd	Foyle Street	86	136
Barnett	W. & R. Ltd	Quay Abercorn		152
Barnett	William	Bennett Street Lower	43	122
Barnett	William T.	Spencer Road	156	175
Barnhill	J. J. S.	Creggan		131
Barnhill	J. J. S.	Foyle Street	20	135
Barnhill	William	Ebrington Street	15	170
Barr	Andrew	Nailor's Row	44	148
Barr	Annie	Nailor's Row	38, 39	148
Barr	Catherine	Fahan Street	108	133
Barr	Daniel	Elmwood Terrace	43	132
Barr	Hamilton	King Street	16	172
Barr	Henry	Pine Street	13	174
Barr	Herbert	Alma Terrace	38	136
Barr	Hugh	Strand Road	87A	157
Barr	James	Elmwood Terrace	2	132
Barr	James	Rossville Street	57, 59	153
Barr	James	Bentley Street	4	165
Barr	John	Fahan Street	111	133
Barr	John	Spencer Road	48	175
Barr	Margaret	Mountjoy Street	4	148
Barr	Michael	Fahan Street	131	133
Barr	Mrs	Creggan Terrace	4	129
Barr	Mrs	Spencer Road	137	175
Barr	Mrs A.	Nailor's Row	42, 43	148
Barr	Neil	Tyrconnell Street	10	158
Barr	Robert	King Street	5	172
Barr	Samuel	Epworth Street	18	163
Barr	Sarah	Creggan Road	18	163
Barr	W. C.	Glen Cottages	2	131
Barr	William	Emerson Street	33	170
Barr	William	Fountain Hill	3	171
Barr	William E.	Marlborough Terrace	14	147
Barr	Andrew	Glasgow Terrace	34	138
Barr	Ernest	Princes Street	9	152
Barr	Hugh	Hawthorn Terrace	9	140
Barr	Joseph	Argyle Street	3	119
Barr	Mrs	Great James Street	63	139
Barr	Neal	Cable Street	11	125
Barr	Sarah	Ann Street	11	119
Barr	Sarah	Brandywell Avenue	17	124
Barr	Thomas	Gresham's Row	4	140
Barr	William	Aubrey Street	9	120

Surname	First Name	Street	House Number	Page Number
Barr & McClements		Ferryquay Gate	1, 3	134
Barrett	Hugh	Carrigans Lane	5	126
Barrett	James	Philips Street	13	151
Barrett	John	Bishop Street	225	123
Barrett	John	Foyle Road	122	136
Barrett	Mary	Abbey Street	45	117
Barrett	Mrs	Bishop Street	217	123
Barrett	Robert	Fountain Street	109	134
Barrett	Thomas	Collon Terrace	7	128
Barrie	H. T. Ltd	Foyle Street	22	136
Barrow	Albert	Corporation Street	7	128
Barton	Bertram	Shipquay Street	8	154
Barton	Irvine	Ferguson Street	51A	134
Barton	James	Bishop Street	201	122
Barton	Peter	Bishop Street	268	124
Barton	William	Quarry Street	22	153
Bateman	A. C.	Strand Road	21	155
Bates	J. P.	Beechwood Avenue	19, Norwood	121
Battisti Bros. Co.		Ferryquay Street	31	134
Baxter	David	Clooney Terrace	35	167
Baxter	David	York Street		176
Baxter	Harold	Abercorn Road	51	118
Baxter	William	Harding Street	12	140
Beale	Albert	Foyle Road	56	136
Beattie	Catherine	Beechwood Avenue	14	121
Beattie	D. H.	Aberfoyle Terrace	35	156
Beattie	Joseph	Clarendon Street	33	127
Beattie	Mrs	Carlisle Road	69	125
Beattie	R. J.	Meadowbank Avenue	35	147
Beattie	William	Fountain Street	39	134
Beatty	Constable John	Rosemount Terrace	6	165
Beatty	James	Bond's Place	4	166
Beatty	Samuel	Nicholson Square	13	149
Beaumont	Colonel	Limavady Road	25	172
Begley	Bernard	Blucher Street	21	124
Begley	Daniel	Fahan Street	105	133
Begley	Francis	Kerr's Terrace	21	162
Begley	Grace	Union Street	21	176
Begley	John	Howard Street	11	141
Begley	John	Duddy's Row	1	169
Begley	John	Violet Street Upper	23	176
Begley	Mrs	Lecky Road	116	144
Begley	Mrs	Union Street	29	176
Begley	Mrs Margaret	Distillery Brae Upper	1	168
Begley	Patrick	Creggan Terrace	1	129
Begley	William	Northland Avenue	22	150
Bell	A & Sons	Ferryquay Street	14	134
Bell	Hugh	Bishop Street	184	123

Surname	First Name	Street	House Number	Page Number
Bell	J.	Carlisle Road	33	125
Bell	John	Creggan Street	27	129
Bell	John	Dark Lane	20	130
Bell	Joseph	Edenmore Street	17	131
Bell	L. H. M.	Sunbeam Terrace	16	122
Bell	Laurence	Union Street	21	158
Bell	Lizzie	Henry Street	10	141
Bell	Miss J.	Foyle Street	19	135
Bell	Miss J.	Hawkin Street	38	140
Bell	Mrs	Duncreggan Road	5	131
Bell	Mrs	Westland Avenue	11	160
Bell	Richard	Epworth Street	5	163
Bell	Robert	Bishop Street	142A	123
Bell	Robert	Fountain Street	53	134
Bell	Robert	Little James Street	15	145
Bell	Robert	Cuthbert Street	24	168
Bell	Robert J.	Ewing Street	27	132
Bell	Samuel	Beechwood Avenue	44	121
Bell	Samuel	Collon Terrace	1 Silverton	128
Bell	Samuel	Nassau Street Upper	33	149
Bell	William H.	Ewing Street	19	132
Bellamy	Mrs	London Street	13	145
Bennett	John	Hawkin Street	26	140
Bennett	Robert	Fountain Place	7	135
Bennett	W. H.	Hawkin Street	24	140
Bennett	William	Governor Road	14	138
Bennett	William H.	Beechwood Avenue	46	121
Best	D. H.	Nicholson Terrace	2	149
Best	David	Sackville Street	19	154
Best	James	Harding Street	20	140
Best	John	Argyle Terrace	34	120
Best	John	Glasgow Terrace	8	138
Best	Joseph S.	Glendermott Road	3	171
Best	Sarah	Florence Street	6	164
Best	William	Argyle Terrace	32	120
Bible	Mrs	Templemore Park	1	158
Bible & Simmons		Diamond	13	130
Bigger	Finlay	Clarendon Street	63	127
Bigger	Mrs	Abercorn Road		117
Bigger	R. A. J.	Francis Street	63	137
Bigger	Mrs	Foyle Road	Riverview	136
Biggers Ltd		Foyle Street	83-89	135
Bigger's Ltd		Sugarhouse lane		158
Bingham	Samuel	College Terrace	7	128
Binks	John T.	Mill Street		173
Birney	Alex	Argyle Street	56	119
Birney	Samuel	Edenmore Street	24	131
Birnie	James	Kennedy Street	1	142
Birnie	John	Harding Street	17	140

Surname	First Name	Street	House Number	Page Number
Black	A. McK.	Marlborough Road	8	147
Black	Charles	Pennyburn	3	151
Black	Douglas	Henry Street	21	141
Black	James	Northland Avenue	1	150
Black	James H. M.	Grove Place	22	139
Black	John	Albert Street	7	118
Black	Joseph	Ferguson Street	38	134
Black	Joseph	Fountain Street	35	134
Black	R. J. & Co.	Foyle Street	68	136
Black	Robert	Wellington Street	20	160
Black	Edward	Strabane Old Road	50	175
Black	John	Moore Street	28	173
Black	Joseph	Meehan's Row	18	173
Black	Mrs	Ebrington Street Lower	6	170
Black	Mrs	Limavady Road	10	173
Black	Robert	Browning Drive	29	166
Black	Robert	Ebrington Street	3	170
Black	Robert	Robert Street	15	174
Black	Robert	Strabane Old Road	29	175
Black	Susan	Duke Street	29	169
Black	William	Moore Street	10	173
Black	William A.	Distillery Lane Lower	10	168
Black	William A.	Primrose Street	17	174
Black	William A.	Spencer Road	111, Victoria Hall caretaker	174
Blackburn	Thomas	Hawthorn Terrace	28	140
Blackmore	G.	Custom House Street	Surveyor's Office	129
Blackmore	George	Mount Street	14	164
Blackwood	David	Fountain Street	62	134
Blad	Captain E. C.	Florence Terrace	20	150
Blair	Andrew	Bishop Street	188	123
Blair	George	Park Avenue	20	151
Blair	James	Glendermott Road	7	171
Blair	James	Moore Street	23	173
Blair	Mary	Ernest Street	14	163
Blair	Miss B.	Spencer Road	35	174
Blair	Robert	Culmore Road	Boomhall	129
Blair	Robert	Strabane Old Road	58	175
Blair	Robert	Violet Street Upper	5	176
Blair	Robert senior	Benvarden Avenue	21	165
Blair	Samuel & Co.	Butcher Street	18	125
Blair	Samuel & Co.	Strand Road	21	155
Blair	Thomas	Clarendon Street	36	127
Blair	William J.	Abercorn Terrace	3	118
Blakely	Fred	Cross Street	23	168
Bleakley	H. R.	Abercorn Road	48	118
Blee	John	Ann Street	27	144
Blee	Joseph	Bishop Street	223	123

Surname	First Name	Street	House Number	Page Number
Blevins	Sergeant J.	Beechwood Avenue	9	121
Blogh	Samuel	Abercorn Road	38	118
Bloomfield	Edwin	Glendermott Road	76	171
Boak	William	Alfred Street	43	165
Boal	Miss	Lorne Terrace	47	118
Boal	Miss	College Terrace	5	127
Boardman	Mrs	Violet Street Lower	7	176
Boardman	Robert	Foyle Street	13	135
Boardman	Samuel	Messines Park	16	128
Boggs	J & Co.	Hawkin Street		140
Boggs	John & Co.	Fountain Street	37	134
Boggs	Samuel	Harvey Street	6	140
Boggs	William	Argyle Street	54	119
Boggs	William	Marlborough Avenue	10	147
Bogle	James	Creggan Road	new basin	163
Bogle	William	Glen Cottages	3	131
Bolton	Samuel	Kennedy Street	19	142
Bonar	James	Fairman Place	11	133
Bond	J. H.	Foyle Street	7	135
Bond	James	Violet Street Lower	53	176
Bond	James H.	Harding Street	23	140
Bond	John	East Avenue	3	170
Bond	Mrs	Artillery Street	1	120
Bond	Mrs	Glasgow Street	1	138
Bond	Mrs	Harding Street	21	140
Bond	Mrs	Benvarden Avenue	39	166
Bond	Thomas	John Street	14	142
Bond	Thomas	Marlborough Avenue	25	147
Bond & Pollock		Butcher Street	2	125
Bones	James	Spencer Road	15	174
Bonner	Agnes	Brook Street Avenue	19	125
Bonner	Bridget	North Street	1	164
Bonner	Edward	Wellington Street	72	160
Bonner	James	Bellevue Avenue	4	121
Bonner	James	Westland Terrace	16	161
Bonner	Manasses	Fahan Street	30	133
Bonner	Margaret	Bishop Street	294	124
Bonner	Margaret	Foyle Road	123	137
Bonner	Mary	Townsend Street	1	158
Bonner	Mary Jane	Gallagher's Square	2	137
Bonner	Michael	Foyle Road	69	136
Bonner	Owen	Fahan Street	19, 21, 23	133
Bonner	Patrick	Union Street	27	176
Bonner	Rev. James	Creggan Street		129
Bonner	Robert	Duddy's Row	8	169
Bonner	Thomas	Spencer Road	162	175
Bonner	William	Nelson Street	28	149
Bonner	William	Cross Street	16	168
Booth	John	Fairman Place	5	133
Booth	Miss	Florence Street	5	163

Surname	First Name	Street	House Number	Page Number
Borland	John	Miller Street	8	147
Borland	M. & Co.	Great James Street	12	139
Borland	Moses	Great James Street	17	139
Borland	William	Great James Street	49	139
Bovaird	Charles	Violet Street Upper	4	176
Bovaird	James	Nassau Street Lower	30	148
Bovaird	W. & Co.	William Street	24	161
Bovaird	William	Marlborough Terrace	2	147
Bovaird	William	Florence Street	1	163
Bowen	W. A.	Foyle Street	7	135
Bowler	Thomas	Sloan's Terrace	6	155
Box	Ernest	Church Wall	3	127
Boyce	Hugh	Deanery Street	31	130
Boyce	Hugh	Rossville Street	20	153
Boyce	Hugh	Cross Street	9	168
Boyce	Josephine E.	Wesley Street	13	165
Boyd	A.	Bishop Street	2	123
Boyd	Alex	Fountain Hill	96	171
Boyd	Alexander	Albert Street	32	118
Boyd	Bertie	Abercorn Road	27	118
Boyd	Charles	Hawkin Street	17	140
Boyd	David	Messines Park	51	128
Boyd	David	George Street	15	138
Boyd	David	Chapel Road	39	167
Boyd	David	Dunfield Terrace	1	169
Boyd	Gerald	Glendermott Road	74	171
Boyd	Hugh	George Street	13	138
Boyd	Hugh	John Street	47	142
Boyd	James	Marlborough Street	39	146
Boyd	James	Market Street	2	147
Boyd	James	Nassau Street Lower	12	148
Boyd	John	Bishop Street	75	122
Boyd	John	Major's Row	7	146
Boyd	John	Columba Terrace	6	168
Boyd	John	Duke Street	55	169
Boyd	John	Fountain Hill	76	171
Boyd	Joseph	Alfred Street	30	165
Boyd	Joseph	Melrose Terrace	10	173
Boyd	Mrs	Governor Road	2A	138
Boyd	Mrs	Marlborough Avenue	2	147
Boyd	Mrs	Mary Street	8	147
Boyd	Mrs	Mountjoy Street	5	148
Boyd	Mrs	Chapel Road	68	167
Boyd	Mrs C.	Marlborough Avenue	23	147
Boyd	Mrs Isabella	Spencer Road	41	174
Boyd	Robert	Hinton Park	1	172
Boyd	Robert A.	Benvarden Avenue	40	166
Boyd	Samuel	Kennedy Street	11	142
Boyd	William	Rosemount Avenue	4	164
Boyd	William E.	Sunbeam Terrace	6	122

Surname	First Name	Street	House Number	Page Number
Boyd & Co.		Strand Road	134	157
Boyd's Hotel		Carlisle Road	49	125
Boylan	Charles	Hawthorn Terrace	20	140
Boylan	John	Walker's Place	28	159
Boyle	Bernard	Tyrconnell Street	20	158
Boyle	Captain R. M.	Strand Road	City Commissioner's Office	156
Boyle	Captain R. M.	Clarence Avenue	10	127
Boyle	Daniel	Wellington Street	23	160
Boyle	Daniel	Dungiven Road	26	170
Boyle	Denis	Custom House Street	Ulster Hotel	129
Boyle	Denis	Guildhall Street	Ulster Hotel	139
Boyle	Dr. A . B.	Pump Street	28	152
Boyle	Frank	Clarendon Street Lower	3	127
Boyle	Hugh	Alfred Street	24	165
Boyle	James	Frederick Street	6	137
Boyle	Jane	St. Columb's Street	1	157
Boyle	John	Elmwood Street	6	132
Boyle	John	Hollywell Street	7	141
Boyle	John	Bluebellhill Terrace	166	144
Boyle	John	Clarke Terrace	240	144
Boyle	John	Limewood Street	21	144
Boyle	John	St. Columb's Wells	64	157
Boyle	John	Epworth Street	17	163
Boyle	M. R.	Cunningham Row	1	129
Boyle	Magnus	The Rock	97	156
Boyle	Margaret	Beechwood Street	6	121
Boyle	Margaret	Corbett Street (Pilot's Row)	3	128
Boyle	Mary	Bishop Street	253	123
Boyle	Mary	Deanery Street	7	130
Boyle	Mary	Edenmore Street	26	131
Boyle	Mary A.	Thomas Street	21	158
Boyle	Mary R.	Bishop Street	27	122
Boyle	Michael	Argyle Street	25	119
Boyle	Miss	Sloan's Terrace	19	154
Boyle	Miss	Benvarden Avenue	5	165
Boyle	Mrs	Kildarra Terrace	3	141
Boyle	Mrs	West-End Terrace	9	161
Boyle	Mrs	William Street	65	161
Boyle	Mrs Mary	Asylum Road	10	120
Boyle	Patrick	Fahan Street	133, 135	133
Boyle	Patrick	Cottage Row	22	164
Boyle	Patrick	Fountain Hill	106	171
Boyle	Patrick	King Street	34	172
Boyle	Robert F.	Westland Villas	5	161
Boyle	William	Bishop Street	237	123
Boyle	William	Blucher Street	36	124

Surname	First Name	Street	House Number	Page Number
Boyle	William	Governor Road	1B	138
Boyle	William	Nassau Street Lower	24	148
Boyle	William	Thomas Street	23	158
Boyle	William	Wellington Street	70	160
Boyle	William	Cross Street	14	168
Brabrook	Charles	Barnewall Place	18	165
Brace	Archibald E.	Margaret Street	19	173
Bracklay	Mrs	Marlborough Street	13	146
Bradford	Miss	Beechwood Avenue	18	121
Bradley	Alex.	Lorne Street	2	145
Bradley	Catherine	Harvey Street	9	140
Bradley	Catherine	St. Columb's Street	7	157
Bradley	Charles	Creggan Street	17A	129
Bradley	Charles	Deanery Street	2	130
Bradley	Charles	Wellington Street	62	160
Bradley	Con	Rossville Street	1, 3	153
Bradley	Con	William Street	49	161
Bradley	Con	William Street	46	161
Bradley	Daniel	Bishop Street	169	122
Bradley	Daniel	John Street	27	142
Bradley	Daniel	Nassau Street Lower	23	148
Bradley	Daniel	St. Columb's Street	6	157
Bradley	Daniel	Union Street	17	158
Bradley	Denis	St. Columb's Street	2	157
Bradley	Edward	Lecky Road	293	143
Bradley	Edward	Lower Road	9	146
Bradley	Francis	Nassau Street Upper	31	149
Bradley	Francis P.	Lecky Road	39	143
Bradley	H.	Spencer Road	48, yard	175
Bradley	Hugh	Bridge Street	59	124
Bradley	James	Governor Road	18	138
Bradley	James	Philips Street	9	151
Bradley	James	Wellington Street	3	160
Bradley	James	Clifton Street	2	167
Bradley	James	Distillery Lane Upper	2	168
Bradley	James A.	Great James Street	26	139
Bradley	Jennie	Eden Place	11	132
Bradley	John	Blucher Street	34	124
Bradley	John	Cedar Street	12	126
Bradley	John	Cooke Street	5	128
Bradley	John	Ewing Street	12	132
Bradley	John	Frederick Street	15	137
Bradley	John	Lecky Road	247	143
Bradley	John	Limewood Street	23	144
Bradley	John	Mountjoy Street	12	148
Bradley	John	May Street	10	173
Bradley	John F.	Limewood Street	38	144
Bradley	Joseph	Creggan		131
Bradley	Joseph	Elmwood Road		132
Bradley	Joseph	Stanley's Walk	37, 38	155

Surname	First Name	Street	House Number	Page Number
Bradley	Margaret	Bluebellhill Terrace	214	144
Bradley	Mary	Long Tower	12	145
Bradley	Miss	Chapel Road	32	167
Bradley	Miss C.	Little James Street	13	145
Bradley	Mrs	Argyle Terrace	3	120
Bradley	Mrs	Stanley's Walk	42	155
Bradley	Mrs	Creggan Road	73	162
Bradley	Mrs	Epworth Street	1	163
Bradley	Mrs	Simpson's Brae	4	174
Bradley	Mrs R. A.	Lecky Road	277	143
Bradley	Neil	Mountain Street	20	173
Bradley	Patrick	Lecky Road	289	143
Bradley	Patrick	Long Tower	78	146
Bradley	Patrick	Margaret Street	10	173
Bradley	Patrick	Simpson's Brae	21	174
Bradley	Philip	Bridge Street	70	125
Bradley	Rev. Hugh	Victoria Place	Parochial House	159
Bradley	Robert	Cedar Street	6	126
Bradley	Robert	New Row	1A	156
Bradley	Robert	Osborne Street	8	164
Bradley	Samuel	Spencer Road	82	175
Bradley	William	Albert Street	13	118
Bradley	William	Bishop Street	165	122
Bradley	William	Bishop Street	190	123
Bradley	William	Governor Road	6	138
Bradley	William	Palace Street	2	151
Bradley	William	Bond's Hill	4	166
Bradley	William J.	Miller Street	21	147
Brady	Alphonsus	Foyle Street	6A	135
Brady	Columba	Waterloo Street	14	159
Brady	Edward	Great James Street	79	139
Brady	Edward	Nailor's Row	21	148
Brady	Hugh	East Wall	5	131
Brady	Hugh	Richmond Street	13	153
Brady	Hugh	Rossville Street	8	153
Brady	Hugh	Waterloo Street	45	159
Brady	Hugh	Westland Avenue	23	160
Brady	J. F.	Artisan Street	17	162
Brady	James	Grafton Avenue	51	120
Brady	James	Bennett Street Upper	11	122
Brady	Mary	Waterloo Street	12	159
Brady	Patrick	Park Avenue	18	151
Brady	William	Waterloo Street	5	159
Braide	George	Bellevue Avenue	14	121
Brandon	Francis	Hogg's Folly	5	141
Brandon	Hugh B. & Co.	Shipquay Street	40	154
Brannigan	Thomas	Francis Street	21	137
Bratton	David	Bond's Street	29	166
Bratton	James	Dungiven Road	87	170

Surname	First Name	Street	House Number	Page Number
Bratton	Mrs	Florence Street	33	170
Bredin	T. F.	Magazine Street	14	146
Bredin	T. F.	Shipquay Street	20, Bank of Ireland	154
Breen	Patrick	Distillery Lane Lower	9	168
Brennan	Catherine	Kildarra Terrace	6	141
Brennan	Hugh	West-End Terrace	3	161
Brennan	John	Bishop Street	59	122
Brennan	John	Kildarra Terrace	10	141
Brennan	Michael	Mount Street	1	164
Brennan	Michael John	Long Tower	67	145
Brennan	Mrs	Bellevue Avenue	27	121
Brennan	Mrs	Foyle Road	105	136
Brennan	Patrick	Marlborough Street	2	147
Brennan	Sarah	Long Tower	11	145
Bresland	James	Cuthbert Street	15	168
Bresland	Robert	Cuthbert Street	6	168
Breslin	Arthur	Bishop Street	39	122
Breslin	Charles	Cable Street	5	125
Breslin	D.	Artisan Street	19	162
Breslin	Daniel	Blucher Street	6	124
Breslin	Daniel	Westland Avenue	20	160
Breslin	James	Castle Gate	1	126
Breslin	James	Chamberlain Street	12A	126
Breslin	James	Messines Park	47	128
Breslin	James	Fahan Street	72A	133
Breslin	James	High Street	12	141
Breslin	James	Nelson Street	12	149
Breslin	James	York Street	23	176
Breslin	John	Deanery Street	35	130
Breslin	John	Howard Street	21	141
Breslin	Margaret	Lecky Road	1	143
Breslin	Mary	Fulton Place	12	137
Breslin	Mary A.	St. Columb's Wells	94	157
Breslin	Mary Anne	Deanery Street	4	130
Breslin	Mrs	Bishop Street	38	123
Breslin	Mrs E.	Victoria Place	2	159
Breslin	Thomas	Mitchelburne Terrace	89	136
Breslin	William	Eden Place	4	132
Breslin	William	Nelson Street	45	149
Breslin Bros.		Sackville Street	17	154
Brewster	F.	Patrick Street	garage	151
Brewster	Frederick	Clarence Avenue	16	127
Brewster	Robert	Foyle Street	39	135
Brewster Ltd		Little James Street	4, 5, 6, 7	145
Brewster's Ltd		William Street	121	161
Broderick	Peter J.	Westland Avenue	28	160
Brogan	Edward	Creggan Road	119	162
Brogan	Pat	Stanley's Walk	22	155
Brogan	Patrick	Lecky Road	stores	143

Surname	First Name	Street	House Number	Page Number
Brogan	Patrick	Lecky Road	stores	143
Brolly	Miss	Riverview Terrace	10	174
Brolly	Mrs	Alma Place	4	119
Brolly	Patrick	Strabane Old Road	5	175
Brolly	Robert	Hamilton Street	1	139
Brolly	Robert	Glendermott Road	21	171
Brookes	John	Browning Drive	7	166
Brothers	Robert	Distillery Brae Upper	5	168
Broughton	J.	Shipquay Street	34, Picture Palace	154
Brown	A. & Sons	Foyle Street	71-79	135
Brown	Andrew	Brandywell Road	20	124
Brown	Andrew	Moore Street	12	173
Brown	Bernard	Glenview Avenue	25	137
Brown	Bridget	Cross Street	24	168
Brown	Daniel	Nassau Street Upper	27	149
Brown	Daniel	Foyleview Terrace	3	156
Brown	David	London Street	5	145
Brown	David	Derry View	4	168
Brown	Edward	Strand Road	34	156
Brown	George	St. Columb's Wells	98	157
Brown	Henry	Benvarden Avenue	12	166
Brown	J. F.	Meadowbank Avenue	24	147
Brown	James	Ann Street	12	119
Brown	James	Creggan Terrace	14	129
Brown	James	Fountain Street	67	134
Brown	James	Glenview Avenue	7	137
Brown	James	Glasgow Terrace	33	138
Brown	James	Philips Street	5	151
Brown	James	New Row	6	156
Brown	James	Emerson Street	16	170
Brown	John	Chamberlain Street	26	126
Brown	John	Messines Park	25	128
Brown	John	Fountain Street	99	134
Brown	John	St. Columb's Wells	71	157
Brown	John	William Street	86, 88	162
Brown	John	Ashfield Terrace	29	162
Brown	Joseph	Fulton Place	21	137
Brown	Joseph	Long Tower	50	146
Brown	Joseph	Strand Road	54	156
Brown	Joseph	Dervock Street	3	168
Brown	Lawrence	Spencer Road	127	175
Brown	Lizzie	Fahan Street	20	133
Brown	Lizzie	Orchard Row	4	150
Brown	Margaret	Mountjoy Street	23	148
Brown	Matthew	Messines Park	17	128
Brown	Matthew	De Burgh Square	4	130
Brown	Michael	Strabane Old Road	98	175
Brown	Mrs	Creggan		131
Brown	Mrs	Fountain Street	46	134

Surname	First Name	Street	House Number	Page Number
Brown	Mrs	Sloan's Terrace	13	154
Brown	Mrs	Strand Road	108	157
Brown	Mrs	St. Columb's Wells	73	157
Brown	Mrs	Rosemount Avenue	15	164
Brown	Mrs Rose	Strabane Old Road	72	175
Brown	Patrick	Messines Park	13	128
Brown	Patrick	Marlborough Terrace	15	147
Brown	Patrick	Quarry Street	12	153
Brown	Patrick	Bentley Street	3	165
Brown	Philip	Stable Lane	1	155
Brown	Robert	Argyle Terrace	12	120
Brown	Robert	Fulton Place	6	137
Brown	Robert	Long Tower	28	146
Brown	Robert	William Street	forge	161
Brown	Robert J.	Violet Street Upper	11	176
Brown	Robert James	Fahan Street	48	133
Brown	Samuel	Bishop Street	181	122
Brown	Samuel	Marlborough Avenue	14	147
Brown	Samuel	Stewart's Terrace	9	155
Brown	Stanley	Bellevue Avenue	13	121
Brown	Sydney	Creggan Road	157	163
Brown	Thomas	Barrack Street	13	120
Brown	Thomas	Bridge Street	27	124
Brown	Thomas	Queen Street	18	153
Brown	Thomas	Waterloo Place	22	160
Brown	William	Messines Park	63	128
Brown	William	Glen Terrace	5	131
Brown	William	Hawthorn Terrace	14	140
Brown	William	Bluebellhill Terrace	150	144
Brown	William J.	Beechwood Avenue	31, Lyndhurst	121
Brown	William J.	Spencer Road	130	175
Brown	Alex	Abercorn Road	2	118
Brown & Co.		Ferryquay Street	23	134
Browne	Arthur	Abercorn Road	39	118
Browne	Dr D. J.	Clarendon Street	49	127
Browne	John	Emerson Street	25	170
Browne	S.	Shipquay Street	8	154
Browne	Sergeant T.	Grafton Street	2	139
Browne	Sergeant T.	Creggan Road	18, R.U.C. Barracks	163
Browne	William	Cedar Street	10	126
Browne	William	Hawthorn Terrace	11	140
Browne	William J.	Clooney Terrace	15	167
Brownell	Jervis	Melrose Terrace	7	173
Brownlow	James	Browning Drive	17	166
Brownlow	James & Co.	Carlisle Road	5	125
Bruce	Miss	Bennett Street Upper	7	122
Bruce	Mrs M.	Foyle Road	113	136
Bryan	Joseph	Ivy Terrace	12	142
Bryans	Joseph	Northland Road	84 (Hilden)	150

Surname	First Name	Street	House Number	Page Number
Bryce & Weston		Strand Road		156
Bryson	George	Cottage Row	4	164
Bryson	Henry	Spencer Road	146	175
Bryson	James	Fairman Place	23	133
Bryson	Michael	Bishop Street	167	122
Bryson	Mrs	Gortfoyle Place	9	171
Bryson	Patrick	Bishop Street	79	122
Bryson	Patrick	Cable Street	3	125
Bryson	Patrick	Henrietta Street		141
Bryson	Samuel	Foyle Street	44	136
Bryson	William	Clooney Terrace	51	167
Bryson	William	Duke Street	60	169
Buchanan	Alex	Lawrence Hill	Foyle College	143
Buchanan	David S.	Meadowbank Avenue	5	147
Buchanan	James	Argyle Street	43	119
Buchanan	James	Garden City		129
Buchanan	James	Linenhall Street Upper	11	145
Buchanan	John	Eden Terrace	12	131
Buchanan	John	Maple Street	3	173
Buchanan	John James	Deanfield	2, Beechmount	168
Buchanan	Mrs	Major's Row	3	146
Buchanan	Mrs	Moore Street	16	173
Buchanan	Mrs M.	Marlborough Street	19	146
Buchanan	R. E.	Templemore Park	6	158
Buchanan	Robert	Miller Street	42	148
Buchanan	Robert	Alfred Street	44	165
Buchanan	Robert	Pine Street	4	174
Buchanan	Thomas H.	Abercorn Road	50	118
Buchanan	William	Alexandra Place	5	119
Buchanan	J.	Strand Road	50	156
Buchanan	Mrs	Grafton Street	25	139
Buchanan & Reid		Shipquay Street	6	154
Buchanan Bros.		Foyle Street	52	136
Buck	R. R. & Sons	Bishop Street	23	122
Buckingham	William	Marlborough Street	42	147
Buckley	Benjamin	Harding Street	3	140
Burke	Alex	Violet Street Lower	23	176
Burke	Alexander	Stanley's Walk	26	155
Burke	Houston	Cuthbert Street	20	168
Burke	James	Aubrey Street	18	120
Burke	James	Epworth Street	4	163
Burke	James	Bond's Street	20	166
Burke	James	Derry View	2	168
Burke	John	Margaret Street	25	173
Burke	John J.	Henry Street	11	141
Burke	John J.	Farney Terrace	3	164
Burke	Leslie	Argyle Terrace	23	120
Burke	Miss K.	Dark Lane	13	130

Surname	First Name	Street	House Number	Page Number
Burke	Mrs	Sugarhouse lane	13	158
Burke	Mrs	Waterloo Street	17	159
Burke	Mrs	Waterloo Street	47	159
Burke	Mrs	Margaret Street	21	173
Burke	Patrick	Donegal Place	22	131
Burke	Patrick	Dungiven Road	2	170
Burke	R. A. & Co.	Foyle Street	20	136
Burke	R. A. & Co.	Quay Queen's	stores	152
Burke	Robert	Barrack Street	11	120
Burke	Samuel	Stewart's Terrace	17	155
Burke	Sergeant J.	Florence Street	21	163
Burke	Thomas	Clarendon Street		127
Burke	Thomas	Eglinton Place	21	132
Burke	William	Margaret Street	12	173
Burnett	James	Mount Street	16	164
Burns	George	Sackville Street	8	154
Burns	Joseph	Mill Street	29	173
Burns	Samuel	Glen Terrace	1	131
Burns	W. J.	Culmore Road	Craiglea	129
Burns	William	Academy Terrace	1	118
Burns	William	Nicholson Square	19	149
Burns	William & Co.	Alma Terrace	43	136
Burns	James	Chapel Road	31	167
Burns	Mary Ann	St. Columb's Wells	116	157
Burns	Miss	Union Street	20	159
Burns & Laird Lines		Water Street		160
Burnside	Alex	Argyle Street	53	119
Burnside	Joseph	Argyle Terrace	35	120
Burnside	Mrs	Barry Street	16	121
Burnside	Mrs	Bond's Street	26	166
Burnside	Mrs E.	Northland Avenue	13	150
Burnside	Walter	Edenmore Street	20	131
Burnside	William	Park Avenue	4	151
Burnside	William	Florence Street	10	164
Burnside	William	Mount Street	6	164
Burnside & Co.		Strand Road	51	155
Burton	William A.	Beechwood Avenue	42	121
Butcher	Joseph	Alma Place	15	119
Butcher	Joseph	Benvarden Avenue	49	166
Butcher	Mary	Elmwood Road	2	132
Butler	Francis	Glasgow Terrace	11	138
Butler	James	Argyle Terrace	9	120
Butler	Jane	Donegal Street	18	163
Butler	M. L.	Waterloo Street	38	159
Butler	Mary	Howard Place	8	141
Butler	Mary Ann	Long Tower	5	145
Butler	Mrs	Tyrconnell Street	19	158
Butler	Richard	Glasgow Street	4	138
Butler	Richard	Glasgow Terrace	15	138

Surname	First Name	Street	House Number	Page Number
Butler	Stephen	Limavady Road	51	172
Butler	William	Argyle Street	12	119
Byrne	Alexander	Marlborough Street	15	146
Byrne	Ellen	Walker's Place	25	159
Byrne	Joseph	Walker's Place	9	159
Byrne	A. & Co.	Butcher Street	10, 12	125
Cabena	Lloyd	Abercorn Road	4	118
Cabena	Thomas	London Street	15	145
Cadden	Francis	Mountjoy Street	24	148
Cadden	James	Alexandra Place	29	119
Cadden	John	Bennett Street Upper	2	122
Cafolla	A.	Spencer Road	1, 3	174
Cafolla & Sons		Duke Street	43	169
Cahill	Mrs P.	Waterloo Street	37	159
Cairns	J. C.	Marlborough Villas	1	146
Cairns	James	Carlin Street	1	166
Cairns	John	Bond's Street	47	166
Cairns	Miss	Riverview Terrace	8	174
Cairns	William	Creggan Road	20	163
Calderwood	Mary A.	Westland Avenue	38	161
Caldwell	David	Alexandra Terrace	44	150
Caldwell	Douglas	Collon Terrace	9	128
Caldwell	E.	Waterloo Place	6	160
Caldwell	Fred	King Street	20	172
Caldwell	George	Florence Street	24	170
Caldwell	James	Carrigans Lane	4	126
Caldwell	James	Union Street	1	175
Caldwell	John	Albert Place	5	119
Caldwell	John	King Street	14	172
Caldwell	Joseph	Henrietta Street	12	141
Caldwell	Martha	Emerson Street	8	170
Caldwell	Miss	Carlisle Road	75½	125
Caldwell	Miss	John Street	52	142
Caldwell	Miss	Shipquay Street	14A	154
Caldwell	Miss	Dervock Street	8	168
Caldwell	Mrs	Bennett Street Upper	10	122
Caldwell	Mrs	Dungiven Road	13	169
Caldwell	Mrs J. H.	May Street	5	173
Caldwell	S. E.	Diamond	9	130
Caldwell	Samuel A.	Aberfoyle Crescent	3	118
Caldwell	William	De Burgh Terrace	11	130
Caldwell	William	Ivy Terrace	9	142
Caldwell	William	Shipquay Street	14A	154
Caldwell & Robinson		Castle Street	11	126
Callaghan	Andrew	West-End Terrace	8	161
Callaghan	James	Fountain Hill	48	171
Callaghan	Michael	Limewood Street	32	144
Callaghan	Miss	Bennett Street Upper	6	122
Callaghan	Patrick	Lecky Road	41	143

Surname	First Name	Street	House Number	Page Number
Callaghan	Timothy	Northland Avenue	24	150
Callan	Joseph	Simpson's Brae	2	174
Callan	Letitia	Bishop Street	251	123
Callen	James	Strabane Old Road	20	175
Callen	James	Strabane Old Road	24	175
Callon	Matthew	Derry View Terrace	8	168
Callon	Sarah J.	Cross Street	39	168
Campbell	A. J.	Lawrence Hill	20	143
Campbell	A. J.	Shipquay Street	25	154
Campbell	A. P.	Bishop Street	2	123
Campbell	Alexander	Matty's Lane	34	158
Campbell	Alexander	Rosemount Avenue	23	164
Campbell	Alexander	Albert Street	17	118
Campbell	Andrew	Fahan Street	102	133
Campbell	Andrew	Philips Street	28	151
Campbell	Andrew	Thomas Street	8	158
Campbell	Annie	Duke Street	6	169
Campbell	David	Lower Road	16	146
Campbell	E. W.	Bishop Street	3	122
Campbell	Edward	Limewood Street	2	144
Campbell	Edward	Mount Street	3	164
Campbell	Eugene	Barry Street	23	121
Campbell	Hannah	Wellington Street	18	160
Campbell	Henry	De Burgh Terrace	2	130
Campbell	James	Hamilton Street	51	140
Campbell	James	High Street	14	141
Campbell	James	Rossville Street	34	153
Campbell	James	Tyrconnell Street	18	158
Campbell	James	Bond's Street	21	166
Campbell	James	Gortfoyle Place	7	171
Campbell	John	Argyle Street	60	119
Campbell	John	Elmwood Terrace	15	132
Campbell	John	Fahan Street	139	133
Campbell	John	Lecky Road	105	143
Campbell	John	Ann Street	31	144
Campbell	John	New Street	6	164
Campbell	John	Strabane Old Road		175
Campbell	John	Violet Street Lower	30	176
Campbell	John	York Street	8	176
Campbell	John A.	Ernest Street	2	163
Campbell	John A.	Dervock Place	8	168
Campbell	Joseph	Argyle Street	13	119
Campbell	Joseph	Philips Street	31	151
Campbell	Joseph	Union Street	15	158
Campbell	Joseph	Wellington Street	16	160
Campbell	Joseph	Rosemount Terrace	9	165
Campbell	Joseph	Bond's Street	3	166
Campbell	Joseph	Duke Street	62	169
Campbell	Joseph	Fountain Hill	1	171
Campbell	Letitia	Wellington Street	50	160

Surname	First Name	Street	House Number	Page Number
Campbell	Margaret	Howard Place	5	141
Campbell	Martin	Garden City		129
Campbell	Mary	Elmwood Terrace	31	132
Campbell	Mary Ann	Rossville Street	70	153
Campbell	Miss	Beechwood Park	100	121
Campbell	Miss	Bennett Street Lower	30	122
Campbell	Miss	Clarendon Street	28	127
Campbell	Miss	Dixon's Close	3	146
Campbell	Miss	Rosemount Terrace	14	165
Campbell	Miss Anne	William Street	103	161
Campbell	Miss M.	Melrose Terrace	3	173
Campbell	Miss M. A.	Diamond	14	130
Campbell	Miss M. E.	Orchard Street	16	151
Campbell	Mrs	Beechwood Avenue	8	121
Campbell	Mrs	Fahan Street	109	133
Campbell	Mrs	Glasgow Street	2	138
Campbell	Mrs	St. Columb's Terrace	85	143
Campbell	Mrs	Lower Road	7	146
Campbell	Mrs	Lower Road	16	146
Campbell	Mrs	Northland Avenue	12	150
Campbell	Mrs	Philips Street	7	151
Campbell	Mrs	Princes Street	29	152
Campbell	Mrs	Westland Avenue	26	160
Campbell	Mrs	Duke Street	20	169
Campbell	Mrs E. J.	Maple Street	4	173
Campbell	Mrs H.	Nicholson Square	3	149
Campbell	Mrs L. E.	Templemore Park	5	158
Campbell	Patrick	Kildarra Terrace	12	141
Campbell	Robert	Victoria Street	8	159
Campbell	Robert J.	Blee's Lane		124
Campbell	Samuel	Aubrey Street	4	120
Campbell	Samuel	Clarence Place	7	127
Campbell	Sydney	Bishop Street	97	122
Campbell	Sydney	Violet Street Upper	31	176
Campbell	Thomas	Margaret Street	15	173
Campbell	W. J.	Melrose Terrace	12	173
Campbell	William	Bishop Street	78	123
Campbell	William	Cottage Row	3	123
Campbell	William	Bridge Street	47	124
Campbell	William	Garden City		129
Campbell	William	Nelson Street	54	149
Campbell	William	Templemore Terrace	1	151
Campbell	William	Thomas Street	3	158
Campbell	William	Ernest Street	21	163
Campbell	William	Clifton Street	1	167
Campbell	William	Duddy's Row	7	169
Campbell	William	Strabane Old Road		175
Campbell	William J.	Riverview Terrace	6	174
Campbell	James	Mitchelburne Terrace	98	136

Surname	First Name	Street	House Number	Page Number
Campbell & Patton		Carlisle Road	42	126
Campbell Bros		Quay Princes		152
Campbell Bros.		Foyle Street	22	136
Canavan	Herbert	Demesne Terrace	13	130
Canavan	Miss	Dungiven Road	77	170
Canney	James	Distillery Lane Upper	4	168
Canning	A.	Foyle Street	45, 47	135
Canning	Alex	Cuthbert Street	7	168
Canning	Alfred	Foyle Road	50	136
Canning	Charles	Glendermott Road	16	171
Canning	Dan	St. Columb's Wells	4	157
Canning	Hannah	William Street	55½	161
Canning	Henry	Nassau Street Upper	12	149
Canning	Hugh	Nailor's Row	47	148
Canning	Hugh	Benvarden Avenue	28	166
Canning	James	Deanery Street	24	130
Canning	James	Quarry Street	16	153
Canning	James	Strand Road	54	156
Canning	James	Lewis Street	28	164
Canning	James	York Street	4	176
Canning	John	Fahan Street	101	133
Canning	John	Park Avenue	22	151
Canning	John	Waterloo Street	42	160
Canning	John	William Street	80	162
Canning	John	Benvarden Avenue	43	166
Canning	John	Bond's Street	5	166
Canning	John	Bond's Street	45	166
Canning	John	Derry View Terrace	3	168
Canning	Joseph	Limewood Street	14	144
Canning	Lily	Ann Street	23	119
Canning	Mary	Bluebellhill Terrace	156	144
Canning	Michael	Osborne Street	4	164
Canning	Mrs	Bishop Street	44	123
Canning	Mrs	Deanery Street	21	130
Canning	Neal	Creggan Road	145	162
Canning	Patrick	Beechwood Street	13	121
Canning	Patrick	Union Street	22	176
Canning	Robert	Bishop Street	187	122
Canning	Samuel	Orchard Row	7	150
Canning	Thomas	Northland Avenue	11	150
Canning	William	Sloan's Terrace	29	155
Canning	William	Walker's Place	27	159
Canning	William	Duke Street	51	169
Canning	William J.	Hollywell Street	13	141
Cannon	Neal	Creggan Road	20	163
Canovan	James	Fahan Street	120	133
Cantell	Thomas	Florence Street	37	170
Carabine	Hugh	Elmwood Street	10	132
Carberry	Rose A.	Stanley's Walk	47	155

Surname	First Name	Street	House Number	Page Number
Carbine	Joseph	Cable Street	15	125
Carbine	Thomas	Lecky Road	253	143
Carey	David	Stable Lane	2	155
Carey	Denis	Howard Street	4	141
Carey	Michael	Cross Street	17	168
Carey	Mrs	Fountain Street	94	135
Carey	Mrs	Long Tower	26	146
Carey	Patrick	Cross Street	21	168
Carey	Samuel	North Street	39	164
Carey	Thomas	Hogg's Folly	12	141
Carey	Thomas	Lower Road	14	146
Cargill	James	Cuthbert Street	18	168
Cargill	Mary Ann	Waterloo Street	53	159
Cargill	Robert	Aubrey Street	12	120
Cargill	Thomas	Hawkin Street	2	140
Cargill	Thomas	Waterloo Street	55	159
Carland	Mrs	Dungiven Road	55, 57	170
Carlin	A.	Water Street	8	160
Carlin	Anthony	Tyrconnell Street	16	158
Carlin	Daniel	Brandywell Road	6	124
Carlin	Daniel	Fahan Street	24	133
Carlin	Daniel	Howard Street	2	141
Carlin	Francis	Nelson Street	59	149
Carlin	Frank	Nelson Street	1	149
Carlin	Frank	Cross Street	29	168
Carlin	Hugh	Creggan Street	lodge	129
Carlin	James	Bishop Street	33	122
Carlin	James	Joseph Street	11	142
Carlin	James	Lecky Road	5	143
Carlin	James	Lecky Road	68	144
Carlin	James	Long Tower	2	145
Carlin	James	Stanley's Walk	43	155
Carlin	James	Stanley's Walk	48	155
Carlin	John	Adam Street	2	118
Carlin	John	Bluebellhill Terrace	146	144
Carlin	Kate	Brandywell Avenue	18	124
Carlin	Laurence	Brook Street Avenue	1	125
Carlin	Maggie	Fahan Street	15	133
Carlin	Manasses	Nailor's Row	18	148
Carlin	Margaret	Chapel Road	46	167
Carlin	Michael	Lecky Road	287	143
Carlin	Michael	Sloan's Terrace	11	154
Carlin	Mrs	Bishop Street	152	123
Carlin	Mrs	Elmwood Terrace	23	132
Carlin	Mrs	Elmwood Street	12	132
Carlin	Mrs	Foster's Terrace	153	143
Carlin	Mrs	Miller Street	2	147
Carlin	Mrs	Nailor's Row	6	148
Carlin	Mrs	Margaret Street	14	173
Carlin	Mrs	Strabane Old Road	11	175

Surname	First Name	Street	House Number	Page Number
Carlin	Neal	Fountain Hill	13	171
Carlin	Neal	Fountain Hill	23	171
Carlin	Patrick	Bishop Street	120	123
Carlin	Patrick	Marlborough Terrace	7	147
Carlin	Rebecca	William Street	10	161
Carlin	Thomas	Sloan's Terrace	26	155
Carlin	Thomas	Cottage Row	34	164
Carlin	Thomas	Margaret Street	18	173
Carlin	W. J.	Nelson Street	33	149
Carlin	William	Fitters Row	267	123
Carlin	William	Foyle Street	7	135
Carlin	William	Lecky Road	55	143
Carlin	William	Friel's Terrace	1	148
Carmichael	R.	Water Street	7	160
Carmichael	W. H.	De Burgh Terrace	Victoria Villa	130
Carnwath	Andrew H.	Bond's Place	6	166
Carnwath	John	Ebrington Street Lower	4	170
Carr	Annie	William Street	53½	161
Carr	Edward	Elmwood Terrace	21	132
Carr	John	Violet Street Lower	55	176
Carr	P. J.	Beechwood Avenue	21, Fairymount	121
Carr	Annie	Corbett Street (Pilot's Row)	8	128
Carr	G. N.	Hawkin Street	29	140
Carr	Hugh	Cross Street	32	168
Carr	John	Glasgow Street	6	138
Carr	Patrick J.	Demesne		130
Carrigan	William	Chapel Road	54	167
Carroll	James	High Street	5	141
Carroll	Paul J.	King Street	48	172
Carruthers	David	Argyle Street	17	119
Carruthers	James	George Street	9	138
Carruthers	John	Harding Street	27	140
Carruthers	John	Creggan Road	123	162
Carruthers	Mary	Creggan Road	135	162
Carruthers	Miss	Collon Terrace	3	128
Carruthers	Moses	Lewis Street	20	164
Carruthers	Mrs	Abercorn Place	3	118
Carruthers	Samuel	East Wall	Y.M.C.A.	131
Carruthers	William	Charlotte Street	3	127
Carson	Constable W. J.	Harding Street	4	140
Carson	James	Park Avenue	26	151
Carson	James	Glendermott Road	23	171
Carson	Patrick	Deanery Street	26	130
Carson	William	Bellevue Avenue	12	121
Carson	William	Ferguson Street	8	134
Carter	Arthur	Deanery Street	52	130
Cartin	Joseph	Foyle Road	108	136

Surname	First Name	Street	House Number	Page Number
Cartin	Michael	Corbett Street (Pilot's Row)	4	128
Cartin	Patrick	Lecky Road	251	143
Carton	J. J.	Prince Arthur Street	factory	152
Carton	J. J.	Pine Street	23, garage	174
Carton	James	Grafton Street	8	139
Carton	James	Clooney Terrace	12	167
Carton	John J.	Ebrington Terrace	15	170
Carton	Margaret	Cross Street	20	168
Carton	Miss	Orchard Row	34	150
Cartwright	E. M.	Great James Street	44	139
Cary	E. G.	Crawford Square	3	128
Casey	Daniel	West-End Park	18	161
Casey	Hugh	Baronet Street	3	120
Casey	Hugh	Clarendon Street	71	127
Casey	James	St. Columb's Wells	53	157
Casey	James	Thomas Street	28	158
Casey	John	Thomas Street	25	158
Casey	M. J. & Co.	William Street	26	161
Casey	Mrs	Marlborough Terrace	17	147
Casey	Mrs Maggie	St. Columb's Wells	46	157
Casey	P. F.	East Wall		131
Casey	Patrick	Laburnum Terrace	17	142
Casey	Thomas	Palace Street	3	151
Cash	Henry	Northland Road	21, gate lodge	150
Cassidy	Denis	Long Tower		145
Cassidy	Denis	Rossville Street	53	153
Cassidy	Hugh	Nassau Street Lower	8	148
Cassidy	James	Corbett Street (Pilot's Row)	9	128
Cassidy	James	Fahan Street	128	133
Cassidy	John	Argyle Terrace	25	120
Cassidy	John	Ivy Terrace	18	142
Cassidy	John	Nassau Street Lower	28	148
Cassidy	John	Wellington Street	45	160
Cassidy	John	Fountain Hill	50	171
Cassidy	Joseph	Spencer Road	114	175
Cassidy	Michael	Harvey Street	13	140
Cassidy	Miss	Bellevue Avenue	29	121
Cassidy	Mrs	Donegal Place	6	131
Cassidy	Mrs	Elmwood Terrace	10	132
Cassidy	Mrs	Hawkin Street	28	140
Cassidy	Patrick	Stewart's Terrace	6	155
Cassidy	Patrick	Wellington Street	39	160
Cassidy	Robert	Violet Street Lower	14	176
Cassidy	Samuel	Epworth Street	23	163
Cassidy	Thomas	Chapel Road	26	167
Cassidy	William	Ivy Terrace	36	142
Cassidy	William	Windsor Terrace	2	162

Surname	First Name	Street	House Number	Page Number
Cassidy & Smith		William Street	58	162
Casson	John J.	Ewing Street	36	133
Casson	Walter	Meehan's Row	8	173
Cassoni & Son		Carlisle Road	26	125
Cathcart	Charles	Epworth Street	14	163
Cathcart	Charles	Cottage Row	36	164
Catherwood	H. M. S.	Diamond	15	130
Catherwood	Messrs.	Foyle Street	11	135
Catterson	Patrick	Lecky Road	26	144
Cauley	Joseph	Dervock Place	4	168
Caulfield	James	Fahan Street	26	133
Caulfield	Manasses	St. Columb's Street	3	157
Caulfield	Mary	Walker's Place	37	159
Caulfield	Owen	Long Tower	23	145
Caulfield	Peter	Sugarhouse lane	7	158
Caulfield	Peter	Thomas Street	4	158
Cavanagh	James	Alexandra Place	17	119
Cavanagh	James	Pine Street	14	174
Cavanagh	John	Messines Park	6	128
Cavanagh	Patrick	Harvey Street	4	140
Cavanagh	Patrick	Lecky Road	70	144
Cavanagh	Thomas	Rossville Street	6	153
Chambers	Alfred	Grafton Street	5	138
Chambers	James	Carrigans Lane	8	126
Chambers	John	Duncreggan Road	3	131
Chambers	Joseph	Abercorn Road	65	118
Chambers	Joseph	Marlborough Street	24	147
Chambers	Joseph	New Market Street		149
Chambers	Matthew	Bishop Street	48	123
Chambers	Miss	Wesley Street	14	165
Chambers	William & Son	Pump Street	19	152
Chambers	Thomas	Wapping Lane	21	159
Chambers & Craig	T. & R. N.	Shipquay Street	33	154
Chapman	William F.	Stewart's Terrace	2	155
Chastellain	Millar	Aberfoyle Crescent	7	118
Cherry	Thomas	Chapel Road	14	167
Cheshire	Mrs	Clooney Terrace	46	167
Cheshire	Percival	Spencer Road	25	174
Christy	John	Clooney Terrace	47	167
Christy	John Ltd	Foyle Street	88, 90	136
Christy	John Ltd	Quay Abercorn	mills	152
Christy	John Ltd	Quay Abercorn	stores	152
Christy	Mrs	Bellevue Avenue	22	121
Clark	Samuel	Sunnyside Terrace	1	123
Clarke	Bernard	Union Street	7	158
Clarke	Francis	Wellington Street	73A	160
Clarke	George	De Burgh Terrace	13	130
Clarke	Henry	Alexandra Place	12	119

Surname	First Name	Street	House Number	Page Number
Clarke	James	Violet Street Upper	13	176
Clarke	James R.	Marlborough Street	21	146
Clarke	John	Dixon's Close	5	146
Clarke	John	Mill Street	25	173
Clarke	John	Violet Street Lower	28	176
Clarke	Joseph	New Street	9	126
Clarke	Miss	Primrose Street	19	174
Clarke	Mrs M. A.	Primrose Street	8	174
Clarke	Patrick	Argyle Terrace	30	120
Clarke	Robert	Cuthbert Street	4	168
Clarke	Thomas	Francis Street	1	137
Clarke	William	Messines Park	38	128
Clarke	William	Henry Street	22	141
Clayton	Robert B.	Creggan		131
Clendinning	Margaret	Hawkin Street	34	140
Clifford	Henry	Bridge Street	50	125
Clifford	Henry	Foyle Road	111	136
Clifford	Henry	Joseph Street	3	142
Clifford	Hugh	Bridge Street	7½	124
Clifford	James	Fahan Street	148	133
Clifford	James	Mitchelburne Terrace	91	136
Clifford	John	New Street	1	128
Clifford	John	Walker's Place	36	159
Clifford	Mrs	Foyle Road	31	136
Clifford	Mrs	Sugarhouse lane	19	158
Clifford	Patrick	Glasgow Terrace	28	138
Clifford	Patrick	Hawthorn Terrace	36	140
Clifford	Patrick	Joseph Street	6	142
Clifford	Samuel	Wesley Street	15	165
Clifford	William	Lecky Road	283	143
Cochrane	Edward	Ferguson Street	49	134
Cochrane	James	McLaughlin's Close	2	134
Cochrane	Mrs	Barrack Street	3	120
Cochrane	Robert	Creggan		131
Cochrane	Robert	Spencer Road	122	175
Cochrane	S,	Bond's Hill	egg store	166
Cochrane	Samuel	Melrose Terrace	18	173
Cochrane	Samuel	Mill Street	garage	173
Cochrane	William	Marlborough Avenue	17	147
Coffey	John	Westland Terrace	12	161
Coghlan	John	Creggan Road	3	162
Cogley	Mark	Waterloo Street	7	159
Cogley	Mark	Waterloo Street	19	159
Cole	Andrew	Strand Road	135	156
Cole	Mrs Sarah	Elmwood Terrace	46	132
Coleman	John	Bluebellhill Terrace	132	144
Colhoun	Adam	Fountain Street	21	134
Colhoun	Annie	Pine Street	17	174
Colhoun	Bridget	Ann Street	1	119
Colhoun	David	Violet Street Lower	21	176

Surname	First Name	Street	House Number	Page Number
Colhoun	Dr. W. P.	Pump Street	24	152
Colhoun	Gerald	Glen Terrace	3	131
Colhoun	Hugh	Clarendon Street	24	127
Colhoun	J.	Deanfield	24, Avondale	168
Colhoun	James	Pitt Street	4	151
Colhoun	James	Ernest Street	23	163
Colhoun	John	North Edward Street	7	149
Colhoun	John	Philips Street	29	151
Colhoun	John	Fountain Hill	68	171
Colhoun	John	Tamneymore		175
Colhoun	John G.	Beechwood Avenue	30	121
Colhoun	Major James	Culmore Road	St. Elmo	129
Colhoun	Miss	Grove Place	16	139
Colhoun	Miss	Marlborough Terrace	25	147
Colhoun	Mrs	Grove Place	18	139
Colhoun	Mrs	Northland Road	19, Alt-an-Righ	150
Colhoun	Mrs E.	Hawkin Street		140
Colhoun	R.	Strand Road Lower	173	156
Colhoun	R.	Bluebellhill Terrace	yard	144
Colhoun	Robert	Messines Park	20	128
Colhoun	Robert	Grafton Street	3	138
Colhoun	Robert	Strand Road	28	156
Colhoun	Robert	Dungiven Road	20	170
Colhoun	Thomas	Orchard Row	23	150
Colhoun	Thomas	Park Avenue	19	151
Colhoun	Thomas	Spencer Road	60	175
Colhoun	William	Major's Row	6	146
Colhoun	William	Mary Street	22	147
Colhoun	William	Florence Street	16	164
Colhoun	William	Benvarden Avenue	36	166
Colhoun	William	Clooney Terrace	4	167
Colhoun	William	Cochrane's Row	3	169
Coll	Mary	Stewart's Terrace	8	155
Coll	Peter	De Burgh Square	10	130
Coll	Charles	Bridge Street	54	125
Coll	Peter	Artillery Street	Synod Hall	120
Coll	George	Margaret Street	6	173
Coll	John	Cottage Row	42	164
Collender	Frederick	Florence Street	4	170
Collins	Daniel	Herbert Street	16	172
Collins	Edward	Collon Terrace	22	128
Collins	Edward	Elmwood Terrace	4	132
Collins	Ellen	Mill Street	27	173
Collins	James	Messines Park	55	128
Collins	John	Lecky Road	94	144
Collins	John	Wellington Street	14	160
Collins	Margaret	Margaret Street	9	173
Collins	Michael	Bishop Street	137	122
Collins	Mrs	Brandywell Avenue	14	124
Collins	Owen	Morrison's Close	1	133

Surname	First Name	Street	House Number	Page Number
Collins	Stephen N.	Glendermott Road	26	171
Collins	Thomas	Lecky Road	31	143
Collins	William	Spencer Road	56	175
Colquhoun & King		Shipquay Street	8	154
Conaghan	Andrew	Orchard Row	32	150
Conaghan	Hannah	Carrigans Lane	6	126
Conaghan	John	Long Tower	71	145
Conaghan	Mrs	Orchard Street	19	151
Conaghan	W. E.	Shipquay Street	27	154
Conaghan	William	Bennett Street Upper	9	122
Conaghan	Catherine	MalvernTerrace	19	169
Conaghan	Charles	Distillery Lane Lower	6	168
Conaghan	Mrs	Margaret Street	3	173
Conaghan	Neal	Duke Street	45	169
Conaghan	Neil	Chapel Road	27	167
Concannon	John	Deanery Street	56	130
Concannon	Mrs E.	St. Columb's Wells	28	157
Condren	James	Argyle Street	27	119
Conlan	Miss	Foyle Street	17	135
Conn	Edward	Dunfield Terrace	3	169
Conn	Joseph	Stewart's Terrace	11	155
Conn	James H.	London Street		145
Conn	James H.	Pump Street	28	152
Connelly	J. & M.	William Street	42, 44	161
Connolly	A. L.	The Rock	103	156
Connolly	Francis	Glendermott Road	10	171
Connolly	John	Fairman Place	20	133
Connolly	Owen	Wesley Street	20	165
Connor	Edward	Long Tower	35	145
Connor	George	Argyle Street	57	119
Connor	Henry	Clarendon Street	29	127
Connor	Hugh	Artisan Street	1	162
Connor	John	Beechwood Park	90	121
Connor	John	Cottage Row	6	164
Connor	Lizzie	Brandywell Road	18	124
Connor	Mrs	Princes Terrace	6	152
Connor	Mrs	Iona Terrace	13	172
Connor	Mrs F.	Albert Street	4	118
Connor	Mrs M.	Strand Road	131	156
Connor	Patrick	Corporation Street	1	128
Connor	Patrick	Lecky Road	74	144
Connor	Patrick	Long Tower	27	145
Connor	Robert	Philips Street	27	151
Connor	Sarah	Wellington Street	33	160
Connor	Thomas	Ferguson Street	43	133
Connor	Thomas	Bluebellhill Terrace	152	144
Connor	Thomas	Cross Street	5	163
Connor	William	Foyle Terrace	117	136
Connor	William	Nassau Street Upper	4	149

Surname	First Name	Street	House Number	Page Number
Conway	Peter	Little Diamond	6	145
Conway	Peter	North Street	17	164
Conway	Rev. Hugh	Creggan Street		129
Conway	Susan	Francis Street	3	137
Cooke	Dr J. G.	Clarendon Street	67	127
Cooke	J. & J.	Quay Queen's	saw mills	152
Cooke	J. & J.	Strand Road	26	156
Cooke	John & Co.	Waterloo Place	13, 14, 15	160
Cooke	Miss	Caw	Caw House	167
Cooke	Mrs	Culmore Road	Troy Hall	129
Cooke	Mrs	Government House		137
Cooke	Robert	Howard Place	1	141
Cooke	Robert	Strand Road	34	156
Cooke	Robert	Bond's Hill	19	166
Cooke	Robert & Co.	Butcher Street	14, 16	125
Cooke	Thomas	Meadowbank Avenue	29	147
Cooke	William	Sunnyside Terrace	Sunnyside house	123
Cooke	William	Bishop Street	85	122
Cooke	J. & J.	Strand Road	98	157
Cooley	Edward	Deanery Place	3	130
Cooley	John	Bishop Street	73	122
Cooley	Michael	Brandywell Avenue	13	124
Cooley	William	Friel's Terrace	2	148
Cooper	Miss	Abercorn Road	16	118
Cooper	Miss	Clarendon Street	48	127
Cooper	Norman	London Street	10	145
Cooper	Robert	Creggan Road	159	163
Cooper	Thomas	Emerson Street	24	170
Copeland	George	Strand Road Lower	155	156
Corbett	David	Foyle Road	9, 10	136
Corbett	J. D.	Deanfield	6	168
Corbett	J. W. & Son	Quay Princes	office	152
Cordiner	Mrs	Abercorn Road	6	118
Cordner	Edward	John Street	49	142
Cordner	Joseph	Pine Street	16	174
Corkey	Henry T.	Meadowbank Avenue	21	147
Corn & Co.		Castle Gate	1	126
Corr	Patrick	Benvarden Avenue	30	166
Cosgrove	Miss	Long Tower	9	145
Cosgrove & Co.		Bishop Street	17, 19	122
Cosgrove & Co.		Society Street	2	155
Costello	Peter	Bond's Hill	1	166
Coulter	John	Westland Avenue	39	160
Coulter	John	Primrose Street	15	174
Coulter	R. A.	Shipquay Street	40	154
Coulter	Thomas M.	West-End Park	12	161
Coulter	William	Alexander Terrace	2	174
Coups	Thomas	Fountain Place	27	135
Courtney	Patrick	Mountjoy Street	22	148

Surname	First Name	Street	House Number	Page Number
Courtney	Patrick	Westland Avenue	14	160
Cousins	Annie	Meehan's Row	4	173
Cowan	John	York Street	15	176
Cowan	Maud	Glendermott Road	78	171
Cowan	Mrs M. A.	Florence Street	1	170
Cowan	Robert	Abercorn Place	2	118
Cowan	William	Messines Park	53	128
Cowell	Rev. E. W.	Spencer Road	109	174
Cowfey	John	Park Avenue	23	151
Cowley	John	Corporation Street	5	128
Cox	Daniel	Long Tower	79	145
Cox	Mrs	Great James Street	74	139
Cox	Mrs	Moore Street	8	148
Coyle	Alexander F.	Elmwood Street	1	132
Coyle	Andrew	Creggan Road	133	162
Coyle	Annie	Union Street	13	176
Coyle	Bernard	Bridge Street	57	124
Coyle	Bridget	St. Columb's Wells	65	157
Coyle	Catherine	Deanery Street	28	130
Coyle	Charles	Spencer Road	118	175
Coyle	Dan	Orchard Street	13	151
Coyle	Daniel	Nassau Street Lower	21	148
Coyle	Daniel	Artisan Street	11	162
Coyle	Denis	Nassau Street Lower	32	148
Coyle	Edward	Hollywell Row	79	143
Coyle	Edward	Rossville Street	44	153
Coyle	Hannah	Thomas Street	9	158
Coyle	Henry	Marlborough Park	57	162
Coyle	Henry	Donegal Street	23	163
Coyle	J. P.	West-End Park	2	161
Coyle	James	Messines Park	49	128
Coyle	James	Fahan Street	91	133
Coyle	James	Lower Road	35	146
Coyle	James	Nassau Street Lower	7	148
Coyle	James	Nassau Street Lower	22	148
Coyle	James	Sugarhouse lane	12	158
Coyle	James	Creggan Road	62	163
Coyle	James	Duke Street	78	169
Coyle	John	Ann Street	5	119
Coyle	John	Ann Street	2	119
Coyle	John	Blucher Street	3	124
Coyle	John	Donegal Place	9	130
Coyle	John	Donegal Place	26	131
Coyle	John	Nassau Street Lower	46	148
Coyle	John	Union Street	4	158
Coyle	John	Creggan Road	165	163
Coyle	John	Strabane Old Road	25	175
Coyle	Manus	Meadowbank Avenue	25	147
Coyle	Mary	Windsor Terrace	7	162
Coyle	Michael	Ivy Terrace	28	142

Surname	First Name	Street	House Number	Page Number
Coyle	Miss	Cochrane's Row	4	169
Coyle	Mrs	Magazine Street Upper	5	146
Coyle	Mrs	Nelson Street	6	149
Coyle	Mrs	Rossville Street	5	153
Coyle	Neal	Ann Street	17	119
Coyle	Neal	Elmwood Street	20	132
Coyle	Patrick	Bishop Street	41	122
Coyle	Patrick	Bridge Street	46	125
Coyle	Patrick	Little James Street	9	145
Coyle	Patrick	Strand Road	39	155
Coyle	Patrick	Spencer Road	111	174
Coyle	Philip	Westland Avenue	10	160
Coyle	Richard	Union Street	18	158
Coyle	Richard	Glendermott Road	48	171
Coyle	Sarah	Irish Street	5	172
Coyle	William	Glasgow Terrace	25	138
Coyle	William	Union Street	8	158
Coyle	William	William Street	119	161
Coyle	William	Artisan Street	10	162
Coyle	William J.	Nassau Street Upper	18	149
Coyle	Robert	Fahan Street	96	133
Cradden	John J.	Spencer Road	11	174
Craig	A. N.	Queen Street	15	153
Craig	Alexander	Beechwood Park	98	121
Craig	Alice	Nassau Street Lower	39	148
Craig	Charles	Bond's Hill	10	166
Craig	David	Queen Street	12	153
Craig	Dr. F. A.	Limavady Road	5, Ard-Cluan	172
Craig	Dr. F. W.	Carlisle Terrace	2	126
Craig	George	Claremont Villas	40, Claremont	150
Craig	Henry	De Burgh Terrace	3	130
Craig	J. R.	Ernest Street	1	163
Craig	James	Governor Road	40	138
Craig	James H.	Spencer Road	125	174
Craig	John	Carrigans Lane	28	126
Craig	Joseph	Spencer Road	76	176
Craig	Mary	Bond's Street	15	166
Craig	Miss	Hawkin Street	37	140
Craig	Miss	Pump Street	23	152
Craig	Miss	Distillery Lane Lower	8	168
Craig	Miss	Limavady Road	47, Clooney cottage	172
Craig	Mrs	Albert Street	36	119
Craig	Robert	Stewart's Terrace	1	155
Craig	Samuel	Strand Road	118	157
Craig	Sergeant S.	Hawkin Street	31	140
Craig	Thomas	King Street	54	172
Craig	William	Argyle Street	6	119
Craig	William	Northland Avenue	14	150

Surname	First Name	Street	House Number	Page Number
Craig	William	Clooney Terrace	10	167
Craig	William J.	St. Columb's Road		172
Craig		Quay Queen's	Engineering Works	152
Craig	Miss L.	Fountain Street	90	135
Craig & Wellwood		Ferryquay Street	15	134
Craig's Engineering Works		Strand Road	76	157
Crainor	Miss	Stanley's Walk	5	155
Craven	Eugene	Elmwood Terrace	35	132
Crawford	Albert	Strabane Old Road	54	175
Crawford	James	Fountain Place	8	135
Crawford	John H.	Victoria Road	7	176
Crawford	Mrs Eva	Montrose Villas	24	150
Crawford	Robert	Carlisle Road	14	125
Crawford	Samuel	King Street	30	172
Crawford	William	De Burgh Terrace	16	130
Crawford	William	Fountain Street	87	134
Crawford	William H.	May Street	9	173
Crawford & Eakin		Foyle Street	60	136
Crawley	James	Fahan Street	36	133
Creany	Miss	Shipquay Street	10	154
Cregan	M. & Co.	Duke Street	14	169
Cregan	Mary	East Wall	4	131
Cregan	Patrick	Strabane Old Road		175
Creighton	Constable	Eden Terrace	8	131
Crerand	George	Rossville Street	43	153
Cresswell	R.	Beechwood Avenue	15, Morass	121
Creswell	Alex	Duke Street	1	169
Creswell	Andrew	Gordon Terrace	1	138
Creswell	Andrew	Linenhall Street Lower	25	145
Creswell	Andrew	Windmill Terrace	33	162
Creswell	John	Linenhall Street Lower	25	145
Creswell	Miss	Sloan's Terrace	36	155
Crichton	Mrs	Kerr's Terrace	17	162
Crilly	John	Fahan Street	28	133
Cripps	Robert S.	Deanfield	5	168
Criswell	Walter	Clarendon Street	44	127
Crockard	James	Iona Terrace	33	172
Crockett	Andrew A.	Templemore Park	7	158
Crockett	Charles	King Street	21	172
Crockett	James	William Street	59	161
Crockett	James	Spencer Road	71	174
Crockett	John	Glasgow Street	5	138
Crockett	Mrs	Glasgow Terrace	29	138
Crockett	Mrs	Glendermott Road	28	171

Surname	First Name	Street	House Number	Page Number
Crockett	Robert	Barry Street	18	121
Crockett	William	Nassau Street Lower	27	148
Crockett	William	Mount Street	10	164
Crockett	Ezekiel	Clarendon Street	21	127
Crockett	John	Clarence Avenue	12	127
Crockett	Robert Wilson	Garden City		129
Crockett	Thomas	Edenmore Street	25	131
Crockett & Guy		Strand Road	11	155
Crolly	John	Bishop Street	157	122
Crolly	John	Caroline Place	23	126
Crolly	John	Nelson Street	66	149
Crommer	Mrs M. E.	Grove Place	22	139
Crook	George F.	Strand Road	2	156
Crooks	Gilbert	Spencer Road	4	175
Crooks	John R.	Fountain Place	17	135
Crooks	Robert J.	Spencer Road	14, 16	175
Crooks	Samuel	Spencer Road	79	174
Crooks	Thomas	Spencer Road	4	175
Crooks	Thomas A.	Spencer Road	6	175
Croom	Miss	Nicholson Terrace	7	149
Crosbie	Dr	Clarendon Terrace	1	127
Cross	Mrs H.	Hawthorn Terrace	24	140
Cross	John	Nassau Street Lower	42	148
Cross	Matilda	Union Street	10	176
Crossan	Annie	Walker's Place	15	159
Crossan	Bernard	Strabane Old Road	78	175
Crossan	Charles	Fahan Street	94	133
Crossan	E.	Fahan Street	75	133
Crossan	Edward	Little Diamond	13, 15	145
Crossan	Edward	Rossville Street	87	153
Crossan	John	Clarke Terrace	230	144
Crossan	John	Princes Street	12	152
Crossan	John	Alfred Street	15	165
Crossan	Margaret	Bishop Street	288	124
Crossan	Miss	Foyle Road	121	136
Crossan	Neal	Bishop Street	239, 241	123
Crossan	Paul	Brook Street Avenue	13	125
Crossan	Thomas	Marlborough Avenue	3	147
Crossan	Thomas	Distillery Lane Lower	5	168
Crowe	Joseph	De Burgh Terrace	12	130
Cruickshank	John	Baronet Street	6	120
Cruickshank	John	Ernest Street	10	163
Crumlish	Jennie	Eglinton Place	1	132
Crumlish	John	Brandywell Avenue	25	124
Crumlish	Joseph	Ewing Street	18	133
Crumlish	Michael	William Street	54	161
Culbert	Walter	Moore Street	29	173
Culbert	Walter	Spencer Road	22	175
Cullen	Alfred	Cottage Row	8	123
Cullen	Charles	Lone Moor		145

Surname	First Name	Street	House Number	Page Number
Cullen	D.	Harvey Street	stables	140
Cullen	Daniel	William Street	90	162
Cullen	Elizabeth	Bishop Street	229	123
Cullen	Hugh	Chamberlain Street	27, 29	126
Cullen	James	Marlborough Avenue	11	147
Cullen	John	Limewood Street	10	144
Cullen	Patrick	Nailor's Row	32	148
Cullen	Phillip	Windsor Terrace	11	162
Cullen	William	Bluebellhill Terrace	222	144
Cullen	William	Nelson Street	57	149
Cullen & Allan		Quay Princes	stores	152
Culley	Harold	Strand Road	49	155
Culley	Mrs E.	Westland Avenue	13	160
Cullimore	Rev. C.	Limavady Road	19, The Rectory	172
Cullinane	Miss	Duke Street	12	169
Cullion	James	Fountain Hill	32	171
Cully	Robert	Stewart's Terrace	10	155
Cummings	Alexander	Spencer Road	31	174
Cummings	Constable	Ernest Street	25	163
Cummings	Thomas	Ashcroft Place	5	165
Cummins	Francis	Miller Street	24	148
Cummins	Mrs	Miller Street	1	147
Cunning	Mrs	Marlborough Park	61	162
Cunningham	Alice	Great James Street	40	139
Cunningham	Daniel	Blucher Street	8	124
Cunningham	David	Cedar Street	2	126
Cunningham	Dr R. W.	Clarendon Street	27	127
Cunningham	Frank	Dervock Place	5	168
Cunningham	H. W.	Clarendon Street	35	127
Cunningham	Harriet	Clooney Terrace	7	167
Cunningham	John	Blucher Street	4	124
Cunningham	Joseph	Long Tower	13	145
Cunningham	Miss E.	Francis Street	49	137
Cunningham	Mrs	Abercorn Terrace	4	118
Cunningham	Mrs	Hempton's Close		134
Cunningham	Mrs	John Street	52	142
Cunningham	Mrs J.	Marlborough Park	65	162
Cunningham	Patrick	Lecky Road	106	144
Cunningham	Patrick	Nailor's Row	49	148
Cunningham	Patrick	Walker's Place	45	159
Cunningham	Patrick J.	Clarence Avenue	5	127
Cunningham	R. A.	Shipquay Place	3	154
Cunningham	R. A.	Queen Street	9	153
Cunningham	Richard	Argyle Street	21	119
Cunningham	T.	Victoria Terrace	11	120
Cunningham	Thomas	Pine Street	5	174
Cunningham	William	Argyle Street	23	119
Cunningham	William	Chapel Road	12	167

Surname	First Name	Street	House Number	Page Number
Cunningham Bros.		William Street	58	162
Curless	Mrs	Long Tower	42	146
Curran	Anthony	Long Tower	44	146
Curran	Bernard	Tyrconnell Street	30	158
Curran	Denis	Miller Street	40	148
Curran	Edward	Glenview Avenue	11	137
Curran	Edward	Governor Road	10	138
Curran	Edward	Rossville Street	30	153
Curran	Francis	Nelson Street	69	149
Curran	Francis	Waterloo Street	63	159
Curran	Fred	Florence Street	35	170
Curran	Harry	Creggan Road	179	163
Curran	Henry	St. Columb's Wells	8	157
Curran	Hugh	Fulton Place	7	137
Curran	Isaac	Dungiven Road	95	170
Curran	James	Nelson Street	21	149
Curran	James	Wellington Street	36	160
Curran	John	Bishop Street	52	123
Curran	John	Richmond Street	10	153
Curran	John	Westland Avenue	27	160
Curran	John	Duke Street	29	169
Curran	John	Walker's Street	1	176
Curran	Joseph	Hamilton Street	22	140
Curran	Mary	Union Street	12	176
Curran	Miss	Victoria Street	20	159
Curran	Mrs	Glenbrook Terrace	14	137
Curran	Patrick	New Street	6	126
Curran	Patrick	Corbett Street (Pilot's Row)	11	128
Curran	Patrick	Glendermott Road	44	171
Curran	Samuel	Cross Street	3	168
Curran	Thomas	Bishop Street	87	122
Curran	Thomas	Sloan's Terrace	25	155
Curran	William	Hamilton Street	17	139
Curran	William	St. Columb's Terrace	83	143
Curran	William	Meehan's Row	14	173
Curry	David	Bellevue Avenue	33	121
Curry	George	Glasgow Terrace	18	138
Curry	Jacob	Emerson Street	22	170
Curry	James	Fountain Place	32	135
Curry	James	Hawkin Street	24	140
Curry	James	Bond's Place	10	166
Curry	John	Emerson Street	17	170
Curry	Lily	Fountain Hill	63	171
Curry	Mary	Alexandra Place	16	119
Curry	Miss	Miller Street	18	148
Curry	Mrs	Dixon's Close	2	146
Curry	Mrs	Stewart's Terrace	14	155
Curry	Mrs	Windmill Terrace	15	162

Surname	First Name	Street	House Number	Page Number
Curry	Mrs	Emerson Street	2	170
Curry	Robert	Barnewall Place	13	165
Curry	Robert	Moore Street	24	173
Curry	Thomas	Strabane Old Road	60	175
Curry	William	Windmill Terrace	25	162
Curry	William J.	Duke Street	77	169
Curtis	H. P.	Diamond	8	130
Curtis	James	Princes Street	4	152
Curtis	Joseph	Violet Street Upper	3	176
Curtis	Patrick	Foyle Road	107	136
Cusack	Robert	Elmwood Street	11	132
Cuthbert	Robert	Beechwood Street	23	121
Cuthbert	Robert	Wellington Street	32	160
Cuthbertson	Samuel	Eden Terrace	3	131
Dale	Samuel	Clooney Terrace	42	167
Dale	Samuel	Ebrington Terrace	1, Clooney Pharmacy	170
Daley	Joseph	Lecky Road	61	143
Dallas	Mrs	Rossville Street	52	153
Dalway	Mrs M.	Grafton Terrace	2	139
Daly	Constable Richard	Nicholson Square	16	149
Daly	Jane	Bridge Street		124
Daly	Joseph	Meave's Row	193	143
Daly	Margaret	Thomas Street	42	158
Daly	Patrick	Beechwood Street	9	121
Daly	Patrick	Long Tower	31	145
Daly	Philip	Orchard Street	6	151
Daly	Robert	St. Columb's Court	1	157
Daly	Thomas	Beechwood Street	21	121
Daly	Thomas	Tyrconnell Street	7	158
Dalzell	James	Robert Street	5	174
Dalzell	Mrs	Strabane Old Road	32	175
Dames	John	Herbert Street	6	172
Danaghy	Patrick	Fountain Hill	98	171
Dane	Mrs	Abercorn Road	61	118
Danker	Solomon	Moat Street	8	148
Darcy	Hugh	Messines Park	43	128
Darlow	George	Philips Street	42	151
Darragh	David	Florence Street	11	170
Darragh	Mrs	Dungiven Road	75	170
Daulton	Eugene	Emerson Street	11	170
David	Currie	Florence Street	17	170
David	George	Aubrey Street	21	120
Davidson	Leslie	Strabane Old Road	56	175
Davidson	Robert	Bond's Hill	23	166
Davidson	Samuel J.	Diamond	13	130
Davies	R. J.	Clarendon Street Lower	2	127
Davin	Thomas	Aberfoyle Terrace	21	156

Surname	First Name	Street	House Number	Page Number
Davis	J. L.	Great James Street	8	139
Davis	James	Pitt Street	2	151
Davis	John	Herbert Street	10	172
Davis	Mrs	Victoria Street	9	159
Davis	R. J.	Great James Street	30	139
Davis	Thomas	Bishop Street	192	123
Davis	Thomas	Ferguson Street	60	134
Davis	William	Foyleview Terrace	6	156
Davis	John	Edenmore Street	6	131
Davis	Mrs A.	Edenmore Street	28	132
Dawson	James	Chamberlain Street	33	126
Dawson	James	Pine Street	23	174
Dawson	Michael	Sydney Terrace	3	139
Deacon	Nurse	Great James Street	39	139
Deane	Catherine	Abbey Street	47	117
Deane	Catherine	St. Columb's Wells	38	157
Deane	David H.	West-End Park	19	161
Deane	James	Nailor's Row	11	148
Deane	Joseph P.	Benvarden Avenue	2B	166
Deane	Miss	Cuthbert Street	3	168
Deane	Mrs H. A.	Shipquay Street	14	154
Deane	Sarah	Nailor's Row	13	148
Deans	Henry	Emerson Street	14	170
Deans	Miss A. R.	Ashcroft Place	3	165
Deans	Sam	King Street	47	172
Deehan	Bernard	King Street	33	172
Deehan	Daniel	Dervock Street	7	168
Deehan	George	Clooney Terrace	24	168
Deehan	Henry	Chapel Road	29	167
Deehan	Hugh	Cross Street	3	163
Deehan	James	Lecky Road	267	143
Deehan	James	St. Patrick Street	11	158
Deehan	Michael	Dungiven Road	16	170
Deehan	Mrs	Osborne Street	21	164
Deehan	Mrs	Irish Street	7	172
Deehan	Neil	St. Columb's Wells	47	157
Deehan	Thomas	Osborne Street	20	164
Deehan	Thomas	King Street	3	172
Deehan	Thomas F.	Pump Street	22	152
Deehan	William	Bishop Street	216	123
Deehan	William	Rossville Street	11	153
Deehan	William	Riverview Terrace	11	174
Deeney	Daniel	Strand Road	120	157
Deeney	Francis	Tyrconnell Street	6	158
Deeney	John	Linenhall Street Lower	25	144
Deeney	Mrs	Creggan Street	15	129
Deeney	Mrs	Elmwood Terrace	20	132
Deeney	Mrs	Violet Street Lower	32	176
Deeney	Patrick	Lecky Road	stores	143

Surname	First Name	Street	House Number	Page Number
Deeney	Philip	Cranagh Terrace	4	142
Deeney	William	Beechwood Street	14	121
Deeny	Charles	Beechwood Street	10	121
Deeny	Daniel	St. Columb's Wells	106	157
Deeny	David	Rossville Street	22	153
Deeny	Edward	West-End Terrace	7	161
Deeny	James	New Row	1	156
Deeny	James	William Street	74	162
Deeny	John	Brandywell Road	26	124
Deeny	John	Foyle View	10	137
Deeny	John	Lower Road	13	146
Deeny	John	Benvarden Avenue	22	166
Deeny	Miss	Creggan Road	64	163
Deeny	William	Blucher Street	1	124
Deeny	William	Pennyburn Terrace	3	151
Deeny	William	New Street	9	164
Deery	John	Matty's Lane	28	158
Deery	John	Walker's Place	42	159
Deery	John	Westland Villas	1	161
Deery	Mrs	Matty's Lane	32	158
Deery	Mrs	Chapel Road	1	167
Deery	Patrick	Argyle Terrace	21	120
Deevine	Phillip	Laburnum Terrace	1	142
Dempsey	Bridget	Bishop Street	248	124
Denning	Robert S.	Bond's Street	14	166
Dennis	Mary	Clooney Terrace	43	167
Desmond	John Ltd.	Victoria Road	2, 4	176
Devenney	Henry	Foyle Road	55	136
Devenny	Mrs	Lecky Road	133	143
Devine	Catherine	Abercorn Road	10	118
Devine	Charles	Abercorn Terrace	2	118
Devine	Charles	Deanery Street	46	130
Devine	Charles	Clarke Terrace	232	144
Devine	Charles	Little Diamond	3	145
Devine	Charles	Dungiven Road	14	170
Devine	D. & Sons	Strand Road	63	155
Devine	Ellen	Linenhall Street Lower	8	145
Devine	James	Elmwood Terrace	36	132
Devine	James	Fountain Hill	108	171
Devine	John	Bishop Street	264	124
Devine	Julia	Westland Terrace	5	161
Devine	Mary	Carrigans Lane	17	126
Devine	Miss D.	Fountain Place	21	135
Devine	Mrs	Bishop Street	118	123
Devine	Mrs	Butcher Street	9A	125
Devine	Mrs	Riverview Terrace	13	174
Devine	Patrick	Argyle Street	61	119
Devine	Patrick	Deanery Street	27	130
Devine	Patrick	Walker's Place	3	159

Surname	First Name	Street	House Number	Page Number
Devine	Rev. Patrick	Victoria Place	Parochial House	159
Devine	Robert	Fountain Place	11	135
Devine	Samuel	Rosemount Avenue	13	164
Devine	Walter	Strand Road	34	156
Devine	William	Deanery Street	1	130
Devine	William	George Street	14	138
Devlin	Andrew	Long Tower	25	145
Devlin	Arthur	Argyle Terrace	29	120
Devlin	Charles	St. Columb's Wells	33	157
Devlin	Hugh	Westland Avenue	34	161
Devlin	James	Creggan Street	43	129
Devlin	James	Limewood Street	5	144
Devlin	John	Long Tower	18	145
Devlin	John	St. Columb's Wells	21	157
Devlin	John	St. Columb's Wells	27	157
Devlin	Michael	Limewood Street	9	144
Devlin	Mrs	Glenbrook Terrace	7	137
Devlin	Mrs	Governor Road	11	138
Devlin	P. A.	Grafton Terrace	5	139
Devlin	William	Nelson Street	67	149
Diamond	Daniel	Bond's Street	36	166
Diamond	Edward	Fountain Hill	122	171
Diamond	Mrs	St. Columb's Wells	54	157
Diamond	Thomas	Wellington Street	68	160
Dick	Joseph	Ivy Terrace	22	142
Dickie	Rev. Knox	Queen Street	Covenanters' Church	153
Dickie	William	Philips Street		151
Dickie	William	Dervock Place	11	168
Dickie	William A.	Great James Street	32	139
Dickson	Arthur E.	Marlborough Street	16	147
Dickson	Arthur E.	Waterloo Place	2	160
Dickson	D.	Limavady Road	21, gate lodge	172
Dickson	F. G.	Shipquay Street	33	154
Dickson	J. A.	Water Street	6	160
Dickson	John	Great James Street	36	139
Dickson	John	Victoria Street	1	159
Dickson	Samuel	Alexandra Place	18	119
Dickson	Samuel	Alfred Street	11	165
Dickson	William	Harding Street	18	140
Dickson	William	Meadowbank Avenue	3	147
Dickson	William C.	Alfred Street	52	165
Diffin	William	Windmill Terrace	32	162
Diggins	William	Grafton Terrace	4	139
Dillon	James	Strabane Old Road	8	175
Dillon	Mrs	Herbert Street	5	171
Dillon	Patrick	Strabane Old Road	10	175
Dillon	William	Fulton Place	18	137
Dinsmore	David	Fountain Street	72	135

Surname	First Name	Street	House Number	Page Number
Dinsmore	James	Kennedy Street	5	142
Dinsmore	Matthew	Bishop Street	128	123
Dinsmore	William	Argyle Street	59	119
Disher	Archibald S.	Duke Street	36	169
Diver	Con	St. Columb's Wells	105	157
Diver	George	North Street	5	164
Diver	James	Barrack Street	4	120
Diver	Mary	Limewood Street	37	144
Diver	Mary A.	St. Columb's Wells	69	157
Diver	Mrs	King Street	40	172
Diver	Patrick	Millar's Close		125
Diver	William	Lecky Road	32	144
Divin	Annie	Bluebellhill Terrace	188	144
Divin	Edward	Nailor's Row	33½	148
Divin	Mrs	Brook Street Avenue	17	125
Divin	William	Bishop Street	72	123
Dixon	Alexander	Glendermott Road	58	171
Dixon	Robert J.	Alfred Street	13	165
Dixon	Samuel	Ebrington Terrace	5	170
Doak	James	Creggan Road	121	162
Doak	John	Lecky Road	127	143
Doak	Mary A.	Bennett Street Upper	23	122
Dobbins	Edward	Little Diamond	1	145
Dobbins	Michael	William Street	61	161
Docherty	Andrew	Abercorn Place	9	118
Docherty	Andrew	Magazine Street	21	146
Dodwell	Mrs	Albert Place	15	119
Dogherty	John	Rosemount Terrace	7	165
Dogherty	Patrick	Sugarhouse lane	17	158
Dogherty	William	Argyle Street	47	119
Doherty	Albert	Glasgow Terrace	30	138
Doherty	Alex	North Street	15	164
Doherty	Andrew	Foyle Street	37	135
Doherty	Andrew	Herbert Street	18	172
Doherty	Anne	North Street	33	164
Doherty	Annie	Laburnum Terrace	16	142
Doherty	Annie	William Street	8	161
Doherty	Annie	Donegal Street	34	163
Doherty	Annie	Cross Street	30	168
Doherty	Bernard	Argyle Street	28	119
Doherty	Bernard	Fahan Street	73	133
Doherty	Bernard	Nelson Street	25	149
Doherty	Bernard	Nelson Street	35	149
Doherty	Bernard	New Market Street	2	149
Doherty	Bernard	Sugarhouse lane	14	158
Doherty	Bernard	Westland Terrace	6	161
Doherty	Bernard	Creggan Road	177	163
Doherty	Bridget	Blucher Street	5	124
Doherty	Bridget	Creggan Road	85	162
Doherty	Cassie	Blucher Street	10	124

Surname	First Name	Street	House Number	Page Number
Doherty	Catherine	Deanery Street	23	130
Doherty	Catherine	Lecky Road	11	143
Doherty	Catherine	Hollywell Row	69	143
Doherty	Catherine	Lecky Road	125	143
Doherty	Catherine	Lecky Road	82	144
Doherty	Charles	Bishop Street	147	122
Doherty	Charles	Glasgow Terrace	36	138
Doherty	Charles	Great James Street	63B	139
Doherty	Charles	Great James Street	65	139
Doherty	Charles	Waterloo Place	11	160
Doherty	Charles	Strabane Old Road	22	175
Doherty	Christopher	Brandywell Avenue	10	124
Doherty	Christopher	Marlborough Avenue	30	147
Doherty	Con	Bishop Street	68	123
Doherty	Daniel	Argyle Street	10	119
Doherty	Daniel	Bishop Street	208	123
Doherty	Daniel	Brook Street Avenue	6	125
Doherty	Daniel	Deanery Street	13, 15	130
Doherty	Daniel	Elmwood Terrace	30	132
Doherty	Daniel	Elmwood Terrace	50	132
Doherty	Daniel	Elmwood Street	22	132
Doherty	Daniel	Quarry Street	6	153
Doherty	Daniel	Rossville Street	72	153
Doherty	David	Long Tower	40	146
Doherty	David	Wellington Street	66	160
Doherty	David	Bond's Street	33	166
Doherty	Denis	Brandywell Avenue	2	124
Doherty	Denis	Foyle Road	114	136
Doherty	E. & Co.	Abercorn Road	39	118
Doherty	Edward	Abbey Street	30	117
Doherty	Edward	Adam Street	7	118
Doherty	Edward	High Street	13	141
Doherty	Edward	Howard Street	3	141
Doherty	Edward	Bluebellhill Terrace	172	144
Doherty	Edward	St. Columb's Wells	122	158
Doherty	Edward	Tyrconnell Street	24	158
Doherty	Edward	West-End Terrace	8	161
Doherty	Edward	Fountain Hill	114	171
Doherty	Edward	Violet Street Lower	16	176
Doherty	Eliza	Nelson Street	8	149
Doherty	Elizabeth	Bridge Street	51	124
Doherty	Elizabeth	Lecky Road	21	143
Doherty	Ellen	Deanery Street	29	130
Doherty	Ellen	St. Patrick Street	6	158
Doherty	Ellen	Waterloo Street	21	159
Doherty	Ellen	Wellington Street	61	160
Doherty	Ellen	Creggan Road	56	163
Doherty	Francis	Blucher Street	7	124
Doherty	Francis	Ivy Terrace	38	142
Doherty	Frank	Bishop Street	116	123

Surname	First Name	Street	House Number	Page Number
Doherty	Frank	Simpson's Brae	8	174
Doherty	George	Fahan Street	134	133
Doherty	George	Fahan Street	152	133
Doherty	George	Lecky Road	151	143
Doherty	George	The Rock	105	156
Doherty	George	Creggan Road	2, 4	163
Doherty	George	Benvarden Avenue	32	166
Doherty	Hannah	High Street	2	141
Doherty	Hannah	Rossville Street	36	153
Doherty	Henry	Glasgow Terrace	26	138
Doherty	Henry	Lecky Road	49	143
Doherty	Henry	Marlborough Street	23	146
Doherty	Henry	Nelson Street	62	149
Doherty	Henry	Epworth Street	21	163
Doherty	Henry	Osborne Street	14	164
Doherty	Henry	Benvarden Avenue	51	166
Doherty	Henry	Chapel Road	30	167
Doherty	Henry	Glendermott Road	98	171
Doherty	Hugh	Ann Street	20	119
Doherty	Hugh	Beechwood Street	5	121
Doherty	Hugh	Creggan Terrace	7	129
Doherty	Hugh	Howard Place	6	141
Doherty	Hugh	Ann Street	7	143
Doherty	Hugh	Nassau Street Lower	43	148
Doherty	Hugh	Rossville Street	61	153
Doherty	Hugh	Sugarhouse lane	21	158
Doherty	Hugh L.	Creggan Road	161	163
Doherty	J.	Bishop Street	134	123
Doherty	J. & Co.	William Street	8	161
Doherty	J. J.	Foyle Street	15	135
Doherty	James	Abbey Street	18	117
Doherty	James	Beechwood Street	19	121
Doherty	James	Bishop Street	231	123
Doherty	James	Bishop Street	274	124
Doherty	James	Butcher Street	13	125
Doherty	James	Deanery Street	19	130
Doherty	James	Deanery Street	54	130
Doherty	James	Demesne Terrace	3	130
Doherty	James	Eglinton Place	11	132
Doherty	James	Eglinton Terrace	11	132
Doherty	James	Elmwood Terrace	13	132
Doherty	James	Elmwood Terrace	41	132
Doherty	James	Fahan Street	86	133
Doherty	James	Ferguson Street	14	134
Doherty	James	Fountain Street	55	134
Doherty	James	Foyle Street	36	136
Doherty	James	Foyle Road	52	136
Doherty	James	Glenview Avenue	21	137
Doherty	James	Hamilton Street	31	140
Doherty	James	Hollywell Street	2	141

Surname	First Name	Street	House Number	Page Number
Doherty	James	Moore Street	1	148
Doherty	James	Friel's Terrace	3	148
Doherty	James	Rossville Street	71	153
Doherty	James	Stanley's Walk	33	155
Doherty	James	St. Columb's Wells	128	158
Doherty	James	Waterloo Place	8	160
Doherty	James	West-End Terrace	2	161
Doherty	James	William Street	17	161
Doherty	James	Creggan Road	147	162
Doherty	James	Barnewall Place	19	165
Doherty	James	Moore Street	21	173
Doherty	James	Union Street	19	176
Doherty	Jane	Bluebellhill Terrace	142	144
Doherty	John	Abbey Street	61	117
Doherty	John	Alexandra Place	31	119
Doherty	John	Ann Street	15	119
Doherty	John	Barry Street	12	121
Doherty	John	Bishop Street	235	123
Doherty	John	Bishop Street	82	123
Doherty	John	Bishop Street	214	123
Doherty	John	Blucher Street	15	124
Doherty	John	Blucher Street	17	124
Doherty	John	Creggan Terrace	15	129
Doherty	John	Fahan Street	44	133
Doherty	John	Fahan Street	110	133
Doherty	John	Foyle Road	75	136
Doherty	John	Glenbrook Terrace	19	137
Doherty	John	Hamilton Street	23	139
Doherty	John	Lecky Road	113	143
Doherty	John	Lecky Road	285	143
Doherty	John	Ann Street	3	143
Doherty	John	Lower Road	1	146
Doherty	John	Richmond Street	16	153
Doherty	John	Sloan's Terrace	17	154
Doherty	John	Stanley's Walk	3	155
Doherty	John	Strand Road	47	155
Doherty	John	Strand Road Lower	165	156
Doherty	John	St. Columb's Wells	25	157
Doherty	John	Sugarhouse lane	15	158
Doherty	John	Wellington Street		160
Doherty	John	Wellington Street	17	160
Doherty	John	William Street	127	161
Doherty	John	William Street	12	161
Doherty	John & Co.	William Street	40	161
Doherty	John J.	Frederick Street	10	137
Doherty	Joseph	Bishop Street	246	124
Doherty	Joseph	Deanery Street	33	130
Doherty	Joseph	Hogg's Folly	3	141
Doherty	Joseph	Meave's Row	195	143
Doherty	Joseph	Bluebellhill Terrace	130	144

Surname	First Name	Street	House Number	Page Number
Doherty	Joseph	Miller Street	22	148
Doherty	Joseph	St. Columb's Wells	100	157
Doherty	Joseph	Tyrconnell Street	13	158
Doherty	Joseph	Union Street	11	158
Doherty	Lawrence	Rossville Street	42	153
Doherty	Leo	Donegal Street	7	163
Doherty	Lizzie	Northland Terrace	4	150
Doherty	Lizzie	Walker's Place	38	159
Doherty	Lizzie	William Street	123	161
Doherty	Lydia	Foyle Road	116	136
Doherty	Maggie	Nailor's Row	12	148
Doherty	Manasses	Bishop Street	80	123
Doherty	Margaret	Abbey Street	24	117
Doherty	Margaret	New Street	2	126
Doherty	Margaret	Fulton Place	14	137
Doherty	Mark	Violet Street Lower	49	176
Doherty	Martha	Spencer Road	138	175
Doherty	Mary	Bishop Street	210	123
Doherty	Mary	Howard Street	22	141
Doherty	Mary	Lecky Road	66	144
Doherty	Mary	Rossville Street	7	153
Doherty	Mary	Waterloo Street	35	159
Doherty	Mary	Bond's Place	3	166
Doherty	Mary A.	Caroline Place	3	126
Doherty	Mary A.	St. Columb's Wells	99	157
Doherty	Mary A.	Violet Street Lower	3	176
Doherty	Mary J.	Lecky Road	86	144
Doherty	Mary J.	Patrick Street	16	151
Doherty	Michael	Ann Street	24	119
Doherty	Michael	Chamberlain Street	31	126
Doherty	Michael	Hollywell Street	11	141
Doherty	Michael	Meave's Row	205	143
Doherty	Michael	Bluebellhill Terrace	176	144
Doherty	Michael	Rossville Street	49	153
Doherty	Michael D.	Bluebellhill Terrace	154	144
Doherty	Miss	Bishop Street	114	123
Doherty	Miss	Lecky Road	37	143
Doherty	Miss	Shipquay Street	18	154
Doherty	Miss	Chapel Road	36	167
Doherty	Miss	Clooney Terrace	5	167
Doherty	Miss	Duke Street	80	169
Doherty	Miss	Fountain Hill	112	171
Doherty	Miss	Walker's Street	7	176
Doherty	Miss R.	Dungiven Road	10	170
Doherty	Mrs	Brook Street Avenue	8	125
Doherty	Mrs	Chamberlain Street	23	126
Doherty	Mrs	Francis Street	41	137
Doherty	Mrs	Frederick Street	8	137
Doherty	Mrs	Glenbrook Terrace	15	137
Doherty	Mrs	Ivy Terrace	21	142

Surname	First Name	Street	House Number	Page Number
Doherty	Mrs	Laburnum Terrace	4	142
Doherty	Mrs	Long Tower	73	145
Doherty	Mrs	Nailor's Row	41	148
Doherty	Mrs	Matty's Lane	30	158
Doherty	Mrs	Walker's Place	48	159
Doherty	Mrs	North Street	27	164
Doherty	Mrs	Osborne Street	13	164
Doherty	Mrs	Clooney Terrace	26	168
Doherty	Mrs	Dungiven Road	79	170
Doherty	Mrs	Glendermott Road	94	171
Doherty	Mrs	King Street	19	172
Doherty	Mrs	Margaret Street	4	173
Doherty	Mrs	Meehan's Row	15	173
Doherty	Mrs	Union Street	11	176
Doherty	Mrs Bridget	Union Street	10	158
Doherty	Mrs J.	Orchard Street	14	151
Doherty	Mrs Mary	Sunbeam Terrace	10	122
Doherty	Mrs Rose	Violet Street Upper	29	176
Doherty	Myles junior	William Street	70	162
Doherty	Neil	Foyle Street	34	136
Doherty	Neil	Henrietta Street	8	141
Doherty	Norah	Great James Street	48	139
Doherty	Norah	William Street	71	161
Doherty	Nurse	Marlborough Avenue	7	147
Doherty	Owen	Moore Street	13	148
Doherty	Owen	Nassau Street Lower	4	148
Doherty	Patrick	Abbey Street	41	117
Doherty	Patrick	Barry Street	1	120
Doherty	Patrick	Edenballymore		131
Doherty	Patrick	Fahan Street	43	133
Doherty	Patrick	Fahan Street	142	133
Doherty	Patrick	Fox's Lane	9	137
Doherty	Patrick	Hamilton Street	3	139
Doherty	Patrick	Hamilton Street	47	140
Doherty	Patrick	Hamilton Street	6	140
Doherty	Patrick	Long Tower	83	145
Doherty	Patrick	Nassau Street Upper	35	149
Doherty	Patrick	Nelson Street	15	149
Doherty	Patrick	Rossville Street	79	153
Doherty	Patrick	Walker's Place	50	159
Doherty	Patrick	William Street	83	161
Doherty	Patrick	William Street	78	162
Doherty	Patrick	Donegal Street	8	163
Doherty	Patrick	Donegal Street	22	163
Doherty	Patrick	Violet Street Lower	44	176
Doherty	Patrick L.	Waterloo Street	4	159
Doherty	Philip	Abbey Street	49	117
Doherty	Philip	Marlborough Avenue	31	147
Doherty	Richard	Creggan Street	25	129
Doherty	Richard	Fountain Street	68	135

Surname	First Name	Street	House Number	Page Number
Doherty	Richard	Hollywell Row	67	143
Doherty	Robert	Corbett Street (Pilot's Row)	13	128
Doherty	Robert	Fountain Street	71	134
Doherty	Robert	Glasgow Street	2	138
Doherty	Robert	Glasgow Terrace	32	138
Doherty	Robert	Margaret Street	23	173
Doherty	Rose	Eglinton Place	1a	132
Doherty	Rose	Frederick Street	5	137
Doherty	Sarah	Chamberlain Street	32	126
Doherty	Sarah	Kennedy Street	18	142
Doherty	Sarah	Lecky Road	131	143
Doherty	Sarah	Philips Street	32	151
Doherty	Susan	New Street	10	126
Doherty	Susan	St. Columb's Wells	110	157
Doherty	Thomas	Abbey Street	32	117
Doherty	Thomas	Beechwood Avenue	2	121
Doherty	Thomas	Caroline Place	9	126
Doherty	Thomas	Stanley's Walk	15	155
Doherty	Vincent	Great James Street	50	139
Doherty	Vincent	Spencer Road	116	175
Doherty	W. J.	Castle Street	10	126
Doherty	William	Adair Street	3	118
Doherty	William	Sunbeam Terrace	8	122
Doherty	William	Bishop Street	130	123
Doherty	William	Bishop Street	134	123
Doherty	William	Caroline Place	17	126
Doherty	William	Corbett Street (Pilot's Row)	16	128
Doherty	William	Eglinton Place	8	132
Doherty	William	Fahan Street	49	133
Doherty	William	Glenbrook Terrace	4	137
Doherty	William	Great James Street	72	139
Doherty	William	Hawthorn Terrace	5	140
Doherty	William	Meave's Row	199	143
Doherty	William	Ann Street	29	144
Doherty	William	Lecky Road	88	144
Doherty	William	Long Tower	64	146
Doherty	William	Strand Road	14	156
Doherty	William	St. Columb's Wells	39	157
Doherty	William	St. Columb's Wells	75	157
Doherty	William	St. Columb's Wells	48	157
Doherty	William	St. Patrick Street	14	158
Doherty	William	Union Street	25	158
Doherty	William	Wapping Lane	9	159
Doherty	William	Artisan Street	12	162
Doherty	William	Ashfield Terrace	41	162
Doherty	William	Creggan Road	48	163
Doherty	William & Sons	Foyle Street	64, 66	136
Doherty & Co.		Butcher Street	4	125

Surname	First Name	Street	House Number	Page Number
Doherty Bros.		Ebrington Terrace	6	170
Dolan	Mary	York Street	1	176
Dolan	Mrs	Strand Road Lower	163	156
Doland	Thomas	Dungiven Road	33	169
Domnitz	Isaac	Fountain Street	27	134
Donaghey	Annie	Donegal Street	27	163
Donaghey	Bernard	Artisan Street	8	162
Donaghey	Edward	St. Patrick Street	1	158
Donaghey	Francis	Wellington Street	47	160
Donaghey	H. & Co.	Water Street	2	160
Donaghey	Hugh	Emerson Street	30	170
Donaghey	Hyland	Melrose Terrace	17	173
Donaghey	J.	Waterloo Place	9	160
Donaghey	James	Creggan Road	115	162
Donaghey	James	Emerson Street	21	170
Donaghey	John	Argyle Terrace	11	120
Donaghey	John	Ivy Terrace	37	142
Donaghey	John	Moore Street	7	173
Donaghey	Joseph	Dungiven Road	69	170
Donaghey	Joseph S.	Dunfield Terrace	35	169
Donaghey	Michael	Dungiven Road	41	169
Donaghey	Mrs	Barry Street	28	121
Donaghey	Mrs	Cedar Street	8	126
Donaghey	Mrs	Fountain Hill	61	171
Donaghey	Patrick	Alexandra Place	21	119
Donaghey	Patrick	Bishop Street	204	123
Donaghey	Philip	Foyle Street	57	135
Donaghey	Samuel	Emerson Street	10	170
Donaghey	Willaim	Mitchelburne Terrace	81	136
Donaghey	William	Violet Street Lower	5	176
Donaghy	James	Violet Street Lower	36	176
Donaghy	John R.	Ewing Street	21	132
Donaghy	Patrick	Northland Terrace	1	150
Donaghy	Patrick	Fountain Hill	96E	171
Donaghy	Robert	Duke Street	52	169
Donaghy	Rose Ann	Hollywell Row	75	143
Donaghy	Thomas	Duke Street	27	169
Donaghy	William	Moore Street	15	173
Donald	Samuel	Messines Park	7	128
Donaldson	A. & S.	Carlisle Road	28	125
Donaldson	Alfred	Northland Avenue	17	150
Donaldson	David	Bennett Street Lower	55	122
Donaldson	Henry	Beechwood Avenue	70	121
Donaldson	Henry	Shipquay Street	32	154
Donaldson	John	Beechwood Avenue	60	121
Donaldson	Mrs	Sunbeam Terrace	13	122
Donaldson	Mrs	Hawkin Street	30	140
Donaldson	Robert	Garden City		129
Donaldson	William G.	Aubrey Street	2A	120
Donaldson	William G.	Aubrey Street	2	120

Surname	First Name	Street	House Number	Page Number
Donnell	Charles	Aubrey Street	10	120
Donnell	Charles	Nicholson Terrace	14	149
Donnell	Charles	Pine Street	9	174
Donnell	J.	Shipquay Place	Guildhall (Accountant)	154
Donnell	John	Elmwood Terrace	26	132
Donnell	John C.	Duncreggan Road	8, Millerfield	131
Donnell	Marshall	Caw	Owenmore	167
Donnell	Miss	Nicholson Terrace	10	149
Donnell	Mrs	Argyle Terrace	27	120
Donnell	Mrs	Crawford Square	5	128
Donnell	William J.	Crawford Square	7	128
Donnell	H. A.	Claremont Street	1	127
Donnell	James	Clarence Avenue	1	127
Donnell	James & Son	Castle Street	2	126
Donnell	S. & W. J.	Castle Street	2	126
Donnell	Thomas	Cable Street	1	125
Donnell	William	Henry Street	18	141
Donnell	John	Glendermott Road	70	171
Donnelly	Agnes	Glendermott Road	8B	171
Donnelly	Annie	St. Columb's Terrace	91	143
Donnelly	Francis	Ivy Terrace	35	142
Donnelly	James	Aberfoyle Terrace	7	156
Donnelly	Joseph	Gortfoyle Place	2	171
Donnelly	Margaret	High Street	6	141
Donnelly	Michael	Sloan's Terrace	18	155
Donnelly	Miss	Bishop Street	118	123
Donnelly	Miss Mary A.	Henrietta Street	17	141
Donnelly	Mrs	Clarence Avenue	6	127
Donnelly	Mrs	Wells Street Terrace	3	160
Donnelly	Mrs	Melrose Terrace	21, Ebrington post office	173
Donnelly	Mrs M.	John Street	13	142
Donnelly	Mrs M.	John Street	2	142
Donnelly	Mrs M.	Foyle Road	1	136
Donnelly	Patrick	John Street	25	142
Donnelly	Patrick	Sloan's Terrace	14	155
Donnelly	Patrick	Glendermott Road	56	171
Donnelly	Samuel	Bishop Street	255	123
Donnelly	William J.	Lecky Road	78	144
Donohoe	Mrs Jane	Miller Street	19	147
Donohue	Catherine	Wellington Street	11	160
Donohue	Thomas	Wellington Street	7	160
Donoughue	James F.	Brook Street	2	125
Donovan	Michael	Messines Park	1	128
Doogan	Annie	St. Columb's Street	4	157
Dooley	Edward	Lecky Road	102	144
Dooley	Robert	Wells Street Terrace	2	160
Doran	Daniel	Fountain Hill	5	171
Doran	Francis	Fountain Hill	11	171

Surname	First Name	Street	House Number	Page Number
Doran	Mrs	Spencer Road	65	174
Doran	Mrs Ellen	Fountain Hill	19	171
Doran	Patrick	Orchard Row	18	150
Doran	Rose	Harvey Street	8	140
Doran	Thomas	Linenhall Street Lower	27	145
Dorian	John	Artisan Street	16	162
Dorrian	Arthur	Argyle Terrace	14	120
Dorrian	James	St. Columb's Terrace	93	143
Dorrian	Maurice	Abercorn Road	43	118
Dorrian	Maurice	Strand Road	13	155
Dorrian	Maurice	Victoria Road	3	176
Dorrian	Mrs	Stanley's Walk	10	155
Dougan	Thomas	Nailor's Row	20	148
Dougan	William	Great James Street	25	139
Dougherty	Alfred	Argyle Terrace	39	120
Dougherty	Henry	East Wall	5	131
Dougherty	James	Bishop Street	103	122
Dougherty	James	Fountain Place	15	135
Dougherty	James	Lower Road	8	146
Dougherty	Sarah	Park Avenue	2	151
Douglas	Henry	Duke Street	100	169
Douglas	James	Creggan Road	125	162
Douglas	James	Carlin Street	6	167
Douglas	John C.	Simpson's Brae	3	174
Douglas	Minnie	Ebrington Street	21	170
Douglas	Mrs	Spencer Road	133	175
Douglas	Mrs L.	Cedar Street	11	126
Douglas	Thomas	Fountain Place	14	135
Douglas	William	Nicholson Square	11	149
Douglas	William	Ernest Street	9	163
Dowding	Edward F.	Alfred Street	18	165
Dowds	George	Foyle View	7	137
Dowds	S.	Deanfield	12, Lincombe	168
Dowds	Samuel Ltd	Waterloo Place	21	160
Dowds	William	Marlborough Terrace	24	147
Downes	James	Wesley Street	11	165
Downes	William	Stewart's Terrace	15	155
Downey	George	Ewing Street	24	133
Downey	John	Lecky Road	7	143
Downey	John	Orchard Row	28	150
Downey	Margaret J. A.	Orchard Row	8	150
Downey	Mary	Mountjoy Street	26	148
Downey	Miss	Elmwood Terrace	14	132
Downey	Mrs	Rossville Street	41	153
Downey	Rose A.	Nelson Street	5	149
Downey	Thomas	Creggan Street	51	129
Downs	John	King Street	52	172
Doyle	Fred	Donegal Street	33	163
Doyle	George	Bridge Street	64	125

Surname	First Name	Street	House Number	Page Number
Doyle	Patrick	Donegal Street	30	163
Duddy	Alexander	Hayesbank Terrace	47	167
Duddy	Bernard	Cranagh Terrace	1	142
Duddy	Charles	Fahan Street	116	133
Duddy	Daniel	Caroline Place	15	126
Duddy	Henry	York Street	11	176
Duddy	Isaac	Foyle Street	45, 47	135
Duddy	James	Mill Street	28	173
Duddy	John	Fahan Street	126	133
Duddy	John	Fountain Place	7½	135
Duddy	Joseph	Mountain Street	24	173
Duddy	Matilda	Mill Street	24	173
Duddy	Michael	Hamilton Street	45	140
Duddy	Mrs	Fahan Street	104	133
Duddy	Mrs	King Street	25	172
Duddy	Patrick	Northland Avenue	4	150
Duddy	Patrick	Thomas Street	11	158
Duddy	Patrick	King Street	8	172
Duddy	Robert	High Street	10	141
Duddy	Robert	Orchard Street	10	151
Duddy	Samuel	Alfred Street	32	165
Duddy	Sarah	Corbett Street (Pilot's Row)	14	128
Duddy	Thomas	Eglinton Place	13	132
Duddy	William	Eglinton Place	5	132
Duddy	William	Thomas Street	16	158
Duddy	William	Alfred Street	38	165
Duddy	William	Benvarden Avenue	2	166
Duff	Alexander	Moore Street	30	173
Duff	Alexander	Spencer Road	119	174
Duff	Joseph	Robert Street	22	174
Duff	Robert	Moore Street	11	173
Duff	Robert	Spencer Road	64	175
Duff	Sarah J.	Spencer Road	64	175
Duffy	Andrew	Spencer Road	123	174
Duffy	Ann	Cottage Row	32	164
Duffy	Annie	Governor Road	1	138
Duffy	Annie	Lecky Road	13	143
Duffy	Bernard	William Street	73	161
Duffy	Con	Little Diamond	2	145
Duffy	Edward	Joseph Street	8	142
Duffy	George	Lecky Road	23	143
Duffy	Hugh	Bluebellhill Terrace	164	144
Duffy	Hugh	Union Street	9	158
Duffy	J. P.	Beechwood Street	8	121
Duffy	James	Bishop Street	67	122
Duffy	James	Creggan Street	39	129
Duffy	James	High Street	16	141
Duffy	James	Philips Street	19	151
Duffy	John	Bishop Street	226	123

Surname	First Name	Street	House Number	Page Number
Duffy	John	Brandywell Road	10	124
Duffy	John	Foyle View	3	137
Duffy	John F.	Argyle Street	31	119
Duffy	John H.	Union Street	26	159
Duffy	Joseph	Corbett Street (Pilot's Row)	17	128
Duffy	Margaret	Cable Street	19	125
Duffy	Margaret	Thomas Street	27	158
Duffy	Mary E.	Lecky Road	123	143
Duffy	Michael	Bishop Street	260	124
Duffy	Michael	Brook Street	3	125
Duffy	Miss	Foyle Street	107	135
Duffy	Miss	Foyle Road	34	136
Duffy	Mrs	Elmwood Terrace	47	132
Duffy	Mrs	Marlborough Avenue	19	147
Duffy	Mrs	Nassau Street Upper	25	149
Duffy	Mrs B. T.	Strand Road	141	156
Duffy	Patrick	Argyle Street	36	119
Duffy	Patrick	St. Columb's Wells	88	157
Duffy	Patrick	Wellington Street	24	160
Duffy	Sergeant	Lecky Road	R.U.C. Barracks	144
Duffy	Thomas	Ferguson Street	12	134
Duffy	Thomas	Walker's Place	11	159
Duffy	William	Fitters Row	265	123
Duffy	William	Caroline Place	11	126
Duffy	William	Ewing Street	20	133
Duffy	William	Foyle Street	55	135
Duffy	William	Howard Street	10	141
Duffy	William	Kerr's Terrace	9	162
Dufy	Ellen	Violet Street Lower	10	176
Dugan	M. J.	Bishop Street	49	122
Dugan	Mrs	Carrigans Lane	13	126
Duggan	Bernard	Nicholson Square	2	149
Duggan	Mary A.	Laburnum Terrace	22	142
Dunbar	Hugh	Cooke Street	13	128
Duncan	A.	Foyle Street	13	135
Duncan	Archibald	Clooney Terrace	28	168
Duncan	James	Lewis Street	10	164
Duncan	Miss	St. Joseph's Avenue	5	158
Duncan	Moses	Creggan		131
Duncan	Moses	Kennedy Street	3	142
Duncan	Mrs	Westland Avenue	33	160
Duncan	Thomas	Albert Place	6	119
Duncan	Thomas	Bellevue Avenue	31	121
Duncan	Thomas	Marlborough Street	31	146
Duncan	William	Miller Street	13	147
Duncan	William	Ebrington Gardens		166
Dunleavy	Anthony	Rossville Street	54	153
Dunleavy	Robert	Abercorn Terrace	1	118

Surname	First Name	Street	House Number	Page Number
Dunleavy	Samuel	Princes Street	23	152
Dunleavy	Samuel G.	Creggan		131
Dunlevy	Samuel	Alfred Street	12	165
Dunlevy	Samuel	Spencer Road	forge	175
Dunlop	Andrew	Cooke Street	11	128
Dunlop	Cassie	Fountain Street	33	134
Dunlop	David	Violet Street Lower	41	176
Dunlop	Frank	Orchard Street	2	151
Dunlop	James	Carrigans Lane	24	126
Dunlop	James	Fountain Hill	56	171
Dunlop	Joseph	Creggan Terrace	10	129
Dunlop	Mrs	Lewis Street	14	164
Dunlop	Nenian	Clarendon Street	45	127
Dunlop	Samuel	King Street	24	172
Dunn	John	Sugarhouse lane	11	158
Dunn	Mrs	Brandywell Road	30	124
Dunn	Mrs	Ferguson Street	37	133
Dunn	Robert	Cuthbert Street	29	168
Dunne	Henry	Foster's Terrace	165	143
Dunne	John J.	Ivy Terrace	2	142
Dunne	William	Victoria Terrace	9	120
Dunne	William	Orchard Row	9	150
Dunniece	Charles	Park Avenue	14	151
Dunniece	Edward Hugh	Long Tower	62	146
Dunniece	Hugh	Bennett Street Lower	28	122
Dunniece	Mrs	Princes Street	6	152
Dunnion	Jeannie	Riverview Terrace	4	174
Dunseath	James	Dark Lane	12	130
Dunseath	John	Albert Place	7	119
Durey	R. J.	Bishop Street	92	123
Durnian	Jane	Bishop Street	150	123
Durnian	Julia	Little James Street	9	145
Durnian	Mrs P.	Cranagh Terrace	2	142
Durnion	Edward	Waterloo Street	1	159
Dykes	Sergeant J.	Hawkin Street	12	140
Eadie	I. A.	Lawrence Hill	10, Hillcrest	143
Eagar	J. F.	Shipquay Street	12, Hibernian Bank	154
Eagar	J. F.	Hinton Park	3	172
Eagleson	John	Melrose Terrace	11	173
Eakin	John	Fairman Place	18	133
Earley	Charlie	Little James Street	1	145
Early	Henry	Deanery Street	12	130
Eason	John	Queen Street	Presbyterian Church House	153
Eason & Son		Foyle Street	51B	135
Eaton	Albert E.	Spencer Road	127	175
Eaton	Alexander	Stewart's Terrace	12	155
Eaton	J. Charles	Limavady Road	14, Everest	173
Eaton	John	Limavady Road	18	173

Surname	First Name	Street	House Number	Page Number
Eaton	Thomas	Argyle Terrace	8	120
Eaton	Albert E.	Dungiven Road	67	170
Eaton & Co. Ltd		Duke Street	2, 4	169
Edgar	Hugh A.	Northland Avenue	16	150
Edgar	James	Gordon Place	7	138
Edgar	John	Gordon Place	6	138
Edgar	John	Maple Street	5	173
Edgar	John	Termon Street	3	175
Edgar	Samuel	Windmill Terrace	16	162
Edmiston	Dr Ruth	Crawford Square	8	129
Edmiston	J. J.	Maybrook House, Shantallow		128
Edmiston	Wallace	Crawford Square	8	129
Edmiston & Co.		Shipquay Street	35-37	154
Edwards	Henry G.	Nicholson Terrace	4	149
Edwards	James	Eden Place	17	132
Edwards	Joseph	Tyrconnell Street	21	158
Edwards	Mrs	Clarendon Street	5	127
Edwards	Mrs	Lawrence Hill	3	143
Edwards	Mrs	Bond's Street	40	166
Edwards	Rev. T.	Limavady Road	39, Beech Grove	172
Edwards	Robert J. R.	East Wall	2	131
Edwards	Thomas	Corbett Street (Pilot's Row)	7	128
Edwards	William	Aubrey Street	16	120
Edwards	William	Ivy Terrace	19	142
Elder	John	William Street	30	161
Elder	Matilda	Clarendon Street	37	127
Elder	Miss	Brooke Villas	37	164
Elder	Robert	Duke Street	21	169
Elder	William	Nailor's Row	19	148
Elliot	R. T.	Collon Terrace	Ivy Cottage	128
Elliott	Annie	Aubrey Street	6	120
Elliott	Hugh	Duke Street	56	169
Elliott	James	Ferguson Street	34	134
Elliott	James	Grafton Street	7	138
Elliott	James	Ernest Street	4	163
Elliott	James	Lewis Street	8	164
Elliott	Lawrence	Fountain Hill	25, forge	171
Elliott	Margaret	Irish Street	21	172
Elliott	Mary	Friel's Terrace	4	148
Elliott	Mary	Orchard Lane	3	151
Elliott	Mary	Spencer Road	33	174
Elliott	Mrs	College Terrace	11	128
Elliott	P. H.	Magazine Street	21	146
Elliott	Patrick H.	Queen Street	3	153
Elliott	Rebecca	Bridge Street		124
Elliott	Robert C.	Palace Street		151
Elliott	Thomas	Bishop Street	56	123

Surname	First Name	Street	House Number	Page Number
Elliott	Thomas	Lewis Street	27	164
Elliott	William	Henry Street	20	141
Ellis	Miss	Marlborough Street	32	147
Ellis	Philip	Baronet Street	8	120
Ellis	Philip	Glasgow Terrace	38	138
Ellis	Samuel	Clooney Terrace	45	167
Elvin	Matilda	Chapel Road	48	167
Elvin	Mrs	Argyle Terrace	28	120
Emerson	Miss	Great James Street	65	139
Emery	Andrew & Son	Carlisle Road	11	125
Emery	William N.	Bishop Street	65	122
English	Charles	The Rock	119	156
English	John G.	Marlborough Street	5	146
Epstein	J.	Richmond Street	13	153
Ervine	William	Eglinton Place	6	132
Evans	James	St. Columb's Wells	57	157
Evans	Maurice	Lecky Road	30	144
Evans	William	Lone Moor	Lodge Foyle Hill Hospital	145
Fahy	William	Caroline Place	13	126
Fairlamb	William A.	Chapel Road	18	167
Fairman	Mrs	Waterloo Street	43	159
Fairweather	George	Cuthbert Street	22	168
Falconer	Robert	Garden City		129
Falkoner	Miss E.	Victoria Place	1	159
Faller	Miss T.	Strand Road	12	156
Faller	William	Orchard Street	11	151
Faller	William	Strand Road	12	156
Faller	William	Clifton Street	3	167
Faller	William junior	Duke Street	20	169
Fallon	Head-Constable	College Terrace	13	128
Fanning	J. Russell	Beechwood Avenue	52	121
Fanning	Mrs Mary	Long Tower	21	145
Fanning	P.	Strand Road Lower	157	156
Fanning	Richard	Long Tower	19	145
Fanning & Rice		Foyle Street	25	135
Farley	Professor W. J.	College Avenue	7	150
Farley	Samuel	Florence Street	2	170
Farran	Julia	Westland Avenue	32	161
Farrell	Christopher	Beechwood Avenue	66	121
Farrell	Margaret	Elmwood Terrace	5	132
Farren	Edward	Glasgow Street	5	138
Farren	Ellen	Bluebellhill Terrace	204	144
Farren	John	Mitchelburne Terrace	94	136
Farren	John	Hamilton Street	4	140
Farren	John	Hamilton Street	34	140
Farren	John	Mary Street	10	147
Farren	Mary	Frederick Street	12	137
Farren	Michael	Bishop Street	43	122
Farren	Michael	Bluebellhill Terrace	180	144

Surname	First Name	Street	House Number	Page Number
Farren	Michael	Long Tower	58	146
Farren	Michael	Wells Street Terrace	5	160
Farren	Mrs	High Street	1	141
Farren	Mrs	Walker's Place	29	159
Farren	Mrs	Florence Street	27	170
Farren	Thomas	Cottage Row	5	123
Farren	Thomas	Walker's Street	3	176
Farren	Very Rev. Neal	Sunbeam Terrace	St. Columb's College	122
Farroll	John	Charlotte Crescent	3	155
Faughnan	Thomas	Glendermott Road	13	171
Faulkener	James	Dervock Street	6	168
Faulkiner	James	Bond's Street	8	166
Faulkiner	Miss	Bridge Street	34	124
Faulkiner	Mrs	Violet Street Lower	18	176
Faulkner	Rev. George	Victoria Place	Parochial House	159
Faulkner	Robert	Princes Street	17	152
Faulkner	Robert	Violet Street Lower	22	176
Faulkner	Thomas	Strand Road	125	156
Faulkner	William	Dungiven Road	73	170
Fee	Margaret	Abercorn Road	14	118
Fee	William J. D.	Bishop Street	36	123
Feely	Conbstable J.	Westland Terrace	13	161
Feeney	Denis	Friel's Terrace	7	148
Feeney	James	Violet Street Lower	9	176
Feeney	Mrs	Limavady Road	2, St. Columb's	172
Feeney	Mrs S.	Nailor's Row	10	148
Feeney	William	Harvey Street	5	140
Feeny	Luke	Abercorn Road	40	118
Feeny	M. C.	Castle Street	6	126
Feeny	William	Eden Place	20	132
Feery	Mrs	Governor Road	42	138
Ferguson	Catherine	Nelson Street	60	149
Ferguson	Elizabeth	Baronet Street	2	120
Ferguson	F. N.	Abercorn Road	56	118
Ferguson	Herbert	Shipquay Street	12A	154
Ferguson	Herbert	William Street	39, City Dispensary	161
Ferguson	J.	Fountain Street	70½	135
Ferguson	J.	Dunfield Terrace	37, Bridgeview	169
Ferguson	James	Hollywell Street	4	141
Ferguson	James	Cross Street	25	168
Ferguson	John	Sunbeam Terrace	18	122
Ferguson	John	Nelson Street	58	149
Ferguson	Joseph	Wapping Lane	1	159
Ferguson	Maggie	Brandywell Avenue	7	124
Ferguson	Mary	Argyle Street	16	119
Ferguson	Matilda J.	Dunfield Terrace	23	169
Ferguson	Miss	Aubrey Street	26	120

Surname	First Name	Street	House Number	Page Number
Ferguson	Mrs	Sunnyside Terrace	3	123
Ferguson	Mrs	Fountain Street	2	134
Ferguson	Mrs	Caw		167
Ferguson	Noble	Albert Place	1	119
Ferguson	Robert	Argyle Street	22	119
Ferguson	Rose	Foyle Road	103	136
Ferguson	William	Fountain Street	82	135
Ferrier	James	Mountjoy Street	16	148
Ferris	Andrew	Lower Road	31	146
Ferris	James	Wapping Lane	23	159
Ferris	John	Dark Lane	16	130
Ferris	Joseph	Cooke Street	2	128
Ferris	Rebecca	Bennett Street Upper	23	122
Ferris	Robert	Lower Road	26	146
Ferris	Samuel	Albert Street	30	118
Ferris	William	Hawthorn Terrace	40	140
Ferry	Daniel	Nassau Street Lower	18	148
Ferry	James	Nassau Street Lower	52	148
Ferry	James	Pennyburn	5	151
Ferry	John	Mitchelburne Terrace	95	136
Ferry	Mrs	Foster's Terrace	159	143
Ferry	Samuel	Donegal Street	14	163
Fielding	George	Fountain Street	116	135
Fields	Robert	Carlisle Road	4th Presbyterian Church	126
Findlay	G. P.	Boating Club Lane	1	157
Findlay	Henry	Creggan Road	26	163
Findlay	James	Meadowbank Avenue	27	147
Findlay	Robert	Marlborough Road	3	147
Finlay	Alex	Bentley Street	10	165
Finlay	Edward	Spencer Road	70	175
Finlay	John	Aubrey Street	15	120
Finlay	John	Moore Street	4	173
Finlay	Robert	Linenhall Street Upper	17	145
Finlay	Robert J.	Northland Villas	2	120
Finlay	Robert J.	Strand Road	123	156
Finlay	Thomas	Kennedy Street	17	142
Finlay	William	Argyle Street	34	119
Finlay	William	Argyle Street	40	119
Finlay	William A.	Bentley Street	6	165
Finlay	Ernest	Duke Street	16	169
Finlay	John	Cochrane's Row	5	169
Finlay Bros		Chapel Road	13	167
Finlay Bros.		Carlisle Road	32	125
Finn	Mary	Lecky Road	121	143
Finn	Peter	Florence Street	12	170
Finn	Annie	Nailor's Row	34	148
Finnemore	Joseph	Mountjoy Street	20	148

Surname	First Name	Street	House Number	Page Number
Fiorentian Bros.		Strand Road	31	155
Fisher	Denis	Orchard Row	15	150
Fisher	Jack	North Street	41	164
Fisher	Joseph	Bishop Street	182	123
Fisher	Michael L.	West-End Park	16	161
Fisher	Mrs	Bridge Street	20	124
Fisher	Patrick	Sloan's Terrace	24	155
Fisher Bros		Prince Arthur Street	forge	152
Fitzgerald	Edward	Iona Terrace	21	172
Fitzpatrick	John S.	West-End Park	8	161
Fitzpatrick	Mrs	Edenmore Street	22	131
Fitzpatrick	Mrs	Dungiven Road	51	170
Fitzsimmons	Mrs	Ann Street	7	119
Flanagan	Bernard	Great James Street	5	139
Flanagan	Bernard	Rosemount Avenue	25	164
Flanagan	John	Argyle Street	73	119
Flanagan	John	Kildarra Terrace	9	141
Flanagan	Lizzie	Henry Street	2	141
Flanagan	Mrs	Bennett Street Upper	3	121
Flanagan	Mrs	Charlotte Street	9	127
Flannagan	Daniel	Foyle Road	119	136
Flannery	John	De Burgh Square	5	130
Flannigan	James	Clooney Terrace	13	167
Fleming	George	Spencer Road	52	175
Fleming	John R.	Princes Terrace	3	152
Fleming	Joseph	Lower Road	14	146
Fleming	Marian	Marlborough Street	43	146
Fleming	Miss F.	Gordon Terrace	9	138
Fleming	Percy	Ernest Street	15	163
Fleming	William	Moore Street	9	148
Fleming	William	Cuthbert Street	2	168
Fleming	William A.	Spencer Road	105	174
Fleming	William J.	Rossville Street	83	153
Fleming & Co.		Strand Road	37	155
Fletcher	A.	Victoria Park	15, gate lodge	176
Fletcher	Daniel	Lawrence Hill	8, Strandmore	143
Fletcher	Daniel	Quay Queen's	Public Health Office	152
Fletcher	Henry J.	Harding Street	19	140
Fletcher	Mrs	Benvarden Avenue	47	166
Flood	Anthony	Fahan Street	100	133
Flood	James	Long Tower	36	146
Florintine	S.	Strand Road	87, Avoca	156
Floyd	R. R. A.	Pump Street	7	152
Flynn	Francis	Abercorn Road	53	118
Flynn	James	Marlborough Avenue	15	147
Flynn	Mary Jane	Osborne Street	23	164
Flynn	Mrs	Abercorn Road	11	118
Flynn	Thomas	Brandywell Avenue	5	124
Flynn	Thomas	Park Avenue	7	151

Surname	First Name	Street	House Number	Page Number
Foley	Michael	Northland Avenue	10	150
Forbes	James A.	Fairman Place	19	133
Forbes	Samuel	Bond's Hill	21	166
Forde	Morris	Ernest Street	6	163
Forde	Robert	Edenmore Street	31	131
Forester	John	Grove Place	10	139
Forrester	John	Strand Road	33	155
Forster	Miss laura	Deanfield	7	168
Forster	William	Richmond Street	7	153
Forsythe	John	Marlborough Terrace	8	147
Forsythe	Miss	Asylum Road	5	120
Forsythe	Miss	Bond's Street	51	166
Forsythe	Mrs E.	Sunbeam Terrace	7	122
Forsythe	Robert	Meadowbank Avenue	31	147
Foster	James	Sugarhouse lane	5	158
Foster	James W.	Bishop Street	11	122
Foster	John H.	Shipquay Place	1	154
Foster	John H.	Strand Road	5	155
Foster	Mrs	Richmond Street	9	153
Foster	William	Richmond Street	4	153
Foster	William	Florence Street	2	163
Fox	Bridget	Rossville Street	4	153
Fox	Bridget	William Street	48	161
Fox	John	Deanery Street	20	130
Foy	Susan	Rossville Street	74 & 76	153
Francis	James	Bishop Street	133	122
Francis	John	Patrick Street	2	151
Frankland	John T.	Marlborough Street	33	146
Fraser	Mrs	Charlotte Street	5	127
Frazer	Alfred E. A.	Beechwood Avenue	26, Homefield	121
Frazer	Charles	Robert Street	24	174
Frazer	David	Edenballymore	3	131
Frazer	David	Major's Row	5	146
Frazer	John	Wapping Lane	31	159
Frazer	Rev. James W. S.	Lawrence Hill	14, The Manse	143
Frazer, Mitchell & Co.		Castle Street	2	126
Fredlander	M.	Strand Road Lower	153	156
Frew	A.	Ferryquay Gate	2	134
Friel	Agnes	Ebrington Street	7	170
Friel	Annie	Abbey Street	20	117
Friel	Bella	Fahan Street	144	133
Friel	Bernard	Nelson Street	50	149
Friel	Bernard	Waterloo Street	39	159
Friel	Bridget	Nelson Street	3	149
Friel	Bridget	Stanley's Walk	16	155
Friel	Charles	Foyle Street	29	135
Friel	Daniel	Abercorn Road	9	118
Friel	Daniel	Abercorn Road	42	118

Surname	First Name	Street	House Number	Page Number
Friel	Edward	Clooney Terrace	53	167
Friel	Edward	Duke Street	102	169
Friel	Francis	Ann Street	5	143
Friel	Henry	Edward Street	forge	132
Friel	Hugh	Howard Street	5	141
Friel	James	Nelson Street	49	149
Friel	James	Rossville Street	65	153
Friel	James	Society Street	4	155
Friel	James	Stanley's Walk	30	155
Friel	James	Union Street	5	158
Friel	James	Lewis Street	26	164
Friel	John	Abbey Street	37	117
Friel	John	Abbey Street	39	117
Friel	John	Orchard Street	21	151
Friel	John	Fountain Hill	21	171
Friel	John	Iona Terrace	25	172
Friel	John P.	Rossville Street	14	153
Friel	Joseph	Fahan Street	50	133
Friel	Justin	Fahan Street	154	133
Friel	Manasses	Thomas Street	36	158
Friel	Margaret	Orchard Street	5	151
Friel	Michael	Abbey Street	22	117
Friel	Michael	Duke Street	48	169
Friel	Mrs	Limewood Street	17	144
Friel	Mrs	Waterloo Street	18	159
Friel	Mrs Mary	Lone Moor		145
Friel	Mrs Mary A.	Fulton Place	11	137
Friel	Owen	Waterloo Street	3	159
Friel	Patrick	Hollywell Row	71	143
Friel	Philip	Limewood Street	19	144
Friel	Thomas	Wesley Street	18	165
Friel	William	Fahan Street	97	133
Friel	Daniel	Bennett Street Upper	25	122
Friel	John	Bridge Street	39	124
Friel	Maria	Bishop Street	42	123
Friel	Mrs	Chamberlain Street	12	126
Friel	William	Caroline Place	1	126
Frieslander	Isaac	Barrack Street	15	120
Frieslander	Isaac	Corporation Street	27	128
Frieslander	William	Grove Place	5	139
Frizell	W. A.	Woodleigh Terrace	3	120
Frizzell	Constable J. R.	Creggan Road	81	162
Fry	James	Alfred Street	29	165
Fullerton	Captain D.	Melrose Terrace	13	173
Fullerton	James	Wellington Street	29	160
Fulton	Andrew	Duke Street	67	169
Fulton	J. A,	Deanfield	3	168
Fulton	Joseph senior	St. Columb's Wells	60	157
Fulton	Matthew	Wapping Lane	51	159
Fulton	Mrs	Fountain Street	92A	135

Surname	First Name	Street	House Number	Page Number
Fulton	Mrs	Kennedy Street	13	142
Fulton	Mrs	Florence Street	23	163
Fulton	Robert	Messines Park	9	128
Fulton	Thomas	Edenmore Street	34	132
Fulton	W.	Brooke Villas	29, Lismore	164
Fulton	W. J.	Duke Street	53	169
Fulton	William D.	Glendermott Road	60	171
Funston	Alex	Baronet Street	7	120
Funston	Mrs	Hawkin Street	25	140
Furey	John	Dungiven Road	47	169
Gaff	Robert	Creggan		131
Gaff & McRitchie		Waterloo Place	1	160
Gailey	Miss	Waterloo Place	17	160
Galbraith	Fitzgerald F.	Bond's Hill	15	166
Galbraith	J.	Magazine Street	9	146
Galbraith	John	Benvarden Avenue	35	166
Galbraith	Joseph	Gordon Terrace	12	138
Galbraith	Mrs	Beechwood Avenue	48	121
Galbraith	Nurse	Princes Terrace	9	152
Galbraith	Robert	George Street	16	138
Galbraith	Thomas	Abercorn Road	42	118
Galbraith	Thomas	Great James Street	21	139
Gallagher	Alex	Bentley Street	9	165
Gallagher	Annie	Brandywell Road	1	124
Gallagher	Annie	Friel's Terrace	9	148
Gallagher	Bridget	Rossville Street	81	153
Gallagher	Charles	Foyle Road	72	136
Gallagher	Charles	Grafton Street	15	138
Gallagher	Charles	Hamilton Street	52	140
Gallagher	Charles	Cottage Row	14	164
Gallagher	Charles	The Rock	101	156
Gallagher	Daniel	Barry Street	37	121
Gallagher	Daniel	Carrigans Lane	9	126
Gallagher	Daniel	Elmwood Street	7	132
Gallagher	Daniel	Lecky Road	64	144
Gallagher	Daniel	St. Columb's Wells	120	158
Gallagher	Dominick	Deanery Street	30	130
Gallagher	Dominick	St. Columb's Wells	80	157
Gallagher	Edward	St. Columb's Terrace	99	143
Gallagher	Edward	Ann Street	25	144
Gallagher	Edward	St. Columb's Wells	76	157
Gallagher	Edward	Artisan Street	3	162
Gallagher	Elizabeth	Eglinton Place	16	132
Gallagher	George	Epworth Street	19	163
Gallagher	Henry	Foster's Terrace	185	143
Gallagher	Henry	St. Columb's Wells	104	157
Gallagher	Hugh	Bishop Street	129	122
Gallagher	Hugh	Clarendon Street	39	127
Gallagher	Hugh	Meave's Row	191	143

Surname	First Name	Street	House Number	Page Number
Gallagher	Hugh	Lundy's Lane	3	145
Gallagher	Hugh	Pennyburn	6	151
Gallagher	Isabel	Fountain Hill	40	171
Gallagher	James	Argyle Terrace	1	120
Gallagher	James	Blucher Street	18	124
Gallagher	James	Deanery Place	4	130
Gallagher	James	Edenmore Street	23	131
Gallagher	James	Sloan's Terrace	1	154
Gallagher	James	Sloan's Terrace	38	155
Gallagher	James	Westland Terrace	9	161
Gallagher	James	North Street	31	164
Gallagher	James & Sons	Strand Road	90	157
Gallagher	John	Aubrey Street	22	120
Gallagher	John	Bishop Street	296	124
Gallagher	John	Brandywell Avenue	8	124
Gallagher	John	Creggan Street	41	129
Gallagher	John	Fahan Street	57	133
Gallagher	John	Glenbrook Terrace	9	137
Gallagher	John	Hamilton Street	33	140
Gallagher	John	Bluebellhill Terrace	134	144
Gallagher	John	Sloan's Terrace	15	154
Gallagher	John	Ernest Street	7	163
Gallagher	John	North Street	21	164
Gallagher	John	Park Villas	63	165
Gallagher	John	Fountain Hill	118	171
Gallagher	John E.	West-End Park	20	161
Gallagher	Joseph	Fahan Street	61	133
Gallagher	Joseph	Quarry Street	10	153
Gallagher	Joseph	Westland Avenue	24	160
Gallagher	Joseph	William Street	66	162
Gallagher	Joseph	Creggan Road	103	162
Gallagher	Josephine	Ann Street	1	143
Gallagher	Josephine	Northland Terrace	5	150
Gallagher	Margaret	Foyle Road	106	136
Gallagher	Margaret	Nassau Street Lower	16	148
Gallagher	Margaret	St. Columb's Wells	77	157
Gallagher	Margaret	St. Columb's Wells	82	157
Gallagher	Mary	Bishop Street	131	122
Gallagher	Matilda	Bellevue Avenue	23	121
Gallagher	Michael	Bishop Street	284	124
Gallagher	Michael	Butcher Street	7	125
Gallagher	Miss	Friel's Terrace	6	148
Gallagher	Molly	Grafton Street	6	139
Gallagher	Mrs	Bishop Street	282	124
Gallagher	Mrs	Carlisle Road	75	125
Gallagher	Mrs	Carrigans Lane	7	126
Gallagher	Mrs	New Street	8	126
Gallagher	Mrs	Corporation Street	19	128
Gallagher	Mrs	Fountain Street	96	135
Gallagher	Mrs	Fountain Street	104	135

Surname	First Name	Street	House Number	Page Number
Gallagher	Mrs	Foyle View	8	137
Gallagher	Mrs	Hamilton Street	20	140
Gallagher	Mrs	Miller Street	10	147
Gallagher	Mrs	Herbert Street	13	172
Gallagher	Mrs	Foyle Road	79A	136
Gallagher	Mrs J.	Foster's Terrace	183	143
Gallagher	Patrick	Messines Park	41	128
Gallagher	Patrick	Stewart's Close	2	146
Gallagher	Patrick	Strand Road	56	156
Gallagher	Peter	Argyle Street	39	119
Gallagher	Philip	Wellington Street	75	160
Gallagher	Richard	Francis Street	15	137
Gallagher	Robert	Fountain Street	59	134
Gallagher	Robert	Fountain Street	100, 102	135
Gallagher	Rose	Nelson Street	56	149
Gallagher	Samuel	Fountain Street	86	135
Gallagher	Sarah	Beechwood Street	11	121
Gallagher	Sarah	Frederick Street	11	137
Gallagher	Sarah	Lecky Road	257	143
Gallagher	T.	Quay Queen's	office	152
Gallagher	Thomas	York Street	3	176
Gallagher	Violet	Stewart's Terrace	7	155
Gallagher	William	Chamberlain Street	16	126
Gallagher	William	Fountain Street	49	134
Gallagher	William	Fountain Street	81	134
Gallagher	William	Foyle Terrace	118	136
Gallagher	William	Glenbrook Terrace	16	137
Gallagher	William	Glasgow Terrace	17	138
Gallagher	William	Ivy Terrace	23	142
Gallagher	William	Laburnum Terrace	10	142
Gallagher	William	Orchard Row	31	150
Gallagher	William	Sackville Street	9	154
Gallagher	William	Tyrconnell Street	23	158
Gallagher	William	Wellington Street	59	160
Gallagher	William	Donegal Street	21	163
Gallagher	William	Lewis Street	17	164
Gallagher	William	Bond's Place	11	166
Gallagher	William	Herbert Street	17	172
Gallagher	William G.	Fahan Street	132	133
Gallagher	William J.	Wellington Street	28	160
Gallagher	Winifred	Long Tower	76	146
Gallen	Miss	Butcher Street	2	125
Gallick	Robert	Collon Terrace		128
Gallick	William	Culmore Road	Brookhall Cottage	129
Gallivan	Daniel	Barrack Street		120
Gallivan	Daniel	Bishop Street	107	122
Gallivan	Daniel	Glendermott Road	11	171
Gallon	Elizabeth	Marlborough Terrace	10	147
Galloway	George P.	Marlborough Terrace	19	147

Surname	First Name	Street	House Number	Page Number
Gamble	Alex	Butcher Street	9A	125
Gamble	Constable	Benvarden Avenue	42	166
Gamble	Jane	Ebrington Street Lower	2	170
Gamble	John	Ann Street	3	119
Gamble	John	Hamilton Street	24	140
Gamble	Mary	Abbey Street	51	117
Gamble	Miss M.	Richmond Crescent	2	153
Gamble	Samuel T.	Chamberlain Street	34	126
Gamble	Thomas	Messines Park	26	128
Gamble	W. C.	Duke Street		169
Gamble	William G.	Dungiven Road	63	170
Gamble	Wilson	College Terrace	6	128
Gannon	Edward	Howard Street	25	141
Gardiner	Gilbert	Infirmary Road	gate house	142
Gardiner	Joseph	Bennett Street Lower	35	122
Gardiner	Thomas	Benvarden Avenue	59	166
Gardiner	William	Messines Park	30	128
Gardiner	William	Glasgow Terrace	31	138
Garmany	William	Clooney Terrace	9	167
Garnham	Charles	McLaughlin's Close	5	134
Garvan	Henry	Charlotte Crescent	1	155
Gasser	Joseph	Bennett Street Upper	21	122
Gavigan	Hugh	King Street	22	172
Gavigan	Thomas	Ferguson Street	51	134
Gavin	Patrick	Riverview Terrace	2	174
Gawley	Isabella Victoria	Infirmary Road	Infirmary	142
Gay	George	Butcher Street	3	125
Gaylor	Peter	Strand Road	124	157
Gerraghty	J. C.	Custom House Street	General Post Office	129
Getty	James	Caw	Lisnagowan	167
Gibbons	Charles	Castle Gate	4	126
Gibbons	Charles	Waterloo Street	26	159
Gibbons	James	Fountain Street	108	135
Gibbons	Martha	Fahan Street	156	133
Gibbons	Mrs	Bishop Street	51	122
Gibbons	Samuel	Chapel Road	23	167
Gibson	Daniel	Emerson Street	29	170
Gibson	John	Fahan Street	1	133
Gibson	John	Miller Street	28	148
Gibson	Joseph	Hinton Park	11	172
Gibson	Miss	Union Street	19	158
Gibson	Susan	Windsor Terrace	6	162
Gibson	William	Edenmore Street	19	131
Gibson	William	Emerson Street	5	170
Gibson	William	Emerson Street	18	170
Giffen	Miss	Diamond	12	130
Gilbert	James	Laburnum Terrace	9	142
Gilbey	W. & A.	Shipquay Street	26	154

Surname	First Name	Street	House Number	Page Number
Gilchrist	James	Glenbrook Terrace	2	137
Gilchrist	Joseph	Dark Lane	3	129
Gilchrist	Thomas J.	Woodleigh Terrace	4	120
Gildea	John	Spencer Road	142	175
Gilfillan	George	Ernest Street	12	163
Gilfillan	J. A,	Bond's Hill	20	166
Gilfillan	J. A.	Foyle Street	45, 47	135
Gilfillan	James	Aubrey Street	28	120
Gilfillan	Miss	Foyle View	9	137
Gilfillan	Mrs	Collon Terrace	16	128
Gilfillan	William	Marlborough Street	9	146
Gill	Edward	Violet Street Lower	25	176
Gill	John	Linenhall Street Lower	33	145
Gillan	William	Bridge Street	53	124
Gillanders	James	Nicholson Square	24	149
Gillen	Charles	Caroline Place	21	126
Gillen	Edward	Ferguson Street	54	134
Gillen	Hugh	Union Street	13	158
Gillen	James	William Street	21	161
Gillen	John	Harvey Street	12	140
Gillen	Mary A.	Caroline Place	19	126
Gillen	Michael	Abbey Street	34	117
Gillen	Mrs	Primrose Street	14	174
Gillen	Patrick	Bishop Street	98	123
Gillen	Patrick	Cable Street	7	125
Gillespie	Arthur	Rosemount Avenue	7	164
Gillespie	Daniel	Elmwood Terrace	45	132
Gillespie	Daniel	Rosemount Avenue	7	164
Gillespie	Edward	Deanery Street	32	130
Gillespie	Hugh	Bridge Street	14	124
Gillespie	James	Academy Terrace	6	118
Gillespie	James	Long Tower	16	145
Gillespie	James	Marlborough Terrace	5	147
Gillespie	John	Hogg's Folly	11	141
Gillespie	John	Brooke Villas	33	164
Gillespie	Mrs	Carrigans Lane	10	126
Gillespie	Mrs	Orchard Row	27	150
Gillespie	Robert	Donegal Place	3	130
Gillespie	Robert H.	Laburnum Terrace	12	142
Gillespie	Stephen	Lecky Road	107	143
Gillespie	Thomas	Ashfield Terrace	47	162
Gillespie	Thomas	Fountain Hill	33	171
Gillespie	William	Mitchelburne Terrace	96	136
Gillespie	William	Fox's Lane	6	137
Gillespie	William	Foyleview Terrace	16	156
Gillian	Michael	Cuthbert Street	17	168
Gillies	J. B.	Clarendon Street	23	127
Gilliland	David	Barry Street	22	121
Gilliland	Frank	Culmore Road	Brookhall	129

Surname	First Name	Street	House Number	Page Number
Gilliland	John	Argyle Terrace	33	120
Gilliland	Miss	Limavady Road	7, Friarsfield	172
Gilliland	Mrs	Cuthbert Street	27	168
Gilliland	Mrs R. K.	Strand Road	130	157
Gilliland	R. K.	Culmore Road	Ardcaen	129
Gilliland	S. & Sons	Quay Queen's		152
Gilliland	S. & Sons Ltd.	Strand Road	126	157
Gilloway	George	Clooney Terrace	55	167
Gilmartin	James	Bishop Street	109	122
Gilmour	Bryce	Hawkin Street	18	140
Gilmour	James	Aubrey Street	20	120
Gilmour	Miss	Spencer Road	150	175
Gilmour	Mrs	Clarendon Street	3	127
Gilroy	John	Bishop Street	154	123
Gilvarrie	Margaret	Fahan Street	85	133
Gilvary	Owen	Philips Street	35	151
Ginn	William	Derry View Terrace	1	168
Given	Alex	Nelson Street	27	149
Given	J. M.	Deanfield	14, Laurelvale	168
Given	John	Marlborough Avenue	35	147
Given	Thomas	Long Tower	30	146
Givin	James	Glenbrook Terrace	20	137
Glacken	Letitia	Wesley Street	16	165
Glackin	Patrick	Carrigans Lane	21	126
Glass	D.	Orchard Street	24	151
Glass	David	Spencer Road	129	175
Glass	James	Carlisle Road	63-65	125
Glass	Joseph	Glen Terrace	2	131
Glass	Mrs	Nicholson Square	20	149
Glass	William	King Street	38	172
Glendinning	Arthur E.	Grafton Street	12	139
Glendinning	J. C.	Crawford Square	11	129
Glendinning	James	Clarendon Street	14	127
Glendinning	James	Ewing Street	22	133
Glendinning	James	Waterloo Place	12	160
Glenn	Charles	Lecky Road	135	143
Glenn	John	Glasgow Terrace	37	138
Glenn	John	Lecky Road	119	143
Glenn	John	St. Joseph's Avenue	3	158
Glenn	John	Emerson Street	19	170
Glenn	Joseph A.	Violet Street Lower	1	176
Glenn	Mrs	Windsor Terrace	5	162
Glenn	Mrs	Bond's Street	17	166
Glenn	Patrick	Union Street	16	158
Glenn	Richard	Albert Place	18	119
Glenn	Robert	Fountain Street	57	134
Glenn	Robert	Orchard Street	25A	151
Glenn	Robert	Dervock Street	9	168
Glenn	Thomas	Dungiven Road	35	169
Glenn	William	Creggan Road	22	163

Surname	First Name	Street	House Number	Page Number
Glenn	William	Bond's Hill	14	166
Glenn	William	Dungiven Road	43	169
Glenn	David	Herbert Street	12	172
Glover	Ellen	Bridge Street	52	125
Gobb	Joseph	Ernest Street	18	163
Godfrey	Alex	Emerson Street	20	170
Godfrey	Edward	Corporation Street	11	128
Godfrey	James	Violet Street Lower	50	176
Golden	W. J.	Chamberlain Street	28	126
Golden	William J.	Chamberlain Street	14	126
Goligher	A. T.	Ebrington Terrace	8	170
Goligher	J. H.	Templemore Park	3	158
Goligher	James	London Street	14	145
Goligher	Matthew	Gordon Terrace	5	138
Goligher	Matthew	Society Street	11	155
Goligher	Mrs	Mrs C. F. Alexander's Memorial Cottages	5	126
Goligher	Mrs	Clarendon Street	20	127
Gomez	Francis	Glenbrook Terrace	26	137
Good	Robert P.	Victoria Road	5	176
Goodman	A. S.	Collon Terrace	15	128
Goodman	Alban	Collon Terrace	19	128
Goodman	Wesley	Collon Terrace	6	128
Goorwitch	N.	Strand Road	29	155
Gordon	C. W.	Alexandra Terrace	42	150
Gordon	E.	New Market Street	7, 8	149
Gordon	Ephraim	Sunbeam Terrace	12	122
Gordon	Ernest	Creggan		131
Gordon	George	Clooney Terrace	1	167
Gordon	Mary Jane	Glendermott Road	2	171
Gordon	R. D.	Lawrence Hill	22, Kona Vista	143
Gordon	Sarah	Friel's Terrace	8	148
Gordon	Thomas & Son	Diamond	12	130
Gordon	William	Alexandra Place	20	119
Gordon	William C.	Chapel Road	58	167
Gordon	William C.	Iona Terrace	17	172
Gordons Ltd		Carlisle Road	2, 4, 6	125
Gorman	Catherine	John Street	27	142
Gorman	Elizabeth	Simpson's Brae	6	174
Gorman	James	Glasgow Street	1	138
Gorman	Sam	Margaret Street	13	173
Gorman	William	Barnewall Place	12	165
Gormley	Daniel	St. Patrick Street	2	158
Gormley	Edward	Strabane Old Road	18	175
Gormley	John	Carrigans Lane	1	126
Gormley	John	Carlin Street	4	167
Gormley	Joseph	Sloan's Terrace	16	155
Gormley	Miss	Harvey Street	15	140
Goss	Herbert	Cochrane's Row	2	169
Goss	Patrick	William Street	115	161

Surname	First Name	Street	House Number	Page Number
Goudie	Agnes	Foyle Road	71	136
Goulding	W. & H. M.	Foyle Street	16	135
Gourlay	William	Glendermott Road	24	171
Gourley	Alex	Meehan's Row	21	173
Gourley	John	Irish Street	4	172
Gourley	William	Hamilton Street	37	140
Gourley	William J.	Alfred Street	39	165
Gover	Daniel	Henry Street	2	141
Graham	Alex	Claremont Villas	30	150
Graham	Alexander	Strand Road	39	155
Graham	Daniel	Fahan Street	14	133
Graham	David	Little James Street	3	145
Graham	David	Fountain Hill	86	171
Graham	George	Bond's Hill	17	166
Graham	James	Mountjoy Terrace	4	118
Graham	John	Aubrey Street	11	120
Graham	John	Maybrook House, Shantallow	gate lodge	128
Graham	John	Spencer Road	120	175
Graham	Mrs	Mrs C. F. Alexander's Memorial Cottages	6	126
Graham	Peter	Limewood Street	8	144
Graham	Robert	Spencer Road	134	175
Graham	Samuel	Albert Place	13	119
Graham	Sarah	Foyle View	2	137
Graham	Thomas	Chapel Road	22	167
Gransden	Miss E.	Crawford Square	23	129
Gransden	S. H.	Pump Street	3	152
Grant	A. B. & Sons	Park Villas		165
Grant	Con	Meave's Row	187	143
Grant	Edward	Foyle Street	105	135
Grant	Margaret	Eglinton Place	23	132
Grant	Miss L.	Tyrconnell Street	15	158
Grant	Mrs	Victoria Place	3	159
Grant	Patrick	Ferguson Street		133
Grant	John	Sunbeam Terrace	15	122
Grant	Patrick	Bishop Street	140	123
Grant	Patrick	Chamberlain Street	20	126
Grant	William	Bishop Street	106	123
Grant	William & Co.	Bishop Street	104	123
Grant Brothers		Barrack Street	17	120
Gray	Ernest J.	Richmond Crescent	1	153
Gray	Fanny	Benvarden Avenue	27	165
Gray	John	Benvarden Avenue	33	166
Gray	Joseph	Edenballymore		131
Gray	Joseph	Glasgow Street	4	138
Gray	Robert	Glenbrook Terrace	3	137
Gray	Robert	Alexandra Terrace	46	150
Gray	Robert	Lewis Street	6	164
Gray	William	New Street	12	128

Surname	First Name	Street	House Number	Page Number
Greaney	J. E.	Barry Street	10	121
Greaves	Thomas	Spencer Road	32	175
Green	Charles	Bishop Street	178	123
Green	James	Fahan Street	118	133
Green	James	William Street	84	162
Green	John	Fahan Street	122	133
Green	John	Thomas Street	13	158
Green	Mrs L.	Creggan Street	21	129
Green	P.	Northland Avenue		150
Green	Patrick	Rossville Street		153
Green	Patrick	St. Columb's Wells	59	157
Green	Patrick	William Street	48	161
Green	Peter	Fahan Street	32	133
Green	Rebecca	Nelson Street	42	149
Green	Patrick	Fahan Street	125	133
Greenway	Henry	Edenmore Street	4	131
Greepe	Harold	Beechwood Avenue	56	121
Greer	George	Strand Road	34	156
Greer	James	Iona Terrace	19	172
Greer	Margaret	Henry Street	12	141
Greer	Rev. J. C.	Edenbank	58	150
Greer	Robert	Fountain Street	11	134
Greer	Stewart	Woodleigh Terrace	1	120
Greer	William	Cedar Street	7	126
Gregg	A. U.	Browning Drive	13	166
Gregg	J. A. U.	Foyle Street	10	135
Gregson	Robert H.	West-End Park	7	161
Greives	Miss	Foyle Road	30	136
Grenaway	Mrs Annie	North Street	35	164
Grennell	A. P. J.	Castle Street		126
Grennell	A. P. J.	Shipquay Street	12, Hibernian Bank	154
Grieve	John	Alexander Terrace	1	174
Grieve	Thomas	Violet Street Lower	43	176
Grieves	Mrs	Clifton Street	8	167
Griffeths	Jane	Primrose Street	27	174
Griffin	Miss	Great James Street	75	139
Griffin	Peter	Gallagher's Square	9	137
Griffin	Peter	William Street	117	161
Griffin	Sergeant A.	Bishop Street	127	122
Griffin	Rose	Rossville Street	34	153
Griffins	Thomas	Quarry Street	15	153
Griffith	John	Chapel Road	28	167
Griffith	Mrs	Donegal Place	1	130
Griffiths	James	Beechwood Avenue	10	121
Griffiths	James	St. Columb's Wells	109	157
Griffs	Henry E.	Clooney Terrace	57	167
Grimes	Hannah	Dervock Place	6	168
Grimes	William B.	Benvarden Avenue	23	165
Grumley	Mrs	Elmwood Terrace	39	132

Surname	First Name	Street	House Number	Page Number
Gunns	Hannah	Stanley's Walk	46	155
Gurney	Hugh	Blee's Lane		124
Gurney	Hugh	Charlotte Street	7	127
Gurney	Hugh	Charlotte Street	18	127
Gurney	Hugh	Glen Terrace	8	131
Gurney	Hugh	Nassau Street Upper	13	149
Gurney	Hugh	Creggan Road	18	163
Gurney	Hugh	Lewis Street	1	164
Gurney	Isaac	Park Avenue	9	151
Gurney	James	Cottage Row	20	164
Gurney	John	London Street	20	145
Gurney	Mary	Creggan Road	143	162
Gurney	William	Lower Road	3	146
Guthrie	Edward	Stanley's Walk	13	155
Guthrie	Thomas	Duncreggan Road	9	131
Guthrie	William	Alma Terrace	42	136
Guy	Andrew	Aubrey Street	19	120
Gwyn & Young		Strand Road	10	156
Hackett	Annie	Cottage Row	28	164
Hagan	Bernard	St. Columb's Wells	89	157
Hagan	George	Florence Street	20	164
Hagan	James	Donegal Street	9	163
Hagan	John	Foyleview Terrace	5	156
Hagan	John	Osborne Street	19	164
Hagan	Joseph	Long Tower	38	146
Hagan	Miss	Fox's Lane	1	137
Hagan	Mrs	Edenmore Street	18	131
Haire	Albert	Benvarden Avenue	1	165
Haire	Edward	Glen Cottages	1	131
Haire	Samuel	King Street	50	172
Haire	Samuel	Melrose Terrace	16	173
Haire	Thomas	St. Mary's Terrace	35	167
Halferty	Edward	Alexandra Place	26	119
Halferty	Miss	Long Tower	81	145
Hall	Alex	Melrose Terrace	14	173
Hall	J. B. & Co.	Great James Street	2, 3	139
Hall	James B.	Asylum Road	7	120
Hall	Miss	Asylum Road	6	120
Hamill	James	Long Tower	46	146
Hamill	James	Windmill Terrace	18	162
Hamill	Michael	Linenhall Street Upper	13	145
Hamill	Mrs	Ferguson Street	24	134
Hamill	Robert	Bellevue Avenue	2	121
Hamill	Robert	Ferguson Street	28	134
Hamill	Trafford	Fountain Place	6	135
Hamilton	Alexander	New Street	10	128
Hamilton	Andrew	Victoria Park	9	176
Hamilton	Charles	Albert Place	14	119
Hamilton	Charles	Creggan Road	75	162

Surname	First Name	Street	House Number	Page Number
Hamilton	David	Henry Street	16	141
Hamilton	Elizabeth J.	Mountain Street	1	173
Hamilton	Ellen	Violet Street Upper	19	176
Hamilton	Ernest	Great James Street	43	139
Hamilton	G. J.	Castle Street	3	126
Hamilton	George	Eglinton Place	17	132
Hamilton	Henry S. & Co.	Foyle Street	32	136
Hamilton	Hugh	Violet Street Upper	17	176
Hamilton	J. & Sons	John Street	44, 46, 50	142
Hamilton	J. A.	Waterloo Place	1	160
Hamilton	J. A.	Marlborough Street	71, Westcote	146
Hamilton	James	Aberfoyle Crescent	5	118
Hamilton	James	Albert Street	19	118
Hamilton	James	Alexandra Place	14	119
Hamilton	James	Bennett Street Lower	51	122
Hamilton	James	Blee's Lane		124
Hamilton	James	Charlotte Street	11	127
Hamilton	James	Fountain Street	77	134
Hamilton	James	Fountain Street	76	135
Hamilton	James	Lecky Road	123	143
Hamilton	James	Lawrence Hill	15, Ferndale	143
Hamilton	John	Lawrence Hill	6	143
Hamilton	Joseph	Wellington Street	12	160
Hamilton	Matthew	William Street	111	161
Hamilton	Miss	Clarence Avenue	2	127
Hamilton	Miss	Fountain Street	92	135
Hamilton	Mrs	Bellevue Avenue	26	121
Hamilton	Mrs	Marlborough Avenue	28	147
Hamilton	Mrs	Caw	Bayview House	167
Hamilton	Mrs L.	Rossville Street	75	153
Hamilton	R. E.	Culmore Road	Hillmount	129
Hamilton	Robert	Henry Street	15	141
Hamilton	Robert	Cuthbert Street	9	168
Hamilton	S.	Culmore Road	Fairymount	129
Hamilton	S. A.	Spencer Road	87	174
Hamilton	Thomas	Abercorn Road	13	118
Hamilton	Thomas	Beechwood Avenue	7	121
Hamilton	Thomas	Bishop Street	86	123
Hamilton	Thomas	Wapping Lane	41	159
Hamilton	William	Frederick Street	2	137
Hamilton	William	Great James Street	53	139
Hamilton	William	Lawrence Hill	4, Inglenook	143
Hamilton	William	Ernest Street	24	163
Hamilton	William & Co.	William Street	43	161
Hamilton	William A.	Melrose Terrace	4	173
Hamilton & Semple		Spencer Road	40	175
Hampsey	Bernard	Bluebellhill Terrace	140	144
Hampsey	William	Spencer Road	67	174
Hampsey	James	Dunfield Terrace	29	169

Surname	First Name	Street	House Number	Page Number
Hampsey & Co.		Duke Street	8	169
Hampton	John	Fountain Street	75	134
Hands	John	St. Joseph's Avenue	1	158
Hanna	Ernest	Victoria Street	3	159
Hanna	James L.	Ivy Terrace	26	142
Hanna	John L.	John Street		142
Hanna	John W.	Glen Cottages	4	131
Hanna	Robert	Philips Street	20	151
Hanna	David	Argyle Street	30	119
Hannaway	Francis	Stanley's Terrace	4	145
Hannaway	James	Brandywell Road	22	124
Hannaway	Joseph	Long Tower	77	145
Hannaway	William	Brandywell Road	11	124
Hannigan	David	Adam Street	5	118
Hannigan	Edward	Bishop Street	240	124
Hannigan	Michael	Duddy's Row	2	169
Hannigan	Mrs	New Row	2	156
Hannigan	Thomas	Harding Street	35	140
Hannigan	Thomas	Violet Street Upper	10	176
Hannigan	William	Cochrane's Row	7	169
Hannon	Mrs	Elmwood Terrace	24	132
Hannon	Mrs	Union Street	22	159
Hants	Mrs	High Street	2	141
Harding	Isabel	Abbey Street	36	117
Hargan	Robert	Chapel Road	4	167
Harkin	Bernard	Donegal Street	41	163
Harkin	Catherine	Bishop Street	143	122
Harkin	Charles	Violet Street Lower	42	176
Harkin	Cornelius	Fahan Street	87	133
Harkin	Daniel	Barry Street	4	121
Harkin	Daniel	Wellington Street	26	160
Harkin	F. J.	Shipquay Street	24	154
Harkin	Francis J.	Bayview Terrace	3	120
Harkin	Hugh	New Street	4	128
Harkin	J.	Waterloo Street	59	159
Harkin	James	Argyle Street	8	119
Harkin	James	Bishop Street	113	122
Harkin	James	Hollywell Street	9	141
Harkin	James	Limewood Street	28	144
Harkin	James	Northland Avenue	9	150
Harkin	James	Thomas Street	12	158
Harkin	James	Donegal Street	35	163
Harkin	James	Cottage Row	38	164
Harkin	Joe	Nailor's Row	45	148
Harkin	John	Barry Street	9	120
Harkin	John	Creggan Terrace	3	129
Harkin	John	Francis Street	13	137
Harkin	John	Rossville Street	25	153
Harkin	John	St. Columb's Wells	97	157
Harkin	Michael	Farney Terrace	1	164

Surname	First Name	Street	House Number	Page Number
Harkin	Miss	Lecky Road	76	144
Harkin	Misses	Chapel Road	2	167
Harkin	Mrs	Joseph Street	10	142
Harkin	Mrs	Stanley's Walk	9	155
Harkin	Patrick	Bishop Street	90	123
Harkin	Patrick	Eden Place	18	132
Harkin	Patrick	Lecky Road	stores	143
Harkin	Patrick	Sir E. Reid's Market	4	154
Harkin	Patrick	Stanley's Walk	6	155
Harkin	Patrick	Tyrconnell Street	29	158
Harkin	Patrick	Lewis Street	30	164
Harkin	Thomas	North Edward Street	9	149
Harkin	William	Lecky Road	51	143
Harkin	William	Sloan's Terrace	22	155
Harkins	Hugh	Ernest Street	22	163
Harkins	Mrs	Waterloo Street	45	159
Harley	Bernard	New Street	5	164
Harley	Denis P.	Glendermott Road	8A	171
Harley	John	Foyle Road	76	136
Harley	John	Grove Place	3	139
Harley	Mrs	Creggan Road	89	162
Harley	Robert	Garden City		129
Harper	Hugh	Bond's Street	23	166
Harper	James Ltd	Duke Street	37	169
Harper	John	Limavady Road	17	172
Harper	Robert J.	Alexandra Place	19	119
Harper	Samuel	Foyle Road	36	136
Harper	W. J.	Ferguson Street	10	134
Harper	William	Nailor's Row	36	148
Harper & Petticrew		Waterloo Place	1	160
Harries	Ernest G.	Bishop Street	3	122
Harrigan	James	Beechwood Street	16	121
Harrigan	James	St. Patrick Street	4	158
Harrigan	John	Alma Place	7	119
Harrigan	John	Infirmary Road		142
Harrigan	Mark	St. Columb's Wells	51	157
Harrigan	Mrs	Sloan's Terrace	4	155
Harrigan	Patrick	Dungiven Road	24	170
Harrigan	William	Bishop Street	183	12
Harrion's Motor Mart		Foyle Street	22	136
Harris	John	Kerr's Terrace	25	162
Harris	Joseph	Fountain Place	26	135
Harris	William J.	North Edward Street	10	149
Harris	William J.	Strand Road	45	155
Harrison	David	Alexandra Place	13	119
Harrison	W. M.	Lower Road	27	146
Harrison	William	Spencer Road	26	175
Harrison & Co.		John Street	31, 33, 35	142

Surname	First Name	Street	House Number	Page Number
Harron	Catherine	Meehan's Row	11	173
Harron	George	Lower Road	29	146
Harron	James	Marlborough Avenue	37	147
Harron	Mrs	Meehan's Row	16	173
Hart	Lieutenant-Colonel G. V.	Culmore Road	Ballynagard	129
Harte	Constable T.	Elmwood Terrace	49	132
Harte	John	Windmill Terrace	19	162
Harte	Maggie	Waterloo Street	25	159
Harte	Mrs	Mount Street	12	164
Harte	Robert	Beechwood Street	26	121
Harte	Thomas	Ewing Street	8	132
Harte	William	Ewing Street	14	132
Harte	William	Foyle Road	57	136
Harten	Thomas	Rossville Street	33	153
Hartin	John	Henry Street	4	141
Hartin	William	George Street	7	138
Harvey	Daniel	Miller Street	12	147
Harvey	F. R.	Magazine Street	21	146
Harvey	Henry	Abercorn Road	22	118
Harvey	J. G. M.	Northland Road	66, Greglorne	150
Harvey	J. G. M. & Son	Custom House Street		129
Harvey	J. G. M. & Son	Shipquay Place	7	154
Harvey	John	Ewing Street	23	132
Harvey	Mrs	Ivy Terrace	24	142
Haslett	Alexander	Northland Road	15, Maplemount	150
Haslett	Mrs	Clooney Terrace	37	167
Haslett	Mrs	Maple Street	2	173
Haslett	Ralph	Duke Street	61	169
Haslett	Ralph	Violet Street Upper	27	176
Haslett	Thomas	Bishop Street	141	122
Haslett Bros.		Abercorn Road		118
Hassan	Daniel	Fox's Lane	8	137
Hassan	Isabel	Carrigans Lane	11	126
Hassen	Bridget	Creggan Terrace	16	129
Hassen	James	Bishop Street	179	122
Hasson	Bernard	Lecky Road	263	143
Hasson	Catherine	Walker's Place	49	159
Hasson	Daniel	Bridge Street	55	124
Hasson	Ellen	Moore Street	16	148
Hasson	George	Howard Street	26	141
Hasson	James	Tyrconnell Street	32	158
Hasson	Miss Jeannie	Bishop Street	69	122
Hasson	Patrick	Moore Street	10	148
Hasson	Samuel	Spencer Road	58	175
Hasson	Thomas	Bishop Street	270	124
Hasson	Thomas	Hogg's Folly	18	141
Hastings	J. R.	Caw	Seymour House	167

Surname	First Name	Street	House Number	Page Number
Hastings	J. R. & Co.	Foyle Street	63, 65, 67	135
Hastings	Mrs	Foyle Road	62	136
Hastings	Thomas	Mitchelburne Terrace	80	136
Haswell	Mrs	Primrose Street	12	174
Hatrick	Alex	Bond's Street	2	166
Hatrick	Joshua	Creggan		131
Haughey	Mrs	Asylum Road	3	120
Haughey	Robert	Barry Street	17	121
Hawkins	Frederick	Gordon Terrace	15	138
Hawthorne	John	Windmill Terrace	2	162
Hawthorne	Mrs M.	Abercorn Road	57	118
Hay	Moses	Hawkin Street		140
Hay	Philip	Edenmore Street	13	131
Hay	William	Spencer Road	85	174
Hayes	Joseph	Ernest Street	8	163
Hayes	W. J.	Spencer Road	68	175
Hayward	Joseph	Bond's Street	35	166
Hazlett	James	Foyle Road	73	136
Healy	Agnes	Pine Street	6	174
Healy	Catherine	Long Tower	48	146
Healy	James	Lecky Road	43	143
Healy	Patrick	Duncreggan Road	2	131
Healy	Patrick	Wellington Street	9	160
Healy	William	Barry Street	30	121
Heaney	Bernard	Margaret Street	11	173
Heaney	Bernard	Spencer Road	23	174
Heaney	David	Benvarden Avenue	25	165
Heaney	David	Tamneymore		175
Heaney	Denis	Benvarden Avenue	4	166
Heaney	John	Benvarden Avenue	18	166
Heaney	Margaret	Clooney Terrace	44	167
Heaney	Miss	Clooney Terrace	11	167
Heaney	Mrs	King Street	56	172
Heaney	Patrick	Governor Road	15	138
Heaney	W. J.	Mountjoy Terrace	2	118
Heaney	William J.	Moore Street	37	173
Heath	Mrs	Creggan Road	28	163
Heatley	George J.	Great James Street	28	139
Heatley	S.	Society Street	5	155
Heatley	Samuel	Fountain Street	107	134
Hedley	David	Glenview Avenue	28	137
Heeney	John	Miller Street	6	147
Hegarty	Charles	Brook Street Avenue	16	125
Hegarty	Charles	Eglinton Terrace	9	132
Hegarty	Charles	Marlborough Terrace	16	147
Hegarty	Daniel	Fahan Street	8	133
Hegarty	Edward	Alfred Street	35	165
Hegarty	Ellen	Nailor's Row	4	148
Hegarty	F. J.	Abercorn Road	25	118
Hegarty	George	Albert Street	18	118

Surname	First Name	Street	House Number	Page Number
Hegarty	George	Chapel Road	44	167
Hegarty	Hugh	McLaughlin's Close	1	134
Hegarty	Hugh	St. Columb's Wells	31	157
Hegarty	Hugh	Wellington Street	74	160
Hegarty	Hugh	William Street	73½	161
Hegarty	James	Lecky Road	122	144
Hegarty	James	Limewood Street	30	144
Hegarty	James	St. Columb's Wells	85	157
Hegarty	John	Eglinton Place	18	132
Hegarty	John	High Street	18	141
Hegarty	John	Walker's Place	41	159
Hegarty	John	Creggan Road	169	163
Hegarty	Joseph	Ebrington Street Lower	1A	170
Hegarty	Margaret	Long Tower	52	146
Hegarty	Mary	St. Columb's Terrace	81	143
Hegarty	Miss	Long Tower	68	146
Hegarty	Miss	Lower Road	37	146
Hegarty	Miss R.	Waterloo Street	36	159
Hegarty	Mrs	Waterloo Street	32	159
Hegarty	Mrs	Corbett Street (Pilot's Row)	1	128
Hegarty	Mrs D. M.	Carlisle Road	71	125
Hegarty	Mrs E.	Fahan Street	150	133
Hegarty	Patrick	Foyle Street	33	135
Hegarty	Patrick	Park Avenue	11	151
Hegarty	Patrick	Rossville Street	69	153
Hegarty	Patrick	Westland Avenue	3	160
Hegarty	Thomas	Harding Street	6	140
Hegarty	Thomas	Donegal Street	4	163
Hegarty	Thomas	Alfred Street	54	165
Hegarty	William	Adam Street	6	118
Hegarty	William	Lecky Road	92	144
Hegarty	William	Westland Avenue	2	160
Hegarty	William	William Street	20	161
Hegarty	William	Alfred Street	6	165
Hempton	James & Co.	Shipquay Street	13	154
Henderson	A. M.	Eden Terrace	2	131
Henderson	D. & Co.	Sackville Street	11	154
Henderson	J. T.	Spencer Road	91	174
Henderson	James	Clooney Terrace	8	167
Henderson	John	Clarendon Street	26	127
Henderson	John	Foyle Street	7	135
Henderson	John	Lecky Road	33	143
Henderson	John	Gortfoyle Place	8	171
Henderson	Patrick	Abbey Street	16	117
Henderson	Robert	Society Street	9	155
Henderson	S.	Foyle Street	111-113 Anchor Line	135
Henderson	Samuel	Great James Street	20	139

Surname	First Name	Street	House Number	Page Number
Henderson	Samuel	Moat Street	2	148
Henderson	W. C.	Demesne Terrace	1	130
Heney	Robert	Rossville Street	26	153
Henry	David	Ewing Street	34	133
Henry	Eliza	Diamond		130
Henry	Hamilton	Ewing Street	5	132
Henry	Hugh	Edenmore Street	29	131
Henry	John	Lower Road	2	146
Henry	John J.	Moore Street	5	173
Henry	Robert	Collon Terrace	4	128
Henry	Thomas	Nicholson Square	18	149
Henry	Thomas	Creggan Road	18, Ivy Cottage	163
Henry	William	Kennedy Street	20	142
Henry	William	Lower Road	4	146
Henry & Co.		Duke Street	96	169
Hepburn	William	Eden Terrace	16	131
Hepburn	William	Shipquay Street	8	154
Hepsley	W. H.	Beechwood Avenue	22	121
Herbert	James	Ferguson Street	1	133
Hernon	Neil	Bishop Street	97	122
Heron	Margaret K.	Ferguson Street	58	134
Heron	Mrs	Orchard Row		150
Herr	Louis	Butcher Street	1	125
Herr	Louis	Diamond	17	130
Herrirty	Patrick	Tyrconnell Street	26	158
Herron	Denis	William Street	91	161
Heslip	W. J.	Claremont Villas	34, Ardavon	150
Hetherington	Dr.	Lawrence Hill	13	143
Hetherington	J. J.	Clooney Terrace		167
Hetherington	J. J.	Dungiven Road	1, 3	169
Hetherington	J. J.	Spencer Road	168	175
Hickey	William	Laburnum Terrace	15	142
Higgins	David	Henry Street	8	141
Higgins	Edward	Wellington Street	52	160
Higgins	James	Florence Street	13	170
Higgins	John	Nelson Street	55	149
Higgins	Lizzie	Bishop Street	111	122
Higgins	Mary	Orchard Row	39	150
Higgins	P. F. & Sons	Foyle Street	45, 47	135
Higgins	Patrick	Fulton Place	9	137
Higgony	Miss L.	Waterloo Street	30	159
Hill	Arthur	Fountain Hill	84	171
Hill	Constable S. D.	Florence Street	11	163
Hill	Jack	Brooke View	51	165
Hill	Miss	Marlborough Street	22	147
Hill	Mrs	Mount Street	20	164
Hill	Sergeant H.	Academy Terrace	7	118
Hill	John James	Bayview Terrace		120
Hill & Co.		Spencer Road	27, 29	174
Hillen	Charles	Ann Street	10	119

Surname	First Name	Street	House Number	Page Number
Hillen	James	Nelson Street	4	149
Hillen	Sarah	Ann Street	16	119
Hilliard	Rev. G. C. B.	Diamond	10	130
Hinds	Walter	Carlin Street	9	166
Hines	Albert E.	Iona Terrace	23	172
Hipps Ltd		Strand Road	10	156
Hobbs	Mrs E. G.	Clarendon Street	42	127
Hogan	Edward	Stanley's Walk	44	155
Hogan	James	St. Patrick Street	8	158
Hogan	Laurence	Alma Terrace	40	136
Hogan	Laurence	Great James Street		139
Hogan	William	Howard Street	19	141
Hogg	John	Glasgow Street	6	138
Hogg	Robert	Mitchelburne Terrace	82	136
Hogg	Robert P.	Caw	Elstow	167
Hogg & Mitchell		Great James Street		139
Hogg & Mitchell		Little James Street		145
Hogg & Mitchell		Sackville Street	10, 12, 14	154
Holland	Mrs	Ivy Terrace	25	142
Holland	Thomas	Kennedy Street	2	142
Hollingsworth	Elizabeth	Fulton Place	13	137
Hollingsworth	Ellen	Dunfield Terrace	19	169
Hollingsworth	John	Spencer Road	98	175
Holloway	William	Orchard Row	22	150
Holman	William H.	Aberfoyle Terrace	19	156
Holmes	David	Cooke Street	14	128
Holmes	James	Barry Street	21	121
Holmes	John	Bishop Street	199	122
Holmes	John	Fountain Street	13	134
Holmes	John	Quarry Street	20	153
Holmes	Miss	Northland Road	31	150
Holmes	Miss H.	Clyde Street	1	153
Holmes	Miss K.	Glasgow Street	3	138
Holmes	Mrs	Primrose Street	31	174
Holmes	Mrs M.	King Street	17	172
Holmes	Robert	Charlotte Street	12	127
Holmes	Robert	Princes Street	19	152
Holmes	Robert	Ashfield Terrace	31	162
Holmes	Robert	New Street	12	164
Holmes	Samuel	Charlotte Place	6	127
Holmes	Samuel	Northland Terrace	10	150
Holmes	William	Abercorn Road	Gate Lodge	117
Holmes	William	Lower Road	6	146
Holmes	Mrs	Windmill Terrace	17	162
Holmes, Mullin & Dunn		Edward Street	store	132

Surname	First Name	Street	House Number	Page Number
Holmes, Mullin & Dunn		Quay Princes	store	152
Holmes, Mullin & Dunn		Waterloo Place	5	160
Holmes, Mullin & Dunn		William Street		161
Hone	John	Glendermott Road	102	171
Hone	Patrick	Union Street	16	176
Hone	Thomas	Cross Street	13	168
Hone	William	Dungiven Road	91	170
Hone	William	Riverview Terrace	12	174
Honeyford	Charles	Dungiven Road	29	169
Horner	Mrs Marian	Mountjoy Terrace	5	118
Hosey	Mrs Elizabeth	Dark Lane	21	130
Houston	Connell	Bishop Street	163	122
Houston	Daniel	Elmwood Street	16	132
Houston	David	Miller Street	30	148
Houston	James	Bishop Street	276	124
Houston	John	Alexandra Place	25	119
Houston	Joyce	Northland Avenue	1A	150
Houston	Mary	Elmwood Street	13	132
Houston	Miss	Ebrington Terrace	13	170
Houston	Mrs E.	Wapping Lane	35	159
Houston	Patrick	Alexandra Place	23	119
Houston	Patrick	Limewood Street	15	144
Houston	Robert	Clarence Avenue	17	127
Houston	Robert	Shipquay Street	36	154
Houston	Steven	Limewood Street	24	144
Howard	Denis	Strand Road Lower	147	156
Howard	William	Barnewall Place	6	165
Howatson	George & Co.	Foyle Street	72, 74	136
Howatson	George & Co.	Quay Abercorn	coal yard	152
Howatson	George & Co.	Duke Street	3	169
Howatson	James	Henry Street	19	141
Howatt	John	Great James Street	34	139
Howieson	Grace	Waterloo Street	41	159
Hudson	C. W.	Dungiven Road	gate lodge	170
Hudson	Joseph	Nassau Street Lower	13	148
Hueston	Head-Contable J.	Strand Road	Victoria Police Barracks	156
Huey	Alex	Gordon Terrace	10	138
Huey	William	De Burgh Square	9	130
Huey	William	Governor Road	36	138
Huffington	Albert	Garden City		129
Huffington	William	Miller Street	7	147
Huggins	John J.	Lecky Road		144
Hughes	Catherine	Lecky Road	19	143
Hughes	Edward	Orchard Street	St. Columb's Hall	151
Hughes	Edward	Farney Terrace	5	164

Surname	First Name	Street	House Number	Page Number
Hughes	Edward J.	Nicholson Square	14	149
Hughes	Edward J.	Orchard Street	29	151
Hughes	Fred	Albert Street	20	118
Hughes	Jack	Cochrane's Row	1	169
Hughes	John	Fountain Street	78	135
Hughes	John & Co.	Orchard Street	27	151
Hughes	Robert	Olive Terrace	2	173
Hughes	Samuel	Fountain Street	17	134
Hughes' Academy		Foyle Street	20	136
Hume & Co.		Sackville Street	6	154
Humes	John	Chamberlain Street	10	126
Humes	William	Westland Avenue	35	160
Humphrey	Richard R.	Marlborough Street	73, The Haven	146
Humphreys	Joseph	Mill Street	35	173
Hunt	Henry	Northland Road	82, Myrtle Villa	150
Hunter	Andrew	York Street	28	176
Hunter	Andrew G.	Barry Street	14	121
Hunter	Cunningham	Mary Street	12	147
Hunter	David	Edenmore Street	37	131
Hunter	Douglas	Victoria Street	18	159
Hunter	H.	Waterloo Place	3, 4, Ulster Bank	160
Hunter	Hugh	Northland Avenue	7	150
Hunter	James	Glasgow Terrace	14	138
Hunter	James	Alfred Street	23	165
Hunter	John	Fountain Street	95	134
Hunter	John	Moat Street	7	148
Hunter	Joseph	Hawkin Street	40	140
Hunter	Minnie	Lewis Street	29	164
Hunter	Miss S.	Ebrington Terrace	7	170
Hunter	Mrs	Albert Street	25	118
Hunter	Mrs	Bond's Hill	6	166
Hunter	Robert	Barnewall Place	11	165
Hunter	S. A.	Bishop Street	The Courthouse	123
Hunter	Sam	St. Columb's Court		157
Hunter	Samuel	Ferguson Street	35	133
Hurley	Joseph	Distillery Brae Upper	8	168
Hurst	Miss	Lawrence Hill	26	143
Hussey	William	MalvernTerrace	5	168
Huston	W. E.	Marlborough Street	18	147
Huston	W. E.	Quay Queen's		152
Hutchieson	James	Clooney Terrace	39	167
Hutchins	Frank	Barrack Street	10	120
Hutchinson	Daniel	Wapping Lane	29	159
Hutchinson	James	Spencer Road	73	174
Hutchinson	John	Spencer Road	75	174
Hutchinson	Mrs	Victoria Street	4	159

Surname	First Name	Street	House Number	Page Number
Hutchinson	T.	Messines Park	59	128
Hutchinson	William	Creggan Road	old basin	163
Hutchison	James	Lower Road	24	146
Hutchison	John	Henry Street	3	141
Hutchman	Alexander	Glasgow Terrace	21	138
Hutchman	Frederick	Glasgow Street	3	138
Hutchman	Robert J.	Albert Street	8	118
Hutton	Daniel	Nailor's Row	46	148
Hutton	Edward	Stanley's Walk	12	155
Hutton	Henry	Donegal Street	2	163
Hutton	John	Kildarra Terrace	7	141
Hutton	Julia	St. Columb's Wells	23	157
Hutton	Mrs	Abercorn Road	46	118
Hutton	Mrs	Foyle Road	46	136
Hutton	Mrs	Mountjoy Street	13	148
Hutton	Mrs	Donegal Street	39	163
Hutton	Patrick	East Wall	11	131
Hutton	Peter	Bishop Street	50	123
Hutton	Peter	Bishop Street	96	123
Hutton	Peter	New Market Street	5	149
Hutton	Thomas	Thomas Street	34	158
Huxley & Postlethwaite		Foyle Street	32	136
Hyland	Fred	Shipquay Street	6	154
Hyland	J. & F.	Clarendon Street Lower	4	127
Hyndman	Caldwell	Philips Street	30	151
Hyndman	Frederick E.	Windmill Terrace	31	162
Hyndman	James	Moat Street	1	148
Hyndman	John	Chapel Road	66	167
Hyndman	Mrs	Glen Cottages		131
Hyndman	R. J.	Fountain Place	9	135
Hyndman	Samuel	Ferryquay Street	22	134
Hyndman	Samuel	Linenhall Street Upper		144
Hyndman	W. E.	Epworth Street	20	163
Hyndman	William	Northland Road	23, Carrickmore House	150
Hyndman	William J.	Robert Street	12	174
Hyndman & Smith Ltd		Bank Place		120
Hynes	Joseph	King Street	6	172
Hynes	Miss	Windsor Terrace	4	162
Inglis & Co.		Magazine Street	7	146
Irons	William M.	Northland Road	62	150
Irvine	D. Ltd.	Waterloo Street	42	160
Irvine	D. S.	Mountroyal	3	150
Irvine	James	Fahan Street	70	133
Irvine	Robert	Cross Street	31	168

Surname	First Name	Street	House Number	Page Number
Irvine	Robert Henry	Creggan	Fern Cottage	131
Irvine	William	Clarence Avenue	9	127
Irvine & Co.	William	Foyle Street	62	136
Irvine & Co.		Ferryquay Street	24	134
Irvine & Co.		Ferryquay Street	28	134
Irvine & Co.		Linenhall Street Upper	4	145
Irwin	Alexander	Fountain Hill	34	171
Irwin	Annie	Rossville Street	68	153
Irwin	James	Princes Street	8	152
Irwin	John	Abercorn Road	29	118
Irwin	John	Great James Street	29	139
Irwin	John	Nelson Street	23	149
Irwin	John	Union Street	30	159
Irwin	John	Donegal Street	11	163
Irwin	Mrs	Foyle Road	60	136
Irwin	Patrick	Fahan Street	83	133
Irwin	Patrick	Patrick Street	11	151
Irwin	Patrick	Creggan Road	6	163
Irwin	R. B. W.	Aberfoyle Terrace	27	156
Irwin	Robert	Browning Drive	9	166
Irwin	Samuel	King Street	23	172
Irwin	William	High Street	3	141
Jack	Captain William H.	Eden Terrace	1	131
Jack	Samuel	Melrose Terrace	5	173
Jack	Stewart	Glasgow Street	1	138
Jack	Gilbert	Argyle Terrace	5	120
Jack	Robert A.	Beechwood Avenue	50	121
Jack	Mrs	Park Avenue	15	151
Jack	Samuel	Alfred Street		165
Jack	Samuel A.	Rosemount Terrace	12	165
Jack	William	Ernest Street	13	163
Jack	William	Brooke Villas	39	165
Jack	William H.	Browning Drive	19	166
Jackson	C.	Collon Terrace	Myrtle Cottage	128
Jackson	Daniel	Long Tower	82	146
Jackson	George	Fountain Street	50	134
Jackson	George	Stewart's Close	4	146
Jackson	George	Magazine Street	5	146
Jackson	J. & Son	Prince Arthur Street	stores	152
Jackson	James	Rossville Street	16	153
Jackson	John	Miller Street	34	148
Jackson	John & Son	Little James Street	8	145
Jackson	Joseph A.	Cooke Street	12	128
Jackson	Maggie	Howard Place	4	141
Jackson	Minnie	Claremont Street	4	127
Jackson	Mrs	Albert Street	38	119
Jackson	Mrs	Sloan's Terrace	7	154
Jackson	Mrs	William Street	50	161

Surname	First Name	Street	House Number	Page Number
Jackson	Patrick	Fahan Street	9	133
Jackson	Robert	Clarence Place	3	127
Jackson	Samuel J.	Nicholson Terrace	9	149
Jackson	William	Messines Park	12	128
Jackson	William	Nicholson Square	12	149
Jackson	William G.	St. Columb's Wells	102	157
Jackson's Ltd		Ferryquay Street	36	134
James	Thomas	Great James Street	56	139
Jamieson	D. A.	Spencer Road	9A	174
Jamieson	David A.	Spencer Road	83	174
Jamieson	John S.	New Street	11	128
Jamieson	Miss	Abercorn Place	12	118
Jamieson	Mrs	Olive Terrace	3	174
Jamieson	William	Bayview Terrace	6	120
Jamieson	William	Harding Street	16	140
Jamieson	William	Lewis Street	13	164
Jamieson	Mrs	Ewing Street	26	133
Jamieson	William & Co.	Corporation Street		128
Jamison	Wilhemina	Clooney Terrace	16	167
Jarvis	Thomas	Carlisle Road	52	126
Jarvis	Thomas	Clarence Place	2	127
Jeffares	Rev. William	Browning Drive	11	166
Jefferies	William	Primrose Street	4	174
Jefferson	Norman J.	Barry Street	2	121
Jefferson	Robert E.	Mitchelburne Terrace	99½	136
Jefferson	Robert J.	Gordon Terrace	13	138
Jeffreys	Miss	Fountain Street	48	134
Jenkins	Samuel	Strabane Old Road	19	175
Jennings	Mrs	Garden City		129
Jermany	Mrs M.	Nicholson Square	7	149
Jervis	Andrew	Tamneymore		175
Jervis	William	Fountain Place	4	135
Johnson	Mrs Annie	May Street	12	173
Johnston	Andrew	Northland Road	68, Westbank	150
Johnston	Anthony	Marlborough Park	55	162
Johnston	Catherine	Harding Street	10	140
Johnston	Constable C.	Hayesbank Terrace	57	167
Johnston	Dr J. A. L.	Clarendon Street	19	127
Johnston	Francis	Cable Street	17	125
Johnston	H.	Ferryquay Street	20	134
Johnston	J. V.	Castle Street	4	126
Johnston	J. V.	Browning Drive	23	166
Johnston	James	Creggan Road	69	162
Johnston	James	East Avenue	4	170
Johnston	John	Mount Street	11	164
Johnston	Miss	Marlborough Street	41	146
Johnston	Mrs	Linenhall Street Lower	29	145
Johnston	Mrs	Nailor's Row	29	148
Johnston	Mrs	Mill Street	30	173

Surname	First Name	Street	House Number	Page Number
Johnston	Patrick	Marlborough Avenue	33	147
Johnston	Patrick	St. Columb's Wells	43	157
Johnston	Richard	Nelson Street	44	149
Johnston	Robert	Fountain Street	112	135
Johnston	S.	East Wall		131
Johnston	Samuel	Abercorn Road	36	118
Johnston	Samuel	Stewart's Close	3	146
Johnston	Sergeant J.	Bellevue Avenue	35	121
Johnston	Sergeant J.	Victoria Road	9, Police Barracks	176
Johnston	Thomas	Benvarden Avenue	2	166
Jolliffe	Robert A.	Grafton Street	17	138
Jones	P. C.	Messines Park	33	128
Jones	William	Edenmore Street	7	131
Jones & Lowther		Bishop Street		122
Jordan	Thomas	Messines Park	19	128
Jordan	William	Ebrington Terrace	9	170
Joyce	Thomas	De Burgh Terrace	10	130
Judd	David	Wesley Street	3	165
Judge	E. A.	De Burgh Terrace	7	130
Kane	Alexander	Ferguson Street	44	134
Kane	Constable S.	Malvern Terrace	7	169
Kane	Ellen	Adam Street	3	118
Kane	Francis	Union Street	15	176
Kane	George	Foster's Terrace	169	143
Kane	George	Stanley's Walk	34	155
Kane	Henry	Fitters Row	259	123
Kane	Hugh	Primrose Street	5	174
Kane	James	Barry Street	41	121
Kane	John	William Street	52	161
Kane	Mrs	Magazine Street	6	146
Kane	Patrick	Alfred Street	21	165
Kavanagh	Catherine	Lecky Road	90	144
Kavanagh	Hannah	Fox's Lane	3	137
Kavanagh	Mrs	Pennyburn	1	151
Kayne	John	Epworth Street	2	163
Kealey	Mrs Louisa	Glendermott Road	8C	171
Kearney	Hugh	Creggan Road	181	163
Kearney	Jane	Deanery Street	38	130
Kearney	John	Philips Street	23	151
Kearney	Joseph	Carlin Street	10	167
Kearney	Maggie	Bishop Street	63	122
Kearney	Michael	Westland Villas	3	161
Kearney	Mrs	Thomas Street	32	158
Kearney	Patrick	Chamberlain Street	9	126
Kearney	Patrick	New Market Street	6	149
Kearns	Catherine	Artisan Street	13	162
Keatings	Mrs	Mountjoy Street	7	148
Kee	W. J.	Ernest Street	3	163

Surname	First Name	Street	House Number	Page Number
Keely	Michael	Chapel Road	52	167
Keenan	Daniel	Limewood Street	11	144
Keenan	Daniel	St. Columb's Wells	44	157
Keenan	Daniel	St. Columb's Wells	50	157
Keenan	James	St. Columb's Street	8	157
Keenan	John	Meehan's Row	13	173
Keenan	Michael	Meehan's Row	12	173
Keeny	John	Deanery Street	16	130
Kellett	James F.	Duncreggan Road	12	131
Kellock	Edwin D.	Marlborough Avenue	12	147
Kellock	Edwin David	Strand Road	64	157
Kellock	Mrs	Lorne Terrace	45	118
Kelly	Alex	Governor Road	35	138
Kelly	Bridget	Stanley's Walk	19	155
Kelly	Bridget	Cottage Row	8	164
Kelly	Daniel	Eglinton Place	9	132
Kelly	Daniel	Benvarden Avenue	7	165
Kelly	Daniel	Glendermott Road	82	171
Kelly	Daniel	Spencer Road	50	175
Kelly	Denis	Irish Street	8	172
Kelly	Edward	Argyle Terrace	7	120
Kelly	Edward	Limewood Street	35	144
Kelly	Edward	Lewis Street	32	164
Kelly	Ernest	Barrack Street	1	120
Kelly	Francis	Blucher Street	24	124
Kelly	Francis	Fahan Street	25	133
Kelly	Frank	Bridge Street	9	124
Kelly	Henry	William Street	56	161
Kelly	Hugh	New Street	13	126
Kelly	Hugh	Henrietta Street	9	141
Kelly	Hugh	Strabane Old Road	106	175
Kelly	Hugh M.	Victoria Park		176
Kelly	Hugh M.	Duke Street	98	169
Kelly	J. & J. R.	Clarendon Street	13	127
Kelly	J. Ltd	Quay Princes		152
Kelly	J. Ltd	Duke Street	27	169
Kelly	James	Clarendon Street	1	127
Kelly	James	Creggan Street	1	129
Kelly	James	Fahan Street	112	133
Kelly	James	Moore Street	2	148
Kelly	James	St. Columb's Wells	67	157
Kelly	James	Thomas Street	33, 35	158
Kelly	James	Chapel Road	16	167
Kelly	James	Fountain Hill	67	171
Kelly	James	Strabane Old Road	88	175
Kelly	James J.	West-End Park	14	161
Kelly	John	Marlborough Avenue	34	147
Kelly	John	Sackville Street	factory	154
Kelly	John	St. Columb's Wells	130	158
Kelly	John	Chapel Road	40	167

Surname	First Name	Street	House Number	Page Number
Kelly	John	Glendermott Road	8B	171
Kelly	John	King Street	35	172
Kelly	John	Riverview Terrace	1	174
Kelly	John Ltd	Foyle Street	54	136
Kelly	Joseph	Albert Place	2	119
Kelly	Joseph	Bennett Street Upper	17	122
Kelly	Margaret	Rossville Street	39	153
Kelly	Margaret	Strabane Old Road	13	175
Kelly	Mary	Rossville Street	29	153
Kelly	Michael	Argyle Street	71	119
Kelly	Michael	Argyle Street	2	119
Kelly	Michael	Creggan Terrace	18	129
Kelly	Michael	Benvarden Avenue	8	166
Kelly	Miss	Violet Street Lower	45	176
Kelly	Miss B.	William Street	27A	161
Kelly	Miss C.	Derry View Terrace	4	168
Kelly	Mrs	Foyle Alley	2	135
Kelly	Mrs	Mountjoy Street	18	148
Kelly	Mrs	Nailor's Row	31	148
Kelly	Mrs	West-End Terrace	9	161
Kelly	Mrs	Creggan Road	163	163
Kelly	Mrs	Duddy's Row	5	169
Kelly	Mrs	Ebrington Street	9	170
Kelly	Mrs	Strabane Old Road	104	175
Kelly	Mrs E.	Fountain Street	42	134
Kelly	Mrs E.	Distillery Brae Upper	4	168
Kelly	Owen	Elmwood Terrace	6	132
Kelly	P. S.	Edenballymore		131
Kelly	Patrick	Bridge Street	60	125
Kelly	Patrick	New Street	5	126
Kelly	Patrick	Eglinton Place	25	132
Kelly	Patrick	Nailor's Row	23	148
Kelly	Patrick	Wellington Street	31	160
Kelly	Patrick	Alfred Street	50	165
Kelly	Patrick	Spencer Road	25	174
Kelly	Philip	Carlisle Road	19	125
Kelly	Philip	Carlisle Road	31A	125
Kelly	Philip	Custom House Street		129
Kelly	Philip	Duke Street	104	169
Kelly	Rev. James	Queen Street	16	153
Kelly	Rev. P.	Chapel Road	Parochial House	167
Kelly	Robert	Argyle Street	35	119
Kelly	Robert	Brook Street Avenue	20	125
Kelly	Robert	Cooke Street	4	128
Kelly	Robert	Edenmore Street	16	131
Kelly	Rose	Laburnum Terrace	13	142
Kelly	Thomas	Argyle Street	9	119
Kelly	Thomas	Miller Street	32	148
Kelly	Thomas	Shipquay Street	8	154

Surname	First Name	Street	House Number	Page Number
Kelly	William	New Market Street		149
Kelly	William	North Edward Street	2	149
Kelly	William	Chapel Road	60	167
Kelly & Son		Foyle Street	31	135
Kelpey	Miss	Ferguson Street	42	134
Kelpie	Joseph	Carrigans Lane	27	126
Kelpie	Patrick	Clarke Terrace	246	144
Kelso	John D.	Beechwood Avenue	80	121
Kenendy	Francis M.	Marlborough Street	34	147
Kennedy	Andrew D.	Foyle Street	39	135
Kennedy	D.	Duke Street	94	169
Kennedy	Elizabeth	Benvarden Avenue	45	166
Kennedy	F.	Rosemount Avenue	2, Fairview	164
Kennedy	Hugh	Bridge Street	42	125
Kennedy	James	Alexandra Place	8	119
Kennedy	James	Argyle Terrace	15	120
Kennedy	John Bond	Bond's Hill	29	166
Kennedy	Marshall	Great James Street	22	139
Kennedy	Matthew	Henry Street	24	141
Kennedy	Miss M.	Sloan's Terrace	20	155
Kennedy	Miss M.	Distillery Brae Upper	6	168
Kennedy	Mrs	Shipquay Street	18	154
Kennedy	Mrs	Simpson's Brae	11	174
Kennedy	Mrs Isabel	Kennedy Place	9	142
Kennedy	Patrick	Glenbrook Terrace	22	137
Kennedy	Rev. W. M.	Crawford Square	22	129
Kennedy	Robert	Bennett Street Lower	45	122
Kennedy	Rose	Thomas Street	26	158
Kennedy	S. M. & Co.	Great James Street	2	139
Kennedy	S. M. & Co.	Magazine Street	16	146
Kennedy	Samuel	Meadowbank Avenue	23	147
Kennedy	Sarah	Ashcroft Place	7	165
Kennedy	Sergeant G.	Hayesbank Terrace	53	167
Kennedy	Sergeant George	Victoria Road	9, Police Barracks	176
Kennedy	Thomas	Ann Street	8	119
Kennedy	Thomas	College Terrace	10	128
Kennedy	William	Strand Road	34	156
Kennedy	William J.	Argyle Street	18	119
Kenney	Mary	Thomas Street	10	158
Kent	Mrs	John Street	52	142
Kenwall	Robert A.	Nassau Street Lower	5	148
Keogh	Agnes	St. Columb's Wells	93	157
Keogh	Andrew	Linenhall Street Upper	7	144
Keogh	Mrs	Abbey Street	53	117
Keohane	Dr. W. P.	Great James Street	24	139
Keown	John	Corporation Street	15	128
Keown	Martha	Strand Road	134	157
Keown	William	Clarence Avenue	3	127

Surname	First Name	Street	House Number	Page Number
Kerigan	Francis	Hamilton Street	7	139
Kerlin	Patrick	Rossville Street	23	153
Kernaghan	Joseph	Fountain Street		134
Kerr	Andrew	Mitchelburne Terrace	83	136
Kerr	Charles	Limavady Road	49	172
Kerr	John	Bishop Street	211	123
Kerr	John	North Street	19	164
Kerr	John L.	Simpson's Brae	7	174
Kerr	Joseph	Bennett Street Upper	3½	121
Kerr	Matthew	Abercorn Road	39	118
Kerr	Michael	Deanery Street	18	130
Kerr	Miss	Carlisle Road	51	125
Kerr	Mrs	Nassau Street Upper	11	149
Kerr	Robert	Argyle Street	48	119
Kerr	Robert	Northland Avenue	15	150
Kerr	Robert	Emerson Street	15	170
Kerr	Samuel	Governor Road	39	138
Kerr	William J.	Patrick Street	8A	151
Kerr & Co.		London Street	18	145
Kerr & Simpson		Strand Road	53	155
Kerrigan	Edward	Spencer Road	112	174
Kerrigan	John	Bluebellhill Terrace	220	144
Kerrigan	Michael	Tyrconnell Street	28	158
Kerrigan	Mrs	Bond's Hill	9	166
Kewell	Mrs	Pine Street	25	174
Keys	David	York Street	20	176
Keys	James	Bishop Street	266	124
Keys	James	Caroline Place	7	126
Keys	James	Lewis Street	15	164
Keys	James H.	Spencer Road	94	175
Keys	John	Spencer Road	164	175
Keys	Joseph	Strabane Old Road	15	175
Keys	Miss	Lewis Street	18	164
Keys	Patrick	Long Tower	80	146
Keys	R.	Strand Road	134	157
Keys	R. & Co.	Quay Queen's	timber yard	152
Keys	R. & Co.	Strand Road	122	157
Keys	R. F.	Limavady Road	20, Rathowen	173
Keys	Robert & Co.	Waterloo Place	10	160
Keys	Samuel	Dunfield Terrace	5	169
Keys	Thomas	Abercorn Place	6	118
Keys	Thomas	Fahan Street	99	133
Keys	Thomas	Marlborough Road	7	147
Keys	Thomas	Spencer Road	46	175
Keys & Fraser		Barrack Street	18	120
Kidd	James	Argyle Street	49	119
Kidd	James	Dunfield Terrace	33	169
Kidd	Mrs	Bennett Street Lower	53	122
Kieley	James	Chapel Road	24	167
Kilbride	Thomas P.	Sunnyside Terrace	2	123

Surname	First Name	Street	House Number	Page Number
Kildea	James	Hamilton Street	10	140
Kildea	Mrs	Westland Terrace	3	161
Kildea	Patrick	Blee's Lane		124
Kildea	Thomas	Blee's Lane		124
Kilgore	James	Messines Park	27	128
Kilgore	James E.	Bellevue Avenue	3	121
Kilgore	John	Bentley Street	7	165
Kilgore	Joseph	Primrose Street	2	174
Kilgore	Mark	Cochrane's Row	6	169
Kilgore	Mrs	Mary Street	18	147
Kilgore	Mrs	Barnewall Place	2	165
Kilgore	Mrs	Primrose Street	7	174
Kilgore	Richard	Ferguson Street	50	134
Kilgore	Robert	Alma Place	14	119
Kilgore	Robert	Major's Row	1	146
KIlgore	William	Diamond	9A	130
Kilgore	William	Mount Street	18	164
KIlgore	William	Bond's Street	34	166
Kilkey	Gertrude	Brandywell Road	5	124
Kilkie	John	Violet Street Lower	13	176
Killen	Dr. J. W.	Lawrence Hill	32	143
Killen	Henry	Fahan Street	140	133
Killen	Mrs	Bennett Street Upper	23	122
Kilpatrick	Joseph	King Street	29	172
Kilpatrick	Robert	Argyle Street	42	119
Kimmitt	E.	Shipquay Street	20, Bank of Ireland	154
Kincade	G.	Strand Road	34	156
Kincade	George	Garden City		129
Kincai & Campbell		Rosemount Avenue	21	164
Kincaid	Andrew	Grove Place	9	139
Kincaid	John	Grafton Terrace	3	139
Kincaid	John	Harding Street	14	140
Kincaid	John	Rosemount Avenue	9	164
Kincaid	John J.	Rosemount Avenue	21	164
Kincaid	Mrs	Fairman Place	21	133
Kincaid	William	Fairman Place	13	133
Kincaid & Campbell		Pump Street	11	152
Kinch	Miss	Mrs C. F. Alexander's Memorial Cottages	4	126
King	James	Strand Road	37	155
King	Mrs	Nelson Street	17	149
King	R. A.	Bishop Street	186	123
King	Samuel	Glasgow Terrace	12	138
King	Samuel	Violet Street Lower	29	176
King	Very Rev. Dean	Bishop Street	30, The Deanery	123
King	William	Pine Street	7	174

Surname	First Name	Street	House Number	Page Number
King	William	York Street	2	176
Kingsbury	George	Messines Park	40	128
Kinnear	Mrs	Strand Road	77	156
Kinnear	Mrs	Rosemount Terrace	5	165
Kinnear	Mrs	Spencer Road	72	175
Kinsella	Michael	Lecky Road	59	143
Kirby	Miss	Abercorn Road	35	118
Kirby	Mrs	Marlborough Street	17	146
Kirke	Samuel A.	Fountain Street	105	134
Kirkland	George	Marlborough Avenue	1	147
Kirkpatrick	Mrs	Diamond	11	130
Kirkwood	N.	Richmond Street	2	153
Kitchen	John	Florence Street	24	164
Kitchen	Samuel	Florence Street	19	170
Kitson	Joseph	Barry Street	19	121
Kitson	Robert J.	Ashcroft Place	1	165
Kivlehan	James	William Street	31	161
Knox	A. J. S.	Shipquay Street	Provincial Bank	154
Knox	Elizabeth E,	Templemore Park	9	158
Knox	Hugh	Northland Road	11, Ard-na-Loc	150
Knox	J. B.	Melrose Terrace	6	173
Knox	J. M. C.	East Wall	2	131
Knox	James	Gordon Place	3	138
Knox	James	Windmill Terrace	30	162
Knox	Mrs	Marlborough Street	3	146
Knox	S. D.	Academy Road	1A	118
Knox	Thomas	Harding Street	1	140
Knox	Thomas	Hawkin Street	36	140
Knox	William	Argyle Street	62	119
Knox	William	Dark Lane	23	130
Knox, Gilliland & Babington		Castle Street	4	126
Kydd	Ernest	Grafton Street	33	139
Kydd	John	Northland Terrace	9	150
Kyle	Ellen	Joseph Street	2	142
Kyle	James	Dungiven Road	34	170
Kyle	James	Violet Street Upper	1	176
Kyle	James P.	Marlborough Road	6	147
Kyle	John	St. Patrick Street	5	158
Kyle	Mrs	Governor Road	13	138
Kyle	Mrs	Philips Street	1	151
Kyle	Robert	The Rock	121	156
Kyle	William	Harding Street	9	140
Kyle	William	Dixon's Close	4	146
Kyle	William	Nassau Street Upper	1	149
Lafferty	Annie	Eglinton Place	2	132
Lafferty	John	Pitt Street	6	151
Lafferty	John	Rossville Street	37	153
Lafferty	Joseph	Sloan's Terrace	2	155

Surname	First Name	Street	House Number	Page Number
Lafferty	Margaret	Foyle Road	70	136
Lafferty	Miss A.	Bridge Street	7	124
Lafferty	Robert	Windmill Terrace	20	162
Laird	David	Lewis Street	23	164
Laird	James	Nicholson Square	6	149
Laird	Mrs	Creggan Road	66	163
Laird's Stores		Princes Street	5	152
Lamb	George	College Avenue	6	150
Lamberton	Joseph	Donegal Street	32	163
Lamberton	Mrs	Osborne Street	22	164
Lamberton	Robert	Nelson Street	51	149
Lane	H. & Co.	Cochrane's Row	coal yard	169
Lane	Henry & Co.	Quay Princes	office and coal yard	152
Lang	John	Bishop Street	H. M. Prison	123
Lang	Mrs	Clooney Terrace	41	167
Lappin	John	Alfred Street	19	165
Lappin	John	Margaret Street	20	173
Lapsley	J. H.	Clooney Terrace	22	167
Lapsley	John	Aubrey Street	3	120
Lapsley	R. J.	Clooney Terrace	16, shop	167
Lapsley	Samuel E.	Victoria Street	13	159
Lapsley	William	Aubrey Street	13	120
Lapsley	William	Fountain Street	70	135
Large	George	Orchard Row	5	150
Larkey	Mrs	Long Tower	75	145
Larkin	John	Barrack Street	16	120
Larmour	James	Fahan Street	22	133
Larmour	James	Nailor's Row	3	148
Larmour	Norah	Nailor's Row	1, 2	148
Latimer	Constable	Eden Terrace	6	131
Latimer	Robert A.	Duke Street	50	169
Latimer	Robert A.	Duke Street	62	169
Latta	Thomas	Stewart's Terrace	19	155
Laughlin	Susan	Moore Street	13	173
Laughlin	William	Bellevue Avenue	7	121
Laughlin	William	Ewing Street	16	132
Laverty	George	Governor Road	1A	138
Laverty	George	Lecky Road	111	143
Laverty	Hector	Ferguson Street	16	134
Laverty	Mrs	Mary Street	6	147
Laverty	Patrick	Bishop Street	209	122
Laverty	Robert	Mary Street	14	147
Lavery	Joseph	Philips Street	3	151
Law	Miss H. E.	Strand Road	34	156
Lawrence	Maggie	Orchard Lane	2	151
Lawrenson	Rev. L. R.	Diamond	10	130
Lawry & Porter Ltd		Bishop Street		122
Layng	Dr.	Academy Road	Foyle College	118

Surname	First Name	Street	House Number	Page Number
Leach	Mrs	Pine Street	12	174
Leach	William	Herbert Street	11	172
Leavy	Mrs	Epworth Street	27	163
Lecky	James	Marlborough Road	5	147
Lecky	James	St. Joseph's Avenue	2	158
Lecky	Michael	Elmwood Terrace	27	132
Lecky	Robert	William Street	63	161
Lee	Alexander	Great James Street	12	139
Lee	John	Argyle Street	7	119
Lee	Joseph	Abercorn Road	37	118
Lee	Mrs	Orchard Row	21	150
Lee	Robert	Sackville Street	7	154
Leeke	Joseph	Benvarden Avenue	17	165
Leeke	Joseph	Olive Terrace	4	174
Leinster	A.	Limavady Road	45, Lisowen	172
Leinster	The Misses	Clooney Park East	1, Avanmore	172
Leinsters Brothers	& Staveacre	Bellevue Avenue		121
Leitch	James	Barnewall Place	17	165
Lemon	Alex	Beechwood Avenue	29, Everest	121
Lemon	George	Duncreggan Road	14	131
Lemon	Joseph	Ferryquay Street	28	134
Lemon	S.	Bishop Street	2	123
Lemon	S.	Demesne Terrace	9, Westbrook	130
Leonard	Arthur	Foyle Road	68	136
Leonard	David	Society Street	13	155
Leonard	James	Glendermott Road	90	171
Leonard	Margaret	Nelson Street	32	149
Leonard	Robert	Abercorn Road	33A	118
Leonard	Thomas	Park Avenue	13	151
Leslie	James	Dark Lane	18	130
Leslie	John	Clooney Terrace	34	167
Leslie	Margaret	Hawkin Street	42	140
Leslie	Mrs	Moore Street	14	173
Lewis	A.	Beechwood Avenue	23, Sunnyholme	121
Lewis	A. E.	Shipquay Street	14	154
Lewis	Hugh	Corporation Street	29	128
Lewis	Robert	Nelson Street	20	149
Lewis	T. G.	Foyle Street	27	135
Lewis	T. G.	Orchard Street	25	151
Liddel	George	Richmond Street	3	153
Liddy	Mrs	Creggan Terrace	17	129
Lilley	Mies	Westland Avenue	16	160
Limerick	Arthur	Foyle Road	45	136
Limerick	Barry	Strand Road	39	155
Limerick	John	Spencer Road	135	175
Lindsay	David	Infirmary Road	gate lodge	142
Lindsay	Miss	De Burgh Square	3	130
Lindsay	Mrs	Park Avenue	29, Avonmore	151

Surname	First Name	Street	House Number	Page Number
Lindsay	William	Barry Street	31	121
Lindsay	William	Lone Moor	City Cemetery	145
Lipton Limited		Bishop Street	5	122
Lister	George	Glen Terrace	7	131
Liston	Horace	Lower Road	33	146
Little	Henry	Grafton Street	29	139
Little	John	Bennett Street Upper	8	122
Little	John	Hamilton Street	19	139
Little	John	Cuthbert Street	8	168
Little	Mrs	Cuthbert Street	10	168
Little	Robert	Barnewall Place	1	165
Little	Robert A.	Hamilton Street	29	140
Little	W. J. & Co.	Barrack Street	19	120
Little	William	Dervock Place	12	168
Livingstone	Miss	Woodleigh Terrace	2	120
Lloyd	William	Foyle Street	57	135
Lloyd, Attree & Smith		Great James Street	14	139
Loagh	William	Dervock Place	3	168
Lobb	Rebecca	Clarendon Street	32	127
Lochhead	Jane	Clooney Terrace	38	167
Lochrie	Edward	Sunbeam Terrace	5	122
Lochrie	Frederick	Robert Street	3	174
Lockart	Mrs M. A.	Harding Street	25	140
Lofting	R. C.	Castle Street	4	126
Lofting	Ronald C.	Hinton Park	5	172
Logan	James	Grafton Street	1	138
Logan	James	Victoria Street	16	159
Logan	John	Foyle Road	43½	136
Logan	Miss K.	William Street	67	161
Logan	Mrs	Academy Terrace	4	118
Logan	Mrs	Woodleigh Terrace	5	120
Logan	William	Abercorn Road	54	118
Logier	Mrs	Abercorn Road	24	118
Logue	Andrew	Bishop Street	138	123
Logue	Bernard	Magazine Street	21	146
Logue	Bernard	Spencer Road	62	175
Logue	Daniel	Deanery Street	6	130
Logue	David	Barnewall Place	23	165
Logue	Edward	Bluebellhill Terrace	160	144
Logue	Edward	Marlborough Avenue	18	147
Logue	George	Spencer Road	110	175
Logue	H.	Sunbeam Terrace	Gate Lodge	122
Logue	James	Beechwood Street	17	121
Logue	James	Friel's Terrace	5	148
Logue	James	Westland Terrace	4	161
Logue	James	Cuthbert Street	26	168
Logue	John	Alexandra Place	9	119
Logue	John	Chapel Road	10	167
Logue	John	Duke Street		169

Surname	First Name	Street	House Number	Page Number
Logue	John	Florence Street	16	170
Logue	John	Spencer Road	106	175
Logue	John J.	Melrose Terrace	1	173
Logue	Joseph	Harding Street	15	140
Logue	Joseph	Waterloo Street	6	159
Logue	Margaret	Bishop Street	218	123
Logue	Miss	Herbert Street	9	171
Logue	Miss M.	Argyle Street	44	119
Logue	Mrs	Bishop Street	138	123
Logue	Mrs	Fountain Street	19	134
Logue	Mrs	Gresham's Row	2	140
Logue	Mrs	Harvey Street	19	140
Logue	Mrs	Orchard Lane	5	151
Logue	Mrs	Waterloo Street	33	159
Logue	Mrs	Bond's Hill	16	166
Logue	Robert	Bishop Street	84	123
Logue	Robert junior	Albert Place	17	119
Logue	Samuel	Spencer Road	119	174
Logue	Thomas	Melrose Terrace	2	173
Logue	William	Fountain Hill	58	171
Logue	William	King Street	39	172
Logue	William	Robert Street	16	174
Long	Alex	Alma Place	2	119
Long	Andrew	Carlisle Road	75	125
Long	Andrew	Fountain Place	18	135
Long	Edward	Wapping Lane	3	159
Long	Elizabeth	William Street	36	161
Long	James	Bishop Street	206	123
Long	James	Ernest Street	19	163
Long	John	Collon Terrace	5	128
Long	John	Donegal Place	7	130
Long	Moses	Grafton Street	10	139
Long	Mrs	Wapping Lane	14	159
Long	Mrs T.	Lundy's Lane	4	145
Long	Robert	Albert Street	9	118
Long	Samuel	Dark Lane	22	130
Long	William	Ewing Street	31	132
Long	William	George Street	6	138
Long	William	Miller Street	36	148
Longwell	John	Foyle Street	13	135
Longwell	John	Kennedy Street	12	142
Longwell	Mrs	Nicholson Terrace	12	149
Longworth	William	Messines Park	65	128
Looney	Martin	Miller Street	3	147
Lorimer	John	Fountain Place	10	135
Loughead	Samuel	Templemore Terrace	2	151
Loughlan	James	Orchard Row	36	150
Loughlan	Matilda	Moore Street	33	173
Loughlin	Andrew	Wapping Lane	12	159
Loughlin	John	Ivy Terrace	17	142

Surname	First Name	Street	House Number	Page Number
Loughlin	Mrs	Alexandra Place	28	119
Loughlin	Mrs	Demesne Terrace	10	130
Loughlin	Patrick	Stanley's Walk	32	155
Loughlin	Robert	Beechwood Avenue	3, Braeside	121
Loughlin	Robert	Charlotte Street	24	127
Loughlin	Robert	Wapping Lane	6	159
Loughray	Constable S.	Ernest Street	5	163
Loughrey	Andrew	Bishop Street	159	122
Loughrey	Dan	Francis Street	53	137
Loughrey	Edward	Elmwood Terrace	42	132
Loughrey	James	North Edward Street	8	149
Loughrey	John	Park Avenue	24	151
Loughrey	Joseph	Caw	Rosslyn	167
Loughrey	Joseph P.	Linenhall Street Upper	19	145
Loughrey	Miss R.	Academy Terrace	8	118
Loughrey	Mrs	Great James Street	71	139
Loughrey	Mrs	Sloan's Terrace	31	155
Loughrey	Patrick	Rossville Street	46	153
Love	Alex	Victoria Street	12	159
Love	Andrew	Magazine Street Upper	3	146
Love	Annie	North Street	13	164
Love	John	Robert Street	1	174
Love	Mrs	Wapping Lane	27	159
Love	Robert	Glendermott Road	25	171
Love	William	Wapping Lane	8	159
Lovett	John	Edenmore Street	1	131
Lovett	John	Rosemount Terrace	4	165
Lowe	Clifton B.	May Street	8	173
Lowry	David	Spencer Road	46	175
Lowry	John	Clooney Terrace	19	167
Lowther	Annie M.	Clooney Terrace	23	167
Lowther	David E.	Creggan		131
Lowther	Mrs	Bishop Street		122
Lowther	Nixon	Bennett Street Lower	24	122
Lowthers	John	Ewing Street	29	132
Lowthers	Mary	Long Tower	53½	145
Lowthers	Thomas	Derry View	1	168
Lumsden	Henry	Orchard Row	2	150
Lumsden	Mrs	Ivy Terrace	6	142
Lund	Charles J.	Strand Road	60	157
Lusk	James S.	Mountjoy Street	1	148
Lyden	Roger	Foyle Road	65	136
Lynch	Charles	Fahan Street	95	133
Lynch	Daniel	Strand Road	129	156
Lynch	Daniel	St. Patrick Street	7	158
Lynch	David	Major's Row	8	146
Lynch	Edward	Lower Road	27	146
Lynch	F. & Son	Sackville Street	15	154

Surname	First Name	Street	House Number	Page Number
Lynch	Hugh	Hogg's Folly	17	141
Lynch	Hugh	Ann Street	9	143
Lynch	James	Fahan Street	82	133
Lynch	James	Little James Street		145
Lynch	James	Dixon's Close	5	146
Lynch	James	Sloan's Terrace	3, 5	154
Lynch	James	Creggan Road	171	163
Lynch	James	Duke Street	92	169
Lynch	James	Florence Street	6	170
Lynch	James & Co.	Sackville Street	23	154
Lynch	John	Hawthorn Terrace	1	140
Lynch	John	Foster's Terrace	171	143
Lynch	John	Nassau Street Lower	44	148
Lynch	John	St. Columb's Wells	42	157
Lynch	John	Florence Street	10	170
Lynch	John J.	Ebrington Street	19	170
Lynch	John James	Florence Street	23	170
Lynch	Joseph	Millar's Close		125
Lynch	Joseph	Carlisle Pass	2	125
Lynch	Joseph	Henrietta Street	10	141
Lynch	Joseph	Artisan Street	21	162
Lynch	Joseph	Fountain Hill	74	171
Lynch	Joseph Orr	Columba Terrace	5	168
Lynch	Margaret	Bluebellhill Terrace	202	144
Lynch	Mary	Stanley's Walk	1	155
Lynch	Mary	St. Columb's Wells	81	157
Lynch	Matilda	Creggan Road	173	163
Lynch	Matthew	Strand Road	85, Hilden	156
Lynch	Michael	Corporation Street	21	128
Lynch	Miss	Great James Street	27	139
Lynch	Mrs	Bentley Street	2	165
Lynch	Patrick J.	Donegal Place	17	131
Lynch	Robert Rankin	Dunfield Terrace	13	169
Lynch	Samuel	Albert Place	11	119
Lynch	Thomas	Fahan Street	160	133
Lynch	Thomas	Little Diamond	5	145
Lynch	William	William Street	82	162
Lynch	William	Derry View	3	168
Lynch	William J.	Lecky Road	259	143
Lyndsay	A. H.	Shipquay Street		154
Lyndsay	Andrew	Bond's Street	38	166
Lyndsay	George	Messines Park	34	128
Lyndsay	Hugh	Windmill Terrace	13	162
Lyndsay	John	Victoria Road	10	176
Lyndsay	Miss	Donegal Street	5, National School	163
Lyndsay	Robert	Creggan Road	46	163
Lynn	Denis	Fountain Hill	65	171
Lynn	Eugene	Fountain Hill	17	171
Lynn	James	Ferguson Street	55	134

Surname	First Name	Street	House Number	Page Number
Lynn	Mrs	Carlisle Road	34	125
Lynn	Mrs	Rockmount Villas	28	150
Lynn	R. J.	Carlisle Road	54	126
Lyons	Francis J.	Stanley's Walk	41	155
Lyons	Fred	Marlborough Street	77, Beaumont	146
Lyons	James	Lawrence Hill	9, Rosebank	143
Lyons	James	Quay Princes	office	152
Lyons	John	Philips Street	33	151
Lyons	Miss	Castle Street	10	126
Lyttle	Alexander	Benvarden Avenue	26	166
Lyttle	Robert	Charlotte Street	20	127
Lyttle	Robert	College Terrace	9	128
Lyttle	Robert	Westland Terrace	2	161
Macafee	William	Bishop Street	13	122
Macari	L.	William Street	32	161
Macari	Luci	William Street	27	161
Macari	T.	Lecky Road		144
Macari	T. & Co.	Bridge Street		124
Macari	T. & Co.	Carlisle Road	1	125
Macari & Co.		Orchard Street	4A	151
Macartney	A. H.	Foyle Road	79	136
Macaulay	David	Fountain Street	15	134
Macaulay	Miss	De Burgh Terrace	14	130
Macdevette & Donnell		Foyle Street	18	135
Macdonald	Alex	Sunbeam Terrace	4	122
Macdonald	Miss M. C.	Whittaker Street	City Hotel	161
Macdonald	Mrs I.	Bishop Street	74	123
Macdonald	The Misses	Crawford Square	2	128
MacDonnell	Mrs	Collon Terrace	12	128
MacDonnell	Robert	Bank Place	1	120
MacFeely	Rev. W. B.	Chapel Road	Parochial House	167
Machett	Andrew	Pine Street	31	174
Mack	Alexander B.	Abercorn Road	1	117
Mackerel	Herbert	Dungiven Road	93	170
Mackey	David	Society Street	15	155
Mackey	Mrs M.	Aberfoyle Terrace	9	156
Mackey	Samuel	Guildhall Street		139
MacKillip	Miss	Crawford Square	19	129
Macky	Barry	Culmore Road	Belmont	129
Macky	Joseph	Foster's Terrace	179	143
Macky	Miss	Great James Street	19	139
Macky	William J.	Bond's Place	14	166
MacLaughlin	J. L.	Clarendon Street	46	127
MacLaughlin	James	Victoria Park	6	176
MacLaughlin	Mrs	King Street	55	172
Maclean & Reaper		East Wall	6, 7, 8	131
MacLehose	James	Fairman Place	10	133

Surname	First Name	Street	House Number	Page Number
MacMillan	A.	Culmore Road	Shantallow	129
MacNeary	T. A.	Bishop Street	16	123
MacNeary	Thomas A.	Clarendon Street	40	127
Maconnachie	John	Fountain Street	69	134
MacQuaide	Rev. Cn. J. W.	Crawford Square	20	129
Macready	John	King Street	27	172
Macrory	John	Philips Street	36	151
Macrory	Lieutenant-Colonel F. S. N.	Hawkin Street	24	140
Macrory	Mrs	Governor Road	37	138
Macrory	R. V.	Limavady Road	22	173
MacSwiney	W. E.	Shipquay Street	9, Munster & Leinster Bank	154
Madden	Ellen	Sloan's Terrace	21	155
Madden	Patrick J.	Clarendon Street	53	127
Madden	John	Princes Street	16	152
Madden Bros		Foyle Street	3	135
Madden Bros		Patrick Street	8	151
Madden Bros.		Waterloo Place	11	160
Madden Brothers		Waterloo Place	18	160
Madden Mineral Water Co.		Clyde Street		153
Madden's Co.		Queen Street	garage	153
Madill	Mrs	Ferryquay Street	4	134
Madill	Sarah	West-End Park	10	161
Magee	Dr. J. R.	Magazine Street	20	146
Magee	J. Gilbert	Castle Street	7	126
Magee	John	Chapel Road	15	167
Magee	Joseph	Hollywell Street	6	141
Magee	Miss	De Burgh Terrace	4	130
Magee	Mrs	Strand Road	89 (Auburn)	156
Magee	Mrs	Pine Street	22	174
Magee	Patrick	Foyle Road	67	136
Magee	Patrick	Frederick Street	7	137
Magee	Patrick	Mill Street	26	173
Magee	Simon	Bond's Street	39	166
Magilton	William	Foyleview Terrace	4	156
Magirr	Mrs	Bridge Street	61	124
Maguire	Bridget	Joseph Street	9	142
Maguire	Dr E. A.	Clarendon Street	7	127
Maguire	Edward	St. Columb's Wells	124	158
Maguire	Frank	Harding Street	8	140
Maguire	James	Sunbeam Terrace	14	122
Maguire	John	Long Tower	29	145
Maguire	Joseph	Hogg's Folly	8	141
Maguire	Patrick	Spencer Road	74	176
Maguire	Rev. T.	Creggan Street		129
Maguire	William	Fulton Place	1	137
Magwood	Miss	Foyle Road	44	136

Surname	First Name	Street	House Number	Page Number
Mahaffey	Samuel	Lewis Street	11	164
Mahon	Annie	Hogg's Folly	16	141
Mahon	Miss	Hogg's Folly	22	141
Mahon	Thomas	Donegal Place	5	130
Mahon	Joseph	Deanery Street	3	130
Mahony	James	Corporation Street	9	128
Mailey	William J.	Strabane Old Road	76	175
Maitland	Andrew	Clooney Terrace	14	167
Maker	James	Dungiven Road	99	170
Mallet	Bernard	Lecky Road	265	143
Mallett	Hugh	Walker's Place	44	159
Mallett	Jeremiah	St. Columb's Wells	55	157
Mallett	Margaret	Deanery Street	14	130
Mallett	Michael	Walker's Place	24	159
Mallett	Sarah	Lecky Road	35	143
Mallett	Teresa	Wellington Street	19	160
Malley	Patrick & Son	Great James Street	55	139
Mallon	James	Foyle Road	74	136
Malone	James	Garden City		129
Malone	P. L.	Great James Street	10	139
Malseed	Dr. A.	Limavady Road	11, Elmhurst	172
Malseed	J.	Limavady Road	37, Woodville	172
Malseed	Mrs	Marlborough Street	35	146
Malseed	Mrs	Limavady Road	43, Edendale	172
Malseed	R. C. & Co.	Duke Street	62	169
Manning	Mary	Donaghy's Row	2	140
Manning	Mrs M.	Benvarden Avenue	53	166
Manning	Sarah A.	York Street	18	176
Manthorpe	Frederick	Bond's Street	16	166
Marchini	Armandra	Fountain Place	20	135
Margey	Annie	Fahan Street	127	133
Margey	Henry	Governor Road	7	138
Margey	Hugh	Argyle Terrace	17	120
Margey	Margaret	Limewood Street	16	144
Mark	Alderman J.	Carlisle Road	40	125
Marley	Margaret	Deanery Street	17	130
Marley	Richard	Quarry Street	17	153
Marriott	Fred A.	Meadowbank Avenue	22	147
Marshall	Edmond B.	Abercorn Road	12	118
Marshall	James	Spencer Road	43	174
Marshall	John	Governor Road	5	138
Marshall	Miss J.	Charlotte Crescent	2	155
Marshall	Mrs	Mountjoy Terrace	3	118
Marshall	Samuel	Bentley Street	8	165
Marshall	Thomas	Dungiven Road	101	170
Martin	Daniel	Stanley's Terrace	3	145
Martin	Denis	Foyle Street	76, 84	136
Martin	Ernest	Ebrington Street	2	170
Martin	Francis	Chapel Road	64	167
Martin	Frederick	Lawrence Hill	12	143

Surname	First Name	Street	House Number	Page Number
Martin	Hugh J.	Sugarhouse lane	3	158
Martin	Jane	Brandywell Avenue	9	124
Martin	John	Aubrey Street	14	120
Martin	John	Beechwood Avenue	54	121
Martin	John	Bishop Street	232	123
Martin	John	Nelson Street	38	149
Martin	John	Barnewall Place	24	165
Martin	Lizzie	Union Street	28	159
Martin	Martha J.	Charlotte Place	8	127
Martin	Mary	Brandywell Avenue	4	124
Martin	Miss	Bishop Street	29	122
Martin	Miss	Glasgow Terrace	9	138
Martin	Mrs	Lower Road	22	146
Martin	Mrs	Victoria Place	5	159
Martin	Mrs M.	Pump Street	26	152
Martin	Mrs M.	Bond's Street	24	166
Martin	Mrs R.	William Street	69	161
Martin	Mrs R.	Lower Road	20	146
Martin	Richard	Ferguson Street	7	133
Martin	Robert	Edenmore Street	39	131
Martin	Samuel	Brook Street Avenue	18	125
Martin	Samuel	Orchard Row	12	150
Martin	Thomas	Lecky Road	10	144
Martin	William	London Street	9	145
Martin	William	Nassau Street Upper	19	149
Mason	David	Victoria Street	14	159
Mason	Miss	Marlborough Street	45	146
Mason	Mrs	Nicholson Terrace	5	149
Mason	William	Sunbeam Terrace	1	122
Mason	William	Carlisle Road	9	125
Masterton	Edward	Wapping Lane	7	159
Matheson	Duncan A.	Magazine Street Upper	3	146
Mathieson	Roderick	Marlborough Street	26	147
Matthews	Arthur C.	Ferguson Street	30	134
Matthews	James	Bond's Street	41	166
Matthieson	William	Bluebellhill Terrace	184	144
Maughan	James	Glenbrook Terrace	6	137
Maultsaid	Lizzie	Strabane Old Road	68	175
Maxwell	Edward	Browning Drive	21	166
Maxwell	G.	Waterloo Place	20, Northern Counties Hotel	160
Maxwell	George	Custom House Street	Northern Counties Hotel	129
Maxwell	George	Wapping Lane	4	159
Maxwell	J.	Governor Road	43, Ash Villa	138
Maxwell	J. & Co.	Great James Street	39	139
Maxwell	Mrs	Bennett Street Lower	14	122
Maxwell	Mrs	East Wall	9	131
Maxwell	William	Great James Street	37	139

Surname	First Name	Street	House Number	Page Number
May	Thomas	Clarendon Street	59	127
May	Thomas	Great James Street	33	139
May	William	Carrigans Lane	26	126
Mayes	Thomas	Alfred Street	25	165
McAdam	Miss M.	Carlisle Road	77	125
McAdams	John	Garden City		129
McAdams	John	New Street	3	164
McAdams	Thomas	Brandywell Road	32	124
McAdams	William	Pennyburn Terrace	1	151
McAdoo	Mrs	Crawford Square	15	129
McAleaney	Charles	Cottage Row	26	164
McAleney	Charles	Eden Place	10	132
McAleney	Daniel	Lecky Road	110	144
McAlinden	H. & T.	Orchard Street	26	151
McAlindon	Charles	Florence Street	26	164
McAlindon	Hugh	Laburnum Terrace	3	142
McAlister	Con	Benvarden Avenue	15	165
McAllister	Andrew	Henry Street	13	141
McAllister	Con	Bridge Street	48	125
McAllister	Mrs	Beechwood Avenue	62	121
McAnair	Martha	Creggan Road	32	163
McAnair	Rachel	Creggan Road	44	163
McAnally	N. J.	Orchard Street	22	151
McAnaney	Mrs Bridget	Foyle Road	59	136
McAnaney	Mrs T.	Sloan's Terrace	8	155
McAnaney	Robert	Bishop Street	245	123
McAnee	Catherine	Deanery Street	11	130
McAtee	William	Barry Street	33	121
McAteer	Hugh	William Street	76	162
McAteer	Patrick	Hawthorn Terrace	2	140
McAuley	J. L.	Spencer Road	102	175
McAuley	Robert	Carlisle Road	73	125
McBane	James	Cuthbert Street	11	168
McBane	Mrs	Duke Street	86	169
McBay	James	Messines Park	4	128
McBay	William James	Argyle Terrace	20	120
McBennett	Joseph	Epworth Street	11	163
McBirney	Mrs	Gordon Terrace	3	138
McBrearty	Charles	Quarry Street	2	153
McBrearty	Daniel	Lecky Road	109	143
McBrearty	Joseph	Elmwood Street	14	132
McBrearty	Mrs	Beechwood Street	2	121
McBrearty	Patrick	Deanery Street	10	130
McBrearty	Patrick	Gallagher's Square	7	137
McBrearty	Patrick	Lecky Road	100	144
McBride	Catherine	St. Columb's Wells	72	157
McBride	Catherine	Chapel Road	42	167
McBride	Edward	Foyleview Terrace	1	156
McBride	James	Bridge Street	23	124
McBride	James	Duncreggan Road	7, Morven	131

Surname	First Name	Street	House Number	Page Number
McBride	James	Hogg's Folly	20	141
McBride	James	Thomas Street	18	158
McBride	John	Beechwood Street	24	121
McBride	John	Bridge Street	18	124
McBride	John	Gordon Place	8	138
McBride	John	Lecky Road	249	143
McBride	John	Nassau Street Lower	31	148
McBride	John	Wesley Street	17	165
McBride	John H.	Howard Street	8	141
McBride	Martha	Carrigans Lane	2	126
McBride	Mrs	Bishop Street	215	123
McBride	Mrs	Eden Place	2½	132
McBride	Mrs	Fox's Lane	7	137
McBride	Mrs	Howard Street	6	141
McBride	Mrs	Victoria Street	19	159
McBride	Mrs	William Street	19	161
McBride	Mrs	Creggan Road	99	162
McBride	Patrick	King Street	31	172
McBride	Robert	Henry Street	14	141
McBride	Samuel	Gordon Terrace	8	138
McBride	Thomas	Philips Street	34	151
McBride	William	Rosemount Terrace	8	165
McBrien	James	Spencer Road	19	174
McBrien	Margaret	Spencer Road	37	174
McCabe	Charles	Bishop Street	112	123
McCabe	John	Victoria Place	4	159
McCabe	Leo	Carlisle Road	77	125
McCabe	William	Bishop Street	180	123
McCafferty	Annie	Henrietta Street	13	141
McCafferty	Annie	Creggan Road	18	163
McCafferty	B.	William Street	97	161
McCafferty	Bartholomew	Elmwood Terrace	18	132
McCafferty	Catherine	Ferguson Street	2	134
McCafferty	Catherine	Foyle Road	8	136
McCafferty	Charles	Lecky Road	60	144
McCafferty	Daniel	Strabane Old Road	66	175
McCafferty	David	Sloan's Terrace	27	155
McCafferty	George	Stanley's Walk	23	155
McCafferty	Henry	Brandywell Road	17	124
McCafferty	Hugh	Henrietta Street	11	141
McCafferty	J. D. & Sons	Magazine Street	19	146
McCafferty	J. P.	Magazine Street	18	146
McCafferty	James	Donegal Place	2	131
McCafferty	James	Long Tower	56	146
McCafferty	James	Mountjoy Street	11	148
McCafferty	James	Strabane Old Road	2	175
McCafferty	John	Elmwood Street	8	132
McCafferty	John	Lecky Road	store	144
McCafferty	John	Wellington Street	43	160
McCafferty	John	Alfred Street	10	165

Surname	First Name	Street	House Number	Page Number
McCafferty	John J.	Philips Street	15	151
McCafferty	Magdelene	Elmwood Terrace	16	132
McCafferty	Mrs	Blucher Street	22	124
McCafferty	Mrs	Waterloo Street	28	159
McCafferty	Mrs	Gortfoyle Place	4	171
McCafferty	Neal	Donegal Place	21	131
McCafferty	Patrick	Elmwood Terrace	28	132
McCafferty	Patrick	Francis Street	25	137
McCafferty	Patrick	Henrietta Street	16	141
McCafferty	Patrick	Nassau Street Upper	10	149
McCafferty	Thomas	New Street	10	164
McCafferty	William	Cable Street	9	125
McCafferty	William	Bluebellhill Terrace	182	144
McCafferty	William J.	Bayview Terrace	7	120
McCaig	Samuel H.	Messines Park	2	128
McCallig	James	Garden City		129
McCallion	Annie	Cunningham Row	2	129
McCallion	Charles	Bond's Hill	31	166
McCallion	Daniel	Nassau Street Lower	35	148
McCallion	Daniel	Cross Street	2	163
McCallion	Denis	Pennyburn	4	151
McCallion	Edward	Nassau Street Lower	14	148
McCallion	Elizabeth	Osborne Street	2	164
McCallion	George	Beechwood Street	7	121
McCallion	George	Cross Street	1	163
McCallion	James	Creggan Terrace	8	129
McCallion	James	Donegal Street	10	163
McCallion	John	Beechwood Street	15	121
McCallion	John	Limewood Street	12	144
McCallion	Joseph	Nassau Street Upper	14	149
McCallion	Joseph	Donegal Street	31	163
McCallion	Joseph	Osborne Street	17	164
McCallion	Margaret	Fahan Street	5	133
McCallion	Margary	Lewis Street	24	164
McCallion	Mary	Duke Street	19	169
McCallion	Mary A.	Barry Street	11	121
McCallion	Michael	Stanley's Terrace	2	145
McCallion	Mrs	Chamberlain Street	36	126
McCallion	Mrs	Ivy Terrace	31	142
McCallion	Mrs	St. Columb's Wells	19	157
McCallion	Mrs	Osborne Street	15	164
McCallion	Patrick	Abbey Street	3	117
McCallion	Patrick	Argyle Street	4	119
McCallion	Patrick	Beechwood Street	18	121
McCallion	Patrick	Kerr's Terrace	7	162
McCallion	Sarah	Osborne Street	7	164
McCallion	Thomas	Bishop Street	156	123
McCallion	Thomas	Blee's Lane		124
McCallion	Thomas	Elmwood Terrace	7	132
McCallion	Thomas	Tyrconnell Street	31	158

Surname	First Name	Street	House Number	Page Number
McCallion	William	Brook Street Avenue	9	125
McCallion	William	Glenbrook Terrace	12	137
McCallion	William	Princes Terrace	8	152
McCallion	William	Creggan Road	149	162
McCallum	D.	Strand Road	30	156
McCallum	Daniel	Aberfoyle Terrace	25	156
McCamphill	Thomas	Hamilton Street	14	140
McCandless	Ellen T.	Grafton Terrace	1	139
McCandless	H. S.	College Terrace	1	127
McCandless	Herbert	Wesley Street	6	165
McCandless	Margaret	Stewart's Terrace	16	155
McCandless	Mrs	Clarendon Street	38	127
McCandless	Mrs	Lawrence Hill	7	143
McCandless	R. J.	Foyle Street	34	136
McCandless	W. H. B.	Clarendon Street	61	127
McCandless & Piggott		Clarendon Street		127
McCann	H.	Westland Terrace	14	161
McCann	Hugh	Hamilton Street	43	140
McCann	James	Eden Place	2	132
McCann	James	New Row	3	156
McCann	James	Waterloo Street	2	159
McCann	James	Riverview Terrace	15	174
McCann	John	Bishop Street	40	123
McCann	John	Creggan Road	58	163
McCann	Joseph	Walker's Place	39	159
McCann	Lawrence	Queen Street	6	153
McCann	Margaret	Donegal Street	20	163
McCann	Michael	Clarke Terrace	242	144
McCann	Michael	Osborne Street	11	164
McCann	Mrs	Queen Street	6	153
McCann	Thomas	Mountjoy Street	2	148
McCann	Thomas	Rossville Street	10	153
McCarroll	Constable W. J.	Laburnum Terrace	14	142
McCarroll	James J.	Westland Avenue	25	160
McCarron	Charlotte	Bellevue Avenue	1	121
McCarron	James	Bellevue Avenue	6	121
McCarron	James	Hogg's Folly	13	141
McCarron	John	Bishop Street	149	122
McCarron	John	Fahan Street	67	133
McCarron	John	Quarry Street	9	152
McCarron	John	Artisan Street	5	162
McCarron	Michael	Blucher Street	23	124
McCarron	Miss	Foyle Road	110	136
McCarron	Mrs	Frederick Street	13	137
McCarron	Neal	Ferguson Street	47	134
McCarron	Neil	Wellington Street	37	160
McCarron	Owen	Wesley Street	2	165
McCarron	Richard	Howard Place	3	141
McCarron	Robert	Bennett Street Upper	4	122

Surname	First Name	Street	House Number	Page Number
McCarron	Thomas	Orchard Row	35	150
McCarron	Thomas	Margaret Street	7	173
McCarron	William	Philips Street	11	151
McCarron	William	Creggan Road	71	162
McCart	Hugh	Hamilton Street	11	139
McCarter	Alex senior	Glendermott Road	64	171
McCarter	James	May Street	6	173
McCarter	John	Pitt Street	3	151
McCarter	Lizzie	Mill Street	34	173
McCarter	Margaret	Bennett Street Lower	29	122
McCarter	Matthew	King Street	28	172
McCarter	Miss	Nicholson Terrace	1	149
McCarter	Mrs	Ferguson Street	39	133
McCarter	Mrs	Marlborough Avenue	5	147
McCarter	Mrs M.	Demesne Terrace	7, Edernish	130
McCarter	Robert	Culmore Road		129
McCarter	Robert	Edenmore Street	14	131
McCarter	William	Alexandra Place	30	119
McCarter	William	Duncreggan Road	4, Rus-Nurbe	131
McCarter	William	Quay Princes	Burns & Laird Lines	152
McCarter	William	Quay Queen's	Belfast Steamship Co.	152
McCarter	William & Son	Duke Street	39, 41	169
McCarthy	Nicholas	Eglinton Place	7	132
McCartney	A. H.	Dunfield Terrace	41	169
McCartney	Henry	St. Columb's Wells	36	157
McCartney	Hugh	Bishop Street	221	123
McCartney	James	Hawthorn Terrace	10	140
McCartney	John	Alexandra Place	22	119
McCartney	Neil	Mitchelburne Terrace	97	136
McCartney	Robert	Dungiven Road	6	170
McCartney	William	Bishop Street	88	123
McCaughey	Bernard	Marlborough Terrace	23	147
McCaughey & Co.		Carlisle Road	36	125
McCaul	Daniel	Stanley's Walk	39	155
McCaul	James	Tyrconnell Street	4	158
McCaul	Norah	Ebrington Terrace	2	170
McCaul	Francis	Deanery Street	25	130
McCaul	John	Lecky Road	63	143
McCauley	Charles	Florence Street	28	170
McCauley	Francis Leo	Foyle View	4	137
McCauley	James	Abbey Street	26	117
McCauley	James	Philips Street	39	151
McCauley	James	Irish Street	6	172
McCauley	Jane	Foyleview Terrace	7	156
McCauley	John	Meave's Row	189	143
McCauley	John	Donegal Street	13	163
McCauley	Joseph	Cottage Row	30	164

Surname	First Name	Street	House Number	Page Number
McCauley	Michael	Alma Place	1	119
McCauley	Miss	Cunningham Row	3	129
McCauley	Miss	King Street	36	172
McCauley	Mrs	Pump Street	21	152
McCauley	Mrs	Donegal Street	28	163
McCauley	Mrs	Violet Street Lower	46	176
McCauley	Mrs Mary	Donegal Street	19	163
McCauley	Patrick	Mitchelburne Terrace	85	136
McCauley	Thomas	Barry Street	6	121
McCauley	Thomas	Harvey Street	2	140
McCauley	Thomas	Donegal Street	15	163
McCauley	Thomas	Donegal Street	25	163
McCauley	W. J.	Gresham's Row	1	140
McCauley	William	Alma Place	3	119
McCauley	William	Millar's Close		125
McCauley	William	Donegal Street	37	163
McCauley	William	Lewis Street	16	164
McCay	Alex & Co.	Ferryquay Street	21	134
McCay	Alexander	Claremont Villas	32	150
McCay	Alexander & Co.	Pump Street	8	152
McCay	Daniel	Blucher Street	19	124
McCay	Daniel	Elmwood Street	26	132
McCay	Henry Crawford	Shipquay Street	27	154
McCay	James	Duke Street	42	169
McCay	John	Spencer Road	13	174
McCay	Mary	Fahan Street	72	133
McCay	Miss	Hollywell Street	17	141
McCay	Mrs	Creggan Terrace	6	129
McCay	Mrs	Stanley's Walk	45	155
McCay	Mrs	Wellington Street	22	160
McCay	Mrs	Clooney Terrace	31	167
McCay	Owen	Lundy's Lane	5	145
McCay	Peter	King Street	7	172
McCay	William	Bishop Street	290	124
McCay	William	Rossville Street	45	153
McCay	Ellen	Lecky Road	27	143
McChrystal	Mark	Carlin Street	8	167
McChrystall	John	Cross Street	36	168
McClafferty	Hugh	Rossville Street	21	153
McClafferty	John	Lower Road	12	146
McClaffery	John	Wellington Street	40	160
McClay	Allan	Irish Street	22, 23	172
McClay	Allan	Strabane Old Road	23	175
McClay	David L.	College Terrace	2	127
McClay	Henry	Robert Street	2	174
McClay	James	Butcher Street	2A	125
McClay	John	Spencer Road	34	175
McClay	Martha	Fountain Hill	71	171
McClay	Mary A.	Howard Street	17	141

Surname	First Name	Street	House Number	Page Number
McClay	Robert G.	Barnewall Place	15	165
McClay	Samuel	Hayesbank Terrace	61	167
McClay	Stephen	Tamneymore		175
McClay	Thomas	East Avenue	1	170
McClay	Thomas	Irish Street	17	172
McClay	William J.	Spencer Road	32	175
McClay	William James	Moore Street	32	173
McClean	A.	Demesne Terrace	5, Auchinlea	130
McClean	Alexander	College Avenue	4	150
McClean	James	Glasgow Terrace	22	138
McClean	James	Limewood Street	20	144
McClean	Mary	Meave's Row	203	143
McClean	Mrs	Clarence Avenue	4	127
McClean	Mrs	William Street	21½	161
McClean	Mrs	Windmill Terrace	22	162
McClean	Sarah	Rosemount Terrace	3	165
McCleary	Charles	Iona Terrace	1	172
McCleery	Charles	Walker's Place	32	159
McCleery	J. R.	Mountjoy Terrace	9	118
McCleery	James	De Burgh Terrace	6	130
McCleery	Samuel	Argyle Street	14	119
McCleery	William	Templemore Terrace	3	151
McClelland	Edward	Fountain Hill	57	171
McClelland	Edward	Irish Street	2	172
McClelland	Isabella	Violet Street Lower	17	176
McClelland	James	Tamneymore		175
McClelland	James	Violet Street Upper	12	176
McClelland	John	Argyle Street	37	119
McClelland	John	Fountain Place	25	135
McClelland	John	Strabane Old Road	1	175
McClelland	Matthew	Little James Street	9	145
McClelland	Matthew	New Street	4	164
McClelland	Patrick	New Street	3	126
McClelland	R. J.	Florence Street	7	163
McClelland	R. J.	Duke Street	18	169
McClelland	Robert	Cooke Street	1	128
McClelland	W. J. G.	De Burgh Terrace	1	130
McClelland	W. J. G.	Magazine Street	10	146
McClelland	William	Ashcroft Place	8	165
McClelland	William	Dervock Street	10	168
McClements	James	Irish Street		172
McClements	John	Irish Street		172
McClements	Mrs	Bond's Street	18, Dispensary	166
McClements	Mrs	Limavady Road	15, Wellington Villa	172
McClements	R.	Victoria Terrace	8	120
McClements	Samuel	Bond's Street	49	166
McClements	William	Charlotte Place	7	127
McClenaghan	Charles	Bishop Street	242	124
McClenaghan	James	Windmill Terrace	5	162

Surname	First Name	Street	House Number	Page Number
McClenaghan	John	St. Columb's Wells	90	157
McClenaghan	Mrs	Fountain Hill	29	171
McClintock	Catherine	Nelson Street	13	149
McClintock	Francis	Cedar Street	5	126
McClintock	James	Long Tower	43	145
McClintock	John	Bishop Street	161	122
McClintock	Mrs	St. Columb's Terrace	87	143
McClintock	Thomas	Hamilton Street	41	140
McCloskey	Andrew	Marlborough Street	4	147
McCloskey	Andrew	William Street	68	166
McCloskey	Bernard	Long Tower	7	145
McCloskey	Cassie	Northland Road	37	150
McCloskey	Catherine	Bluebellhill Terrace	136	144
McCloskey	Charles	Lecky Road	84	144
McCloskey	Francis	Grafton Avenue	53	120
McCloskey	George	Brook Street Avenue	10	125
McCloskey	Hugh	Hamilton Street	25	140
McCloskey	Isaac	Dungiven Road	11	169
McCloskey	James	Cottage Row	7	123
McCloskey	James	Brook Street Avenue	12	125
McCloskey	James	Nassau Street Lower	3	148
McCloskey	James	Westland Avenue	7	160
McCloskey	James	West-End Terrace	5	161
McCloskey	John	Fahan Street	124	133
McCloskey	John	Ferguson Street	33	133
McCloskey	John	Kildarra Terrace	2	141
McCloskey	John	Hollywell Street	5	141
McCloskey	John	Bluebellhill Terrace	138	144
McCloskey	John	Stanley's Walk	11	155
McCloskey	John	Dungiven Road	83	170
McCloskey	Joseph	Laburnum Terrace	11	142
McCloskey	Mary	Creggan Street	9	129
McCloskey	Michael	Stanley's Walk	25	155
McCloskey	Michael	Waterloo Street	29	159
McCloskey	Michael	Spencer Road	80	175
McCloskey	Minnie	Kildarra Terrace	1	141
McCloskey	Mrs	Creggan Terrace	19	129
McCloskey	Mrs	Laburnum Terrace	2	142
McCloskey	Mrs	Creggan Road	127	162
McCloskey	P.	Duke Street	75	169
McCloskey	Patrick	Bishop Street	89	122
McCloskey	Patrick	Glenview Avenue	3	137
McCloskey	Patrick	Harding Street	33	140
McCloskey	Patrick	Dungiven Road	65	170
McCloskey	The Misses	Carlisle Road	47	125
McCloskey	Thomas	Foyle Road	79A	136
McCloskey	Thomas	Townsend Street	3	158
McCloskey	Thomas	Strabane Old Road		175
McCloskey	William	Foyle Street	109	135
McCloskey	William	Nassau Street Lower	20	148

Surname	First Name	Street	House Number	Page Number
McCloskey	William	Philips Street	38	151
McCloskey	William	Bond's Street	9	166
McCloskie	R. J.	Columba Terrace	8	168
McCloud	William	Benvarden Avenue	37	166
McClune	James	Claremont Street	2	127
McClune	John	Meadowbank Avenue	33	147
McClure	Errnest	Rosemount Terrace	11	165
McClure	Frank	Culmore Road	The Elms	129
McClure	James	Cross Street	40	168
McClure	John	Dervock Street	2	168
McClure	John	Maple Street	1	173
McClure	Miss	Beechwood Avenue	16	121
McClure	Mrs	Great James Street	42	139
McCluskey	Margaret A.	Carlin Street	17	167
McCluskey	Miss	Waterloo Street	8	159
McCoach & Co.		Shipquay Place	4	154
McColgan	J. Ltd	Bishop Street	18, 20	123
McColgan	James	West-End Park	11	161
McColgan	James	Carlin Street	3	166
McColgan	John	Walker's Place	20	159
McColgan	John & Co.	London Street	4, 6	145
McColgan	Joseph	Mary Street	26	147
McColgan	Michael	Wellington Street	34	160
McColgan	Mrs	Demesne Terrace	4	130
McColgan	Mrs	Marlborough Street	50, Ailsa-Boru Villa	147
McColgan	Patrick	Waterloo Street	6	159
McColgan	Robert	Joseph Street	5	142
McColgan	Thomas	Abbey Street	57	117
McColgan	Thomas	Limewood Street	7	144
McComb	John	Alma Place	10	119
McComb	Mrs	Cedar Street	13	126
McComb	James	Moore Street	3	173
McCombe	Mrs M.	Beechwood Avenue	38	121
McCombe	Samuel	May Street	15	173
McConachie	Mrs	Abercorn Road	59	118
McConachie	William	Distillery Brae Lower		168
McConaghey	Matthew	York Street	9	176
McConaghey	Mrs	Caw	Ballyowen	167
McConaghy	James	Park Avenue	17	151
McConnell	Catherine	Abercorn Road	18	118
McConnell	Charles H.	Crawford Square	1	128
McConnell	Constable	Eden Terrace	10	131
McConnell	Henry	Hayesbank Terrace	55	167
McConnell	Hugh	Meehan's Row	2	173
McConnell	J. H.	Foyle Street	13	135
McConnell	James	Brandywell Road	4	124
McConnell	James	Carlisle Road	75	125
McConnell	James	Charlotte Street	4	127
McConnell	James	Violet Street Upper	25	176

Surname	First Name	Street	House Number	Page Number
McConnell	John	Albert Street	1	118
McConnell	John	Mountain Street	23	173
McConnell	John junior	St. Patrick Street	10	158
McConnell	Michael	Nelson Street	7	149
McConnell	Miss	Crawford Square	12	129
McConnell	Miss	Queen Street	8	153
McConnell	Miss	Bond's Street	18, Dispensary	166
McConnell	Miss	Margaret Street	22	173
McConnell	Misses	Spencer Road	117	174
McConnell	Moses	Harding Street	5	140
McConnell	Moses	St. Columb's Wells	62	157
McConnell	Mrs	Alfred Street	33	165
McConnell	Mrs	Duke Street	84	169
McConnell	Robert	Wapping Lane	10	159
McConnell	Rose	Brandywell Avenue	15	124
McConnell	Thomas	Bennett Street Lower	27	122
McConnell	Thomas	Bennett Street Lower	31	122
McConnell	Thomas & Co.	Pump Street	6	152
McConnell	William	Northland Road	35	150
McConnell	William	Emerson Street	27	170
McConnell	J. H.	Culmore Road	Tripoli	129
McConnell & Co.		Foyle Street	8	135
McConnell Bros		Quay Queen's		152
McConnellogue	Andrew	Eden Place	14	132
McConnellogue	D.	Francis Street	35	137
McConnellogue	Daniel	Fitters Row	269	123
McConnellogue	Daniel	Fulton Place	3	137
McConnellogue	Denis	Great James Street	64	139
McConnellogue	Frank	Lecky Road	245	143
McConnellogue	John	Kildarra Terrace	5	141
McConnellogue	Michael	St. Joseph's Avenue	6	158
McConnellogue	Miss B.	Creggan Street	13	129
McConnelogue	Bridget	Wellington Street	10	160
McConnelogue	Michael	Thomas Street	31	158
McConnollogue	William J.	Meadowbank Avenue	17	147
McConomy	Charles	Patrick Street	15	151
McConomy	James	Sugarhouse lane	10	158
McConomy	James	York Street	19	176
McConomy	John	York Street	25	176
McConoway	Mrs	Fahan Street	130	133
McConway	Charles	Lecky Road	217	143
McConway	William	Great James Street	73	139
McCool	Annie	Elmwood Terrace	34	132
McCool	George	Quarry Street	13	153
McCool	John	Hamilton Street	9	139
McCool	John	Pennyburn Terrace	2	151
McCool	Joseph	Shipquay Place	5	154
McCool	Margaret	Foster's Terrace	155	143
McCool	Margaret	Limewood Street	22	144

Surname	First Name	Street	House Number	Page Number
McCool	Miss	Bishop Street	247	123
McCool	Mrs	Orchard Row	25	150
McCool	Mrs	Quarry Street	3	152
McCool	William	Argyle Street	26	119
McCool	William	Creggan Street	33	129
McCool	William	Foyle Street	1	135
McCool	William	Lawrence Hill	30	143
McCool	William	Sackville Street	2	154
McCool	William	Shipquay Place	5	154
McCool	William	Strand Road	17	155
McCool	William	William Street	29	161
McCorkell	George	Hamilton Street	5	139
McCorkell	James	Culmore Road	The Farm	129
McCorkell	John	Fountain Street	93	134
McCorkell	Joseph	Creggan Road	10	163
McCorkell	Mrs	Culmore Road	Hampstead Hall	129
McCorkell	Robert	Barrack Street	9	120
McCorkell	W. H. & Co.	Quay Queen's	stores	152
McCorkell	William & Co.	Strand Road	20	156
McCorkell	William J.	Ivy Terrace	16	142
McCorkell & Co.		Waterloo Place	19	160
McCormack	James	Maybrook Terrace	1	128
McCormack	Mrs	Grove Place	8	139
McCormick	Charles	Castle Street	3	126
McCormick	Charles	Francis Street	27	137
McCormick	Charles	Creggan Road	93	162
McCormick	Frank	Wellington Street	46	160
McCormick	George	Bishop Street	171	122
McCormick	H.	Clarendon Street	25	127
McCormick	Henry	Nailor's Row	22	148
McCormick	John	Fahan Street	129	133
McCormick	John	Lewis Street	33	164
McCormick	Mary	Dungiven Road	4	170
McCormick	Mrs	Aubrey Street	5	120
McCormick	Mrs	Francis Street	29	137
McCormick	Mrs	Bluebellhill Terrace	216	144
McCormick	Mrs	Windsor Terrace	9	162
McCormick	Stanley	Stanley's Walk	28	155
McCourt	Daniel	Eden Place	15	132
McCourt	Daniel	Hollywell Row	73	143
McCourt	Henry	Bellevue Avenue	19	121
McCourt	Hugh	St. Columb's Terrace	97	143
McCourt	J. H.	Bishop Street	49	122
McCourt	James	Fulton Place	2	137
McCourt	Jeremiah	Francis Street	31	137
McCourt	John	Walker's Place	33, 34	159
McCourt	Joseph	Herbert Street	7	171
McCourt	Mrs	Blucher Street	20	124

Surname	First Name	Street	House Number	Page Number
McCourt	Mrs	Wellington Street	49	160
McCourt	Mrs	Wellington Street	58	160
McCourt	Mrs M.	Francis Street	43	137
McCourt	Patrick	Howard Street	18	141
McCourt	Patrick	Lower Road	15	146
McCourt	Patrick	St. Columb's Wells	126	158
McCourt	Patrick	Wellington Street	53	160
McCourt	Thomas	Wellington Street	25	160
McCourt	Thomas junior	Wellington Street	69	160
McCourt	Thomas senior	Wellington Street	73	160
McCourt	William	Great James Street	77	139
McCoy	John	Nicholson Terrace	6	149
McCracken	Joseph	Alma Place	16	119
McCracken	Mrs M.	Grove Place	13	139
McCrea	J. H.	Great James Street	31	139
McCrea	Alex	Cuthbert Street	21	168
McCrea	James	Ivy Terrace	32	142
McCrea	James	Walker's Place	17	159
McCrea	Mrs	Mountain Street	21	173
McCrea	Mrs E.	Clarendon Street	55	127
McCrea & McFarland		Mill Street	yard	173
McCrea & McFarland		Foyle Street	12, 14	135
McCready	Daniel	Distillery Lane Lower	7	168
McCready	Denis	Mill Street	36	173
McCready	Mary A.	Foster's Terrace	173	143
McCready	Peter	Long Tower	33	145
McCrory	Margaret	York Street	6	176
McCrossan	Eliza	Bennett Street Upper	23	122
McCrossan	Harry	Marlborough Terrace	26	147
McCrossan	Patrick	Park Avenue	16	151
McCrossan	William	Fahan Street	138	133
McCrudden	Patrick	Fahan Street	16	133
McCrudden	Patrick	Walker's Place	1	159
McCrum	R. C.	Shipquay Place	6, Northern Bank	154
McCrystal	Mark	North Street	11	164
McCrystal	Mrs	Lecky Road	45	143
McCrystell	Ellen	Alfred Street	20	165
McCullagh	James	Violet Street Lower	33	176
McCullagh	Kathleen	Templemore Park	2	158
McCullagh	Miss	Bishop Street	120	123
McCullagh	Mrs	Alma Place	12	119
McCullagh	Mrs	Myrtle Terrace	70	150
McCullagh	Mrs	Foyleview Terrace	2	156
McCullagh	W. J.	Waterloo Place	16	160
McCullough	S. G. & Co.	Strand Road	7	155
McCully	Mrs	Tyrconnell Street	2	158
McCully	T. & Co. Ltd.	Victoria Road	1	176

Surname	First Name	Street	House Number	Page Number
McCully	Thomas Ltd	Spencer Road	1, 2	175
McCully	William	Argyle Street	41	119
McCurdy	Dr. D. A.	Pump Street	5	152
McCurdy	Dr. W. A.	Pump Street	5	152
McCurdy	Samuel	Beechwood Avenue	72	121
McCurdy	W.	Beechwood Avenue	25. Northcrest	121
McCurdy	William	Princes Terrace	2	152
McCurry	Joseph	Marlborough Street	46	147
McCurry	Joseph	Strand Road	66, 68	157
McCutcheon	George	Bridge Street	49	124
McCutcheon	John	Bishop Street	220	123
McCutcheon	The Misses	Butcher Street	11	125
McCutcheon	The Misses	Carlisle Terrace	1	126
McDaid	Anthony	Strabane Old Road	94	175
McDaid	Bernard	Argyle Street	65	119
McDaid	Bernard	Creggan Street	17	129
McDaid	Denis	Brandywell Avenue	11	124
McDaid	Edward	Wellington Street	15	160
McDaid	Elizabeth	Ann Street	15	144
McDaid	James	Chamberlain Street	22	126
McDaid	James	Eglinton Place	10	132
McDaid	James	Elmwood Terrace	29	132
McDaid	James	Ferguson Street	bakery	134
McDaid	James	Hamilton Street	32	140
McDaid	James	Hawthorn Terrace	34	140
McDaid	James	Lecky Road	295	143
McDaid	James	Lecky Road	28	144
McDaid	James	Bluebellhill Terrace	170	144
McDaid	James	Orchard Street	8	151
McDaid	James	Strand Road Lower	167	156
McDaid	James	Mount Street	19	164
McDaid	Jane	Francis Street	33	137
McDaid	John	Cedar Street	1	126
McDaid	John	Deanery Street	8	130
McDaid	John	Fahan Street	17	133
McDaid	John	Fahan Street	76	133
McDaid	John	Fahan Street	84	133
McDaid	John	Francis Street	11	137
McDaid	John	Creggan Road	109	162
McDaid	Madge	Little James Street	2	145
McDaid	Manus	Rossville Street	73	153
McDaid	Mary	Nailor's Row	14	148
McDaid	Michael	Brook Street Avenue	14	125
McDaid	Michael	New Street	12	126
McDaid	Michael	Hamilton Street	30	140
McDaid	Michael	Windsor Terrace	8	162
McDaid	Miss	Francis Street	19	137
McDaid	Miss	John Street	25	142
McDaid	Miss	Lecky Road	62	144
McDaid	Miss K.	Wesley Street	22	165

Surname	First Name	Street	House Number	Page Number
McDaid	Mrs	Bluebellhill Terrace	218	144
McDaid	Mrs	Northland Avenue	19	150
McDaid	Mrs	Rossville Street	38	153
McDaid	Mrs	Violet Street Upper	21	176
McDaid	Mrs L.	Long Tower	53	145
McDaid	Neil	William Street	26	161
McDaid	Patrick	Foyle Road	112	136
McDaid	Patrick	Alfred Street	8	165
McDaid	Patrick	Caw		167
McDaid	Thomas	Dervock Street	4	168
McDaid	William	Brandywell Avenue	3	124
McDaid	William	Lecky Road	58	144
McDaid	William	Westland Terrace	15	161
McDaid	William	Creggan Road	67	162
McDaide	James	Creggan Street	21	129
McDermid	John	Argyle Street	20	119
McDermott	Ann J.	Stanley's Terrace	1	145
McDermott	Catherine	Ann Street	19	119
McDermott	Catherine	Henrietta Street	6	141
McDermott	Charles	Lecky Road	15	143
McDermott	Charles	Pitt Street	8	151
McDermott	Charles	Wellington Street	41	160
McDermott	Charles	Wellington Street	38	160
McDermott	Daniel	St. Columb's Wells	87	157
McDermott	Denis F.	Mountjoy Terrace	6	118
McDermott	J.	Foyle Street	101	135
McDermott	James	East Wall	3	131
McDermott	James	Howard Street	24	141
McDermott	James	Lecky Road	261	143
McDermott	James	Nailor's Row	33	148
McDermott	James	Shipquay Street	14	154
McDermott	James	Browning Drive	5	166
McDermott	John	St. Columb's Wells	91	157
McDermott	Mary	Beechwood Avenue	6	121
McDermott	Michael	Fahan Street	89	133
McDermott	Michael	Ivy Terrace	1	142
McDermott	Michael	Stanley's Walk	35	155
McDermott	Miss	North Edward Street	3	149
McDermott	Miss	William Street	19	161
McDermott	Miss	Moore Street	22	173
McDermott	Mrs	John Street	43	142
McDermott	Mrs	Marlborough Avenue	9	147
McDermott	Mrs	Bond's Hill	28	166
McDermott	Mrs	Irish Street	18	172
McDermott	Neil	Creggan Road	6	163
McDermott	Patrick	Asylum Road	1	120
McDermott	Patrick	The Rock	95	156
McDermott	Patrick	Margaret Street	16	173
McDermott	Robert	Albert Street	14	118
McDermott	Stephen	Gordon Place	10	138

Surname	First Name	Street	House Number	Page Number
McDermott	William	North Street	23	164
McDermott	Mrs	Clarendon Street	12	127
McDermott & Sterritt		Castle Street	5	126
McDevitt	Denis	Waterloo Street	11, 13	159
McDevitt	J.	Shipquay Street	4	154
McDevitt	James	Rossville Street	82	153
McDevitt	John	Francis Street	55	137
McDevitt	John	St. Columb's Wells	41	157
McDevitt	M. & Co.	Duke Street	38, 40	169
McDevitt	Michael	Columba Terrace	2	168
McDevitt	Mrs	Nicholson Square	5	149
McDevitt	William	Bishop Street	126	123
McDevitt	William	Brandywell Road	2	124
McDevitte	Edward	Fahan Street	69	133
McDevitte & Donnell		Quay Princes		152
McDivette	Michael	Demesne Terrace	2	130
McDonagh	Charles	Brook Street Avenue	15	125
McDonagh	Denis	Duke Street	7	169
McDonagh	Edward	Limewood Street	33	144
McDonagh	Hugh	Waterloo Place	11	160
McDonagh	James	Deanery Street	44	130
McDonagh	Mary	Nelson Street	29	149
McDonagh	Michael	Bennett Street Lower	18	122
McDonagh	Michael	Foyle Road	100	136
McDonagh	Miss	Bond's Place	2	166
McDonagh	Thomas	Kerr's Terrace	15	162
McDonald	D.	Clarendon Street	garage	127
McDonald	Edwin	Clarke Terrace	236	144
McDonald	James	Bishop Street	244	124
McDonald	James	Marlborough Terrace	22	147
McDonald	John	Carrigans Lane	stores	126
McDonald	Miss	Argyle Street	19	119
McDonald	Mrs	Park Avenue	3	151
McDonald	Mrs M. K.	Shipquay Street	6	154
McDonald	Patrick	Joseph Street	4	142
McDonald	Patrick	Duke Street	47	169
McDonald	Terence	William Street	34	161
McDonald Bros. Ltd.		William Street	34	161
McDonald Brothers		Bishop Street	11	122
McDonnell	David	Clarendon Street	69	127
McDonnell	George	Sydney Terrace	1	139
McDonnell	Mrs	Harvey Street	17	140
McDonnell	Robert	Shipquay Street	39, Belfast Bank	154
McDonough	James	Great James Street	68	139
McDowell	Charles	Thomas Street	17	158

Surname	First Name	Street	House Number	Page Number
McDowell	George	Tyrconnell Street	11	158
McDowell	George	Alfred Street	46	165
McDowell	James	Laburnum Terrace	18	142
McDowell	James	Rossville Street	11	153
McDowell	Mary	Fountain Hill	59	171
McDowell	Miss L.	Barry Street	35	121
McDowell	Miss Margaret	Epworth Street	15	163
McDowell	Patrick	Philips Street	17	151
McDowell	T. junior	Strand Road	50	156
McDowell	Thomas	Great James Street	38	139
McDowell	William	Glasgow Terrace	24	138
McDowell	William	Dervock Street	1	168
McEldowney	William	Grafton Street	23	138
McEleney	Michael	Abbey Street	28	117
McEleney	Michael	Rossville Street	62	153
McEleney	Patrick	Bishop Street	102	123
McElhinney	Alexander	Garden City		129
McElhinney	Edward	Aberfoyle Terrace	1, Strandview	156
McElhinney	Frank	Brandywell Avenue	1	124
McElhinney	Frank	Bluebellhill Terrace	224	144
McElhinney	James	Philips Street	26	151
McElhinney	Mark	Philips Street	24	151
McElhinney	Miss	Long Tower	6	145
McElhinney	R.	Northland Road	2, lodge	149
McElhinney	R. A.	Beechwood Avenue	40	121
McElhinney	Samuel	Henrietta Street	15	141
McElhinney	T.	Quay Queen's	workshop	152
McElhinney	T.	Strand Road	52	156
McElhinney	Thomas	De Burgh Square	8	130
McElhinney	Thomas	Marlborough Street	6	147
McElhinney	Thomas	Boating Club Lane		157
McElhinney	Thomas	Florence Street	5	170
McElroy	Samuel	Bishop Street	45	122
McElroy	Thomas	Asylum Road	8	120
McElroy	William	Barnewall Place	10	165
McElroy & Morris		Bishop Street	45	122
McElvenney	Mrs	Primrose Street	6	174
McElvenny	Miss M.	Foyle Road	79A	136
McElwee	Archibald	Albert Street	5	118
McElwee	George	Moore Street	6	173
McElwee	Thomas	Stanley's Walk	27	155
McElwee	William	Bellevue Avenue	15	121
McElwee	William	Bluebellhill Terrace	190	144
McEnaney	Mrs	Bishop Street	185	122
McEvoy	John	Westland Avenue	36	161
McFadden	Arthur	Quarry Street	5	152
McFadden	Bernard	Elmwood Terrace	33	132
McFadden	Bernard	Stanley's Walk	29	155
McFadden	Bridget	Hollywell Street	15	141

Surname	First Name	Street	House Number	Page Number
McFadden	Charles	Bishop Street	212	123
McFadden	Daniel	St. Columb's Wells	83	157
McFadden	James	Eden Place	8	132
McFadden	James	Limewood Street	25	144
McFadden	John	Long Tower	45	145
McFadden	John	Moore Street	14	148
McFadden	John	Nelson Street	18	149
McFadden	John	Duke Street	58	169
McFadden	Joseph	Bishop Street	110	123
McFadden	Michael	Fahan Street	51	133
McFadden	Miss Mary	Bishop Street	252	124
McFadden	Patrick	Lecky Road	3	143
McFadden	William	Argyle Street	63	119
McFadden	William	Brandywell Road	28	124
McFadden	William	Quarry Street	1	152
McFarland	Alexander	Hawkin Street	16	140
McFarland	Daniel	Alma Terrace	39	136
McFarland	Daniel G.	Gordon Terrace	14	138
McFarland	G. & Co.	Foyle Street	82	136
McFarland	James M.	Governor Road	8	138
McFarland	Lady	Strand Road	Aberfoyle	156
McFarland	Mary	Moore Street	8	173
McFarland	Mrs	Bennett Street Lower	39	122
McFarland	Sir B. A. T.	Northland Road	21, Richmond	150
McFarland	Sir B. A. T.	Strand Road	Richmond	156
McFarland	Thomas	Cuthbert Street	19	168
McFarland	William A.	Messines Park	57	128
McFaul	Annie	Meehan's Row	7	173
McFaul	David	Robert Street	4	174
McFaul	James	Fahan Street	71	133
McFaul	Rev. Charles	Chapel Road	Parochial House	167
McFaul	William	Fountain Hill	60	171
McFawn	Samuel	Fountain Place	29	135
McFeely	Daniel	Elmwood Street	4	132
McFeely	Denis	Great James Street	70	139
McFeely	Denis	Chapel Road	19	167
McFeely	John	Bennett Street Lower	16	122
McFeely	John	Westland Avenue	18	160
McFeely	Mary	Benvarden Avenue	10	166
McFeely	Mary A.	Bridge Street	68	125
McFeely	Patrrick J.	Francis Street	59	137
McFeely	D. F.	Strand Road	45	155
McFeely	D. F. & Co	Patrick Street	3, 4	151
McFeeters	James	Ivy Terrace	15	142
McFeeters	James	Ivy Terrace	10	142
McFeeters	Jane	Bishop Street	146	123
McFeeters	Mrs	Blee's Lane		124
McFeeters	Samuel	Fountain Street	106	135

Surname	First Name	Street	House Number	Page Number
McFetridge	Annie	Mrs C. F. Alexander's Memorial Cottages	2	126
McFrederick	Mrs	Hamilton Street	8	140
McGaffigan	John	Nassau Street Upper	23	149
McGahey	Charles	John Street	37, 39	142
McGahey	Charles	Kennedy Street	15	142
McGahey	James	Millar's Close		125
McGahey	James	Clarence Place	4	127
McGahey	Mrs	Fountain Street	54	134
McGahey	Mrs	Hayesbank Terrace		167
McGahey	Robert	Fountain Street	74	135
McGahey	William	Fountain Street	110	135
McGahey	William, J.P.	Fountain Street	43	134
McGandy	Daniel	Bond's Hill	7	166
McGarrigle	Andrew	Robert Street	14	174
McGarrigle	Charles	Moore Street	20	173
McGarrigle	George W.	Spencer Road	96	175
McGarrigle	James	Messines Park	28	128
McGarrigle	James	Tamneymore		175
McGarrigle	Mrs	Barry Street	27	121
McGarrigle	Thomas	Stanley's Walk	18	155
McGarrigle	William	Alma Place	11	119
McGarrigle	William	London Street	16	145
McGarrity	Constable J.	Ivy Terrace	8	142
McGarry	John	Bellevue Avenue	25	121
McGarvey	Catherine	Church Wall	5	127
McGarvey	David	Chapel Road	72	167
McGarvey	David	Robert Street	11	174
McGarvey	Fanny	Argyle Terrace	18	120
McGarvey	Henry	Creggan Road	42	163
McGarvey	James	Foyle Road	120	136
McGarvey	James	Long Tower	51	145
McGarvey	Mrs	Chamberlain Street	6	126
McGarvey	Thomas	Violet Street Upper	7	176
McGarvey	William	Clooney Terrace	18	167
McGaughey	John	Abercorn Road	34	118
McGavigan	James	Ferguson Street	40	134
McGavigan	Patrick	Eglinton Place	3	132
McGaw	James	Carlisle Road	40	125
McGeady	Catherine	Lecky Road	12	144
McGeady	Francis	High Street	8	141
McGeady	James	Hawthorn Terrace	4	140
McGeady	James	William Street	23	161
McGeady	John	Argyle Terrace	6	120
McGeady	John	Chamberlain Street	1	126
McGeady	John	William Street	22	161
McGee	John	Glendermott Road	20	171
McGee	James	Blucher Street	14	124
McGee	John	Clooney Terrace	50	167
McGeehan	Bernard	Henrietta Street	3	141

Surname	First Name	Street	House Number	Page Number
McGeehan	Charles	Clarke Terrace	244	144
McGeehan	James	Francis Street	5	137
McGeehan	James C.	Argyle Street	66	119
McGeehan	John	Chapel Road	21	167
McGeehan	Miss	Cottage Row	2	123
McGeehan	Miss	Ferguson Street	52	134
McGeehan	Mrs	Grafton Avenue	55	120
McGeehan	Neil	Beechwood Street	25	121
McGeehan	Patrick	Nassau Street Upper	17	149
McGeoghegan	Patrick	Fahan Street	146	133
McGeoghegan	Patrick	Rossville Street	9	153
McGeown	John	Rossville Street	24	153
McGettigan	Hugh	Westland Terrace	18	161
McGettigan	James	Governor Road	3	138
McGettigan	Michael	Chamberlain Street	15, 17	126
McGettigan	Mrs	Moore Street	2	173
McGettigan	Rev. J.	Creggan Street		129
McGhee	William J.	Park Avenue	8	151
McGildowny	Rosetta	Ivy Terrace	11	142
McGill	Charles	Fountain Hill	38	171
McGill	Edward	Strabane Old Road	17	175
McGill	John	Fountain Hill	28	171
McGill	Mrs	The Rock	111	156
McGill	Mrs	Herbert Street	1	171
McGill	Patrick	Great James Street	63A	139
McGill	Patrick	Lower Road	39	146
McGill	William	Walker's Place	21	159
McGilligan	John	Lecky Road	124	144
McGilloway	Charles	Brandywell Road	14	124
McGilloway	Daniel	Nassau Street Lower	17	148
McGilloway	James	Maybrook Terrace	3	128
McGilloway	James	Gortfoyle Place	6	171
McGilloway	John	Lecky Road	207	143
McGilloway	John	Sugarhouse lane	17	158
McGilloway	Joseph	Hollywell Street	1	141
McGilloway	Mrs	Windsor Terrace	3	162
McGilloway	Patrick	Thomas Street	30	158
McGilloway	Patrick	Meehan's Row	17	173
McGinley	Alfred	Ebrington Street	5	170
McGinley	Bernard	Abbey Street	63	117
McGinley	Charles	Cross Street	18	168
McGinley	Daniel	The Rock	107	156
McGinley	Edward	Glenview Avenue	15	137
McGinley	Edward	Strand Road	54	156
McGinley	Ellen	Union Street	31	176
McGinley	Grace	Sugarhouse lane	18	158
McGinley	Hugh	Rossville Street	17	153
McGinley	Hugh	Sloan's Terrace	9	154
McGinley	J. & T.	Foyle Street	7	135
McGinley	John	Donegal Place	8	131

Surname	First Name	Street	House Number	Page Number
McGinley	John	Frederick Street	3	137
McGinley	John	Stanley's Walk	2	155
McGinley	John	Bond's Street	1	166
McGinley	Miss	Waterloo Street	33	159
McGinley	Mrs	Clarendon Street	22	127
McGinley	Patrick	Millar's Close		125
McGinley	Patrick	Bridge Street	40	125
McGinley	Patrick	Foyle Street	103	135
McGinley	Patrick	Stanley's Walk	24	155
McGinley	Patrick	Townsend Street	4	158
McGinley	Patrick	William Street	97	161
McGinley	Sarah A.	Meehan's Row	19	173
McGinn	Mrs A.	William Street	27	161
McGinn	Mrs J.	Fountain Hill	26	171
McGinness	Miss	Ferguson Street	57	134
McGinnis	Edward	Benvarden Avenue	11	165
McGinnis	James	Creggan Street	35	129
McGinnis	James	Nelson Street	52	149
McGinnis	John	Clifton Street	6	167
McGinnis	Maria	Hollywell Row	77	143
McGinnis	Michael	Waterloo Street	49	159
McGinnis	Miss S.	William Street	113	161
McGinnis	Mrs	Nelson Street	41	149
McGinnis	Nurse	Bond's Hill	13	166
McGinnis	Patrick	Bluebellhill Terrace	196	144
McGinnis	William	Benvarden Avenue	13	165
McGinnis	Mrs	Violet Street Lower	4	176
McGinnis	Mrs	Collon Terrace	13	128
McGinniss	David	Robert Street	6	174
McGinniss	Edward	Duke Street	3	169
McGinniss	James	Chamberlain Street	4	126
McGinniss	John	Meadowbank Avenue	19	147
McGinniss	John	Wellington Street	71	160
McGinniss	Patrick	Orchard Street	7	151
McGinniss	Thomas	Elmwood Street	5	132
McGinty	Bernard	Long Tower	72	146
McGinty	Edward	High Street	11	141
McGinty	James	High Street	9	141
McGinty	James	Marlborough Street	11	146
McGirr	James	Bishop Street	57	122
McGirr	James	Mitchelburne Terrace	92	136
McGirr	Mrs	Carrigans Lane	23	126
McGirr	Peter	Orchard Street	18	151
McGlinchey	Andrew	Nailor's Row	30	148
McGlinchey	Edward	New Street	7	126
McGlinchey	Edward	Bluebellhill Terrace	148	144
McGlinchey	Henry	Ann Street	23	44
McGlinchey	James	Blucher Street	38	124
McGlinchey	James	Deanery Street	34	130
McGlinchey	James	Nelson Street	65	149

Surname	First Name	Street	House Number	Page Number
McGlinchey	James	Walker's Place	31	159
McGlinchey	Mary A.	Long Tower	20	145
McGlinchey	Michael	Carrigans Lane	19	126
McGlinchey	Miss	Spencer Road	166	175
McGlinchey	Mrs	Brook Street Avenue	2	125
McGlinchey	Mrs	Deanery Street	22	130
McGlinchey	Myles	Long Tower	34	146
McGlinchey	Thomas	Sloan's Terrace	10	155
McGlinchey	William	Creggan		131
McGlynn	Charles	Gortfoyle Place	11	171
McGlynn	Mary	Quarry Street	14	153
McGlynn	Miss	Westland Terrace	7	161
McGoldrick	James	Strabane Old Road	6	175
McGoldrick	John	King Street	32	172
McGonagle	Annie	Ann Street	13	119
McGonagle	Felix	Artisan Street	9	162
McGonagle	Hugh	Great James Street	57	139
McGonagle	Hugh	Bluebellhill Terrace	168	144
McGonagle	Hugh	Primrose Street	10	174
McGonagle	James	Kildarra Terrace	11	141
McGonagle	John	Edenmore Street	1	131
McGonagle	John	Northland Avenue	2A	150
McGonagle	Joseph	Bluebellhill Terrace	228	144
McGonagle	Mary	Lecky Road	47	143
McGonagle	Miss	Stanley's Walk	31	155
McGonagle	Mrs	Bishop Street	196	123
McGonagle	Mrs	Great James Street	74	139
McGonagle	Mrs S.	William Street	37	161
McGonagle	Sarah	Butcher Street	9A	125
McGonagle	William	Ann Street	14	119
McGonigal	Hugh	Miller Street	9	147
McGonigal	Matilda	Stanley's Walk	14	155
McGonigle	Bridget	Fahan Street	74	133
McGonigle	David	Simpson's Brae	13	174
McGonigle	H.	Foyle Street	34	136
McGonigle	Hugh	Violet Street Lower	6	176
McGonigle	James	Windmill Terrace	7	162
McGonigle	John	Clifton Street	4	167
McGonigle	Mrs	Epworth Street	3	163
McGonigle	Sarah	Governor Road	17	138
McGonigle	Thomas	Glendermott Road	52	171
McGonigle	William	Chapel Road	9	167
McGowan	Allan	Fountain Hill	73	171
McGowan	Charles	Abbey Street	12	117
McGowan	Charles	Barnewall Place	25	165
McGowan	Edward	Creggan Road	113	162
McGowan	George	Fountain Street	48	134
McGowan	George	Duke Street	1	169
McGowan	Hugh	Walker's Place	43	159
McGowan	James	Ann Street	19	144

Surname	First Name	Street	House Number	Page Number
McGowan	James	Wellington Street	30	160
McGowan	John	Cuthbert Street	25	168
McGowan	John	Moore Street	27	173
McGowan	Jospeh	Bond's Place	5	166
McGowan	Lawrence	Nelson Street	26	149
McGowan	Maggie	Walker's Place	40	159
McGowan	Michael	Lecky Road	129	143
McGowan	Michael J.	Abercorn Road	63	118
McGowan	Mrs	Fountain Street	55	134
McGowan	Mrs	Lecky Road	120	144
McGowan	Mrs	Moore Street	7	148
McGowan	Patrick	Wellington Street	64	160
McGowan	Patrick	William Street	28	161
McGowan	Patrick J.	Messines Park	44	128
McGowan	Rebecca	Alfred Street	7	165
McGowan	Susan	Wells Street Terrace	4	160
McGowan	Thomas	Spencer Road	148	175
McGowan	William	Alexandra Place	27	119
McGowan	William	Messines Park	32	128
McGowan	William	Moore Street	12	148
McGranaghan	John	Fitters Row	263	123
McGranaghan	John	Bluebellhill Terrace	210	144
McGranaghan	Susan	Gresham's Row	3	140
McGranaghan	William	Hamilton Street	49	140
McGranahan	William	Fahan Street	115, 117	133
McGranery	Daniel	Westland Avenue	6	160
McGrath	J. P.	Marlborough Street	29	146
McGrath	J. P.	New Market Street		149
McGrath	M. P.	Argyle Street		119
McGrath	Michael P.	Argyle Terrace	36	120
McGrath	Mrs	Waterloo Street	27	159
McGreenery	James	Riverview Terrace	3	174
McGregor	Alexander	Victoria Street	2	159
McGregor	William	Barrack Street	5	120
McGrelis	Robert	Foyle Street	58	136
McGrellis	Hugh	Orchard Street	3	151
McGrellis	Mrs	Orchard Row	10	150
McGrenery	Julia	Waterloo Street	4	159
McGrenra	Mrs	Cottage Row	18	164
McGroarty	Mary	St. Columb's Wells	61	157
McGroarty	Patrick	Foyle Road	32	136
McGrorty	Mrs	Creggan Road	107	162
McGrory	Annie	St. Columb's Wells	95	157
McGrory	Bernard	Marlborough Park	63	162
McGrory	Edward	Hawthorn Terrace	18	140
McGrory	Edward	Westland Villas	2	161
McGrory	Edward	Kerr's Terrace	27	162
McGrory	Elizabeth	Donegal Place	16	131
McGrory	F.	Bishop Street	10	123
McGrory	Hugh	Fahan Street	34	133

Surname	First Name	Street	House Number	Page Number
McGrory	James	Eden Place	3	132
McGrory	James	New Street	7	164
McGrory	John	Alma Place	13	119
McGrory	John	William Street	121	161
McGrory	Joseph	Bishop Street	83	122
McGrory	Leo	Cottage Row	24	164
McGrory	Mary A.	Donegal Place	12	131
McGrory	Mary A.	Edward Street	8	132
McGrory	Mrs	Castle Street	8	126
McGrory	Mrs	Creggan Road	8	163
McGrory	Patrick	Mary Street	2	147
McGrory	Sarah	Lewis Street	35	164
McGrory	W. J.	Lundy's Lane	2	145
McGrotty	Edward	Mount Street	4	164
McGuigan	Francis	Fahan Street	2	133
McGuigan	Francis	Fahan Street	2A	133
McGuigan	Patrick	York Street	21	176
McGuiggan	Felix	Fulton Place	8	137
McGuiggan	Lizzie	Fulton Place	4	137
McGuiggan	Margaret	Violet Street Lower	51	176
McGuinness	Archibald	Sunbeam Terrace	3	122
McGuinness	D. D.	St. Columb's Court	5	157
McGuinness	Hugh	Beechwood Avenue	4	121
McGuinness	James	Bishop Street	16	123
McGuinness	James	Osborne Street	3	164
McGuinness	John	Bishop Street	47	122
McGuinness	Mary	Bond's Hill	2	166
McGuinness	Michael	Westland Avenue	4	160
McGuinness	Mrs	Eden Place	12	132
McGuinness	Mrs	Lawrence Hill	18	143
McGuinness	Nellie	Rossville Street	32	153
McGuinness	W. N.	Lawrence Hill	28, Clifton Holme	143
McGuinness	Catherine	Bridge Street	66	125
McGuinness	Robert	Maybrook Terrace	2	128
McGuire	Charles	Abercorn Place		118
McGuire	Charles	Mrs C. F. Alexander's Memorial Cottages	1	126
McGuire	John	Creggan Road	36	163
McGuire	Mrs	Windmill Terrace	23	162
McGuire	Patrick	Spencer Road	48	175
McGuire	Thomas	Hamilton Street	54	140
McGuire	Thomas	Windmill Terrace	8	162
McGurk	James	Glendermott Road	92	171
McGurk	John	Bluebellhill Terrace	192	144
McGurk	Peter	Donegal Place	4	131
McGurnaghan	Nellie	Limewood Street	31	144
McHugh	Alexander	Wapping Lane	49	159
McHugh	Ellen	St. Columb's Terrace	89	143
McHugh	Henry	Donegal Street	1	163

Surname	First Name	Street	House Number	Page Number
McHugh	James	Creggan Road	87	162
McHugh	Joseph	Florence Street	19	163
McHugh	Mary	Dungiven Road	8	170
McHugh	Miss	Chamberlain Street	11	126
McIlaney	Mrs	Creggan Road	175	163
McIlhargey	The Misses	Sunbeam Terrace	11	122
McIlhargy	Mrs K.	Spencer Road	8	175
McIlhinny	S.	Strand Road	93, lodge	156
McIlroy	Robert	Westland Avenue	17	160
McIlroy	W. J.	Dungiven Road	Rossdowney	170
McIlwaine	Crawford	Abercorn Road	19	118
McIlwaine	Robert	Marlborough Street	28	147
McIlwaine	Samuel	Abercorn Road	21	118
McIlwaine	Samuel	Abercorn Road	28	118
McIntosh	W. R.	Baronet Street	5	120
McIntyre	Annie	Wells Street Terrace	1	160
McIntyre	Bernard	Bridge Street	29	124
McIntyre	Bernard	Ferguson Street	56	134
McIntyre	Bernard	Orchard Row	1	150
McIntyre	Bernard	Artisan Street	15	162
McIntyre	Charles	Artisan Street	2	162
McIntyre	Daniel	Abbey Street	43	117
McIntyre	Denis	St. Columb's Wells	74	157
McIntyre	Denis	St. Patrick Street	12	158
McIntyre	Edward	Fahan Street	158	133
McIntyre	Ellen	Creggan Road	50	163
McIntyre	George	Eden Place	16	132
McIntyre	Hugh	Ann Street	4	119
McIntyre	Hugh	Gordon Terrace	4	138
McIntyre	James	Millar's Close		125
McIntyre	John	St. Columb's Wells	29	157
McIntyre	John	Creggan Road	167	163
McIntyre	John	Barnewall Place	4	165
McIntyre	John	Dunfield Terrace	7	169
McIntyre	Joseph	Hamilton Street	15	139
McIntyre	Joseph	Nailor's Row	48	148
McIntyre	Joseph	Spencer Road	38	175
McIntyre	Miss	Artillery Street	2	120
McIntyre	Mrs	Fountain Street	23	134
McIntyre	Mrs	George Street	2	138
McIntyre	Mrs	Glasgow Terrace	19	138
McIntyre	Mrs	Strand Road	55	155
McIntyre	Mrs	King Street	13	172
McIntyre	Patrick	Donegal Place	10	131
McIntyre	Patrick	St. Columb's Wells	84	157
McIntyre	Philip	Alfred Street	42	165
McIntyre	Robert	Magazine Street Upper	Memorial Hall	146
McIntyre	Thomas	Beechwood Avenue	82	121
McIntyre	Thomas	Market Street	4	147

Surname	First Name	Street	House Number	Page Number
McIntyre	William	Chamberlain Street	18	126
McIntyre	William	Donegal Street	6	163
McIntyre	William	Moore Street	17	173
McIntyre	William	Spencer Road	103	174
McIntyre	William	Society Street	15	155
McIntyre, Hogg, Marsh & Co.		Queen Street	shirt factory	153
McIvor	Bernard	Fountain Hill	94	171
McIvor	Edward & Co.	Strand Road	65	155
McIvor	Miss	Glendermott Road	30	171
McKale	Joseph	Hamilton Street	35	140
McKane	John	Abbey Street	31	117
McKane	Joseph	Thomas Street	44	158
McKane	Robert	Emerson Street	28	170
McKane	W. J.	Pine Street	21	174
McKane	William	Clooney Terrace	40	167
McKay	Harry	Brooke Villas	41	165
McKay	Marshall	Termonbacca		137
McKay	Thomas	Limewood Street	36	144
McKeague	James	Mount Street	13	164
McKeague	Patrick	Duke Street	3	169
McKearn	Mary J.	Foyle Road	48	136
McKee	Robert	Edenbank	60	150
McKee	William J.	De Burgh Square	2	130
McKee	James	Clarence Avenue	7	127
McKee	Miss	Lone Moor	Foyle Hill Hospital	145
McKee	Miss K.	Hawkin Street	39	140
McKeegan	Ann Jane	Stewart's Terrace	3	155
McKeegan	David	Pine Street	27	174
McKeegan	Mrs	Orchard Row	17	150
McKeever	Charles	Governor Road	27	138
McKeever	Henry	Bluebellhill Terrace	200	144
McKeever	James	Hamilton Street	26	140
McKeever	John	Creggan Street	7	129
McKeever	John	Hamilton Street	12	140
McKeever	John	Glendermott Road	66	171
McKeever	Maggie	Deanery Street	48	130
McKeever	Michael	Strand Road Lower	159	156
McKeever	Miss	Dungiven Road	5	169
McKeever	Mrs	Elmwood Terrace	17	132
McKeever	Mrs	Cranagh Terrace	3	142
McKeever	Mrs	Little Diamond	4	145
McKeever	Mrs	Strand Road Lower	149	156
McKeever	Thomas	Hamilton Street	18	140
McKeever	William	Brook Street Avenue	4	125
McKeever	William	Hawthorn Terrace	8	140
McKeever	William	Quarry Street	19	153
McKendrick	Charles	Epworth Street	13	163
McKenna	Henry	Stanley's Walk	20	155
McKenna	Henry	Westland Avenue	12	160

Surname	First Name	Street	House Number	Page Number
McKenna	John	William Street	64	162
McKenna	Mrs	Bishop Street	101	122
McKenna	Neil	Marlborough Avenue	32	147
McKenna	Patrick	Rossville Street	85	153
McKenna	Patrick	William Street	105	161
McKenna	Philip	Carlin Street	5	166
McKenna	Sarah	Foyle Street	17	135
McKenzie	Alexander	Florence Street	17	163
McKenzie	Robert	Alfred Street	48	165
McKeon	James	Kildarra Terrace	4	141
McKeown	Hugh	Marlborough Street	14	147
McKeown	James	Rossville Street	48	153
McKeown	John	Castle Gate	3	126
McKeown	John	Grafton Street	4	139
McKeown	John	Olive Terrace	5	174
McKeown	Michael	Richmond Street	15, 17	153
McKeown	Mrs	Beechwood Street	20	121
McKeown & Co.		Ferryquay Street	25	134
McKeown & Co.		Waterloo Street	24	159
McKeown & Co.		William Street	38	161
McKernan	Frank	Fahan Street	11, 13	133
McKerr	Edwin C.	Pump Street	1	152
McKillip	J.	Shipquay Street	39, Belfast Bank	154
McKillip	John	Victoria Park	11	176
McKimm	Mrs	Windmill Terrace	26	162
McKimm	Robert	Orchard Street	9	151
McKinlay	H & Co.	Diamond		130
McKinlay	James	Ferguson Street	59	134
McKinlay	John	Bishop Street	202	123
McKinlay	John	Moore Street	25	173
McKinlay	Lewis	Moore Street	19	173
McKinley	John	Creggan		131
McKinney	Annie	Duke Street	5	169
McKinney	Catherine	Orchard Lane	6	151
McKinney	Charles	Osborne Street	9	164
McKinney	Doctor W. G.	Bond's Hill	30	166
McKinney	Hugh	Tyrconnell Street	1	158
McKinney	James	Ann Street	13	143
McKinney	James	Cross Street	7	168
McKinney	John	Bishop Street	236	124
McKinney	John	Governor Road	19	138
McKinney	John junior	Blucher Street	28	124
McKinney	John senior	Blucher Street	26	124
McKinney	Miss	Bishop Street	234	123
McKinney	Moses	Foyle View	1	137
McKinney	Mrs	Dark Lane	14	130

Surname	First Name	Street	House Number	Page Number
McKinney	P. & Co.	Patrick Street	6, 7	151
McKinney	Patrick	Union Street	2	176
McKinney	Rev. J. W.	Victoria Park	3	176
McKinney	Robert	Alfred Street	41	165
McKinney	Samuel	Moore Street	5	148
McKinney	Thomas	New Street	16	164
McKinney	William	Bishop Street	153	122
McKinney	William	Governor Road	44	138
McKinney	William	Dungiven Road		170
McKinnon	Murdock	Garden City		129
McKnight	John	Cross Street	35	168
McKnight	Samuel	Corporation Street	23	128
McLaren	John	Blucher Street	2	124
McLaren	William	Marlborough Terrace	18	147
McLaren	William & Co.	Strand Road	59 & 61	155
McLaughlin	Alex. H.	Foyle Road	49	136
McLaughlin	Alexander	Creggan		131
McLaughlin	Andrew	Fountain Place	19	135
McLaughlin	Andrew	Hamilton Street	38	140
McLaughlin	Ann	Strabane Old Road	64	175
McLaughlin	Bernard	Bishop Street	93	122
McLaughlin	Bernard	Waterloo Street	9	159
McLaughlin	Bernard	Primrose Street	21	174
McLaughlin	Bridget	Corbett Street (Pilot's Row)	6	128
McLaughlin	Bridget	Morrison's Close	3	133
McLaughlin	Bridget	William Street	60	162
McLaughlin	C.	Richmond Street	8	153
McLaughlin	Catherine	Carrigans Lane	15	126
McLaughlin	Catherine	Fulton Place	20	137
McLaughlin	Catherine	Northland Avenue	23	150
McLaughlin	Charles	Harvey Street	7	140
McLaughlin	Charles	Lecky Road	275	143
McLaughlin	Charles	Linenhall Street Upper	17	145
McLaughlin	Charles	William Street	79	161
McLaughlin	Daniel	Abbey Street	33	117
McLaughlin	Daniel	Cottage Row	12	164
McLaughlin	Daniel	Fountain Hill	15	171
McLaughlin	David	Creggan Road	60	163
McLaughlin	Denis	Lewis Street	4	164
McLaughlin	Dr. J. N.	Queen Street	13	153
McLaughlin	Edward	Cable Street	13	125
McLaughlin	Edward	Creggan Terrace	2	129
McLaughlin	Edward	Creggan Terrace	12	129
McLaughlin	Edward	Elmwood Terrace	44	132
McLaughlin	Edward	Limewood Street	13	144
McLaughlin	Elizabeth	Bishop Street	280	124
McLaughlin	Elizabeth	John Street	23	142
McLaughlin	Eugene	Moore Street	6	148

Surname	First Name	Street	House Number	Page Number
McLaughlin	Francis	Riverview Terrace	7	174
McLaughlin	George	Union Street	7	176
McLaughlin	Hugh	Bishop Street	219	123
McLaughlin	Hugh	Bishop Street	200	123
McLaughlin	Hugh	Lecky Road	stores	143
McLaughlin	Hugh	Nassau Street Upper	3	149
McLaughlin	Hugh	Nelson Street	71	149
McLaughlin	Hugh	Quarry Street	4	153
McLaughlin	Hugh	William Street	75	161
McLaughlin	J.	Richmond Street	6	153
McLaughlin	J.	Limavady Road	4, gate lodge	172
McLaughlin	J. (reps of)	Waterloo Street	57	159
McLaughlin	James	Baronet Street	1A	120
McLaughlin	James	Bishop Street	132	123
McLaughlin	James	Fox's Lane	2	137
McLaughlin	James	Hamilton Street	36	140
McLaughlin	James	High Street	4	141
McLaughlin	James	Mountjoy Street	21	148
McLaughlin	James	The Rock	113	156
McLaughlin	James	Strand Road	116	157
McLaughlin	James	Thomas Street	15	158
McLaughlin	James	Union Street	2	158
McLaughlin	James	Chapel Road	20	167
McLaughlin	James	Cuthbert Street	23	168
McLaughlin	James	Glendermott Road	40	171
McLaughlin	John	Argyle Street	69	119
McLaughlin	John	Bennett Street Upper	5	122
McLaughlin	John	Bishop Street	227	123
McLaughlin	John	Bishop Street	243	123
McLaughlin	John	Corbett Street (Pilot's Row)	15	128
McLaughlin	John	Corbett Street (Pilot's Row)	12	128
McLaughlin	John	Eglinton Terrace	3	132
McLaughlin	John	Fountain Street	84	135
McLaughlin	John	Foyle Street	41	135
McLaughlin	John	Governor Road	2B	138
McLaughlin	John	Hawthorn Terrace	26	140
McLaughlin	John	Joseph Street	1	142
McLaughlin	John	Lecky Road	117	143
McLaughlin	John	Nassau Street Lower	10	148
McLaughlin	John	St. Columb's Wells	103	157
McLaughlin	John	Waterloo Street	34	159
McLaughlin	John	Alfred Street	14	165
McLaughlin	John	Dungiven Road	59	170
McLaughlin	Joseph	Argyle Street	45	119
McLaughlin	Joseph	Beechwood Street	28	121
McLaughlin	Joseph	Brandywell Road	24	124
McLaughlin	Joseph	Creggan Street	31	129
McLaughlin	Joseph	Duke Street	15	169

Surname	First Name	Street	House Number	Page Number
McLaughlin	Lewis	Derry View Terrace	7	168
McLaughlin	Margaret	Fahan Street	27	133
McLaughlin	Margaret	Howard Street	1	141
McLaughlin	Mary	Deanery Place	2	130
McLaughlin	Mary	High Street	7	141
McLaughlin	Mary	Lower Road	14	146
McLaughlin	Mary Ann	Frederick Street	1	137
McLaughlin	Mary E.	Frederick Street	4	137
McLaughlin	Michael	Argyle Terrace	22	120
McLaughlin	Michael	Bishop Street	55	122
McLaughlin	Michael	Fulton Place	19	137
McLaughlin	Michael	Westland Terrace	10	161
McLaughlin	Michael	West-End Terrace	4	161
McLaughlin	Michael A.	Great James Street	69	139
McLaughlin	Miss	St. Columb's Wells	108	157
McLaughlin	Mrs	Ann Street	9	119
McLaughlin	Mrs	Bishop Street	256	124
McLaughlin	Mrs	Great James Street	67	139
McLaughlin	Mrs	Nelson Street	2	149
McLaughlin	Mrs	Thomas Street	7	158
McLaughlin	Mrs	Tyrconnell Street	9	158
McLaughlin	Mrs	Carlin Street	7	166
McLaughlin	Mrs	Fountain Hill	62	171
McLaughlin	Mrs	Fountain Hill	90	171
McLaughlin	Mrs Bridget	Nelson Street	34	149
McLaughlin	Mrs Rose	Park Avenue	1	151
McLaughlin	Mrs S.	Linenhall Street Upper	5	144
McLaughlin	P.	Carlisle Road	45	125
McLaughlin	Pat	Eglinton Place	4	132
McLaughlin	Patrick	Argyle Street	24	119
McLaughlin	Patrick	Chamberlain Street	24	126
McLaughlin	Patrick	Creggan Street	19	129
McLaughlin	Patrick	Dark Lane	10	130
McLaughlin	Patrick	Lecky Road	114	144
McLaughlin	Patrick	Bluebellhill Terrace	212	144
McLaughlin	Patrick	Long Tower	63	145
McLaughlin	Patrick	Nassau Street Lower	15	148
McLaughlin	Patrick	Sugarhouse lane	1	158
McLaughlin	Patrick	Wellington Street	67	160
McLaughlin	Patrick	Lewis Street	31	164
McLaughlin	Patrick	Spencer Road	136	175
McLaughlin	Philip	Eglinton Place	19	132
McLaughlin	Phillip	Stanley's Walk	50, 51	155
McLaughlin	Robert	Donaghy's Row	3	140
McLaughlin	Robert	Gortfoyle Place	1	171
McLaughlin	Thomas	Collon Terrace		128
McLaughlin	Thomas	Elmwood Terrace	48	132
McLaughlin	Thomas	Elmwood Street	9	132
McLaughlin	W. J.	Nassau Street Lower	26	148

Surname	First Name	Street	House Number	Page Number
McLaughlin	William	Bishop Street	99	122
McLaughlin	William	Brook Street	5	125
McLaughlin	William	Creggan Street	49	129
McLaughlin	William	Glenbrook Terrace	21	137
McLaughlin	William	Hollywell Street	10	141
McLaughlin	William	Lecky Road	17	143
McLaughlin	William	Lecky Road	2	144
McLaughlin	William	Lecky Road	34	144
McLaughlin	William	Bluebellhill Terrace	158	144
McLaughlin	William	Nassau Street Lower	50	148
McLaughlin	William	Richmond Street	13	153
McLaughlin	William	Shipquay Street	2	154
McLaughlin	William	The Rock	117	156
McLaughlin	William	William Street	92	162
McLaughlin	William	Ashfield Terrace	33	162
McLaughlin	William	Creggan Road	16	163
McLaughlin	William	Mount Street	15	164
McLaughlin	William	Duddy's Row	3	169
McLaughlin	William	Duke Street	11	169
McLaughlin	William	Violet Street Lower	34	176
McLaughlin Bros.		William Street	33	161
McLean	John	Edenballymore		131
McLehose	James	Dungiven Road	103	170
McLelland	Robert	Ebrington Terrace	14	170
McLenaghan	Robert	Lecky Road	53	143
McLeod	Gilbert	Robert Street	18	174
McLoone	Joseph	Foyleview Terrace	10	156
McLoone	Neil & Co.	Sir E. Reid's Market		154
McLoone	Neill & Co	Linenhall Street Upper		145
McLoone	Neill & Co.	Linenhall Street Upper		144
McLoone	Peter	Union Street	23	158
McLoughlin	Miss	Little James Street	10	145
McLucas	Andrew	Foyle View	5	137
McLucas	Archibald	Wesley Street	7	165
McLucas	John	Donegal Place	24	131
McLucas	Joseph	Foyle View	11	137
McLucas	Joseph	Governor Road	34	138
McLucas	Mrs	Orchard Row	24	150
McLucas	William	Garden City		129
McLure	Donald	Ferguson Street	5	133
McMackin	James	Bennett Street Upper	19	122
McMahon	Hugh	London Street	12	145
McMahon	James	Brandywell Road	23	124
McMahon	John	Donegal Street	43	163
McMahon	Michael	Creggan Terrace	13	129
McMahon	Mrs	North Street	3	164
McManus	Jane	Lecky Road	96	144

Surname	First Name	Street	House Number	Page Number
McManus	John	Bridge Street	11	124
McManus	John	Creggan Road	111	162
McManus	Miss	Marlborough Park	59	162
McManus	Mrs	Hogg's Folly	14	141
McManus	Philip	Foyle Street	5	135
McManus	Richard	Bridge Street	15	124
McManus	Rose	Violet Street Lower	11	176
McMaster	Professor J.	College Avenue	3	150
McMenamin	Edward	Hamilton Street	48	140
McMenamin	Edward	Orchard Street	23	151
McMenamin	Edward	Dungiven Road	23	169
McMenamin	Francis	Bishop Street	262	124
McMenamin	Frank	Bishop Street	124	123
McMenamin	Hugh	Donegal Place	14	131
McMenamin	James	Miller Street	17	147
McMenamin	John	Nailor's Row	35	148
McMenamin	John	Dungiven Road	18	170
McMenamin	John	Union Street	5	176
McMenamin	Lizzie	Foster's Terrace	167	143
McMenamin	Michael	Hamilton Street	46	140
McMenamin	Michael	Limewood Street	27	144
McMenamin	William	Hamilton Street	28	140
McMenemy	John	Iona Terrace	7	172
McMichael	James	De Burgh Square	6	130
McMichael	Samuel	Kerr's Terrace	19	162
McMichael	Samuel	Glendermott Road	22	171
McMichael Bros		Sackville Street	8	154
McMillan	Andrew D.	Florence Street	4	164
McMillan	Charles	Creggan Road	83	162
McMillan	David	New Street	4	126
McMillan	Neil	Messines Park	3	128
McMonagle	Charles	Joseph Street	7	142
McMonagle	Denis	St. Columb's Wells	30	157
McMonagle	J.	Magazine Street Upper	5	146
McMonagle	James	Nelson Street	53	149
McMonagle	John	Butcher Street	15	125
McMonagle	John	Butcher Street	cellar	125
McMonagle	John	Eden Place	7	132
McMonagle	Miss	Kennedy Place	3	142
McMonagle	P.	Magazine Street	1	146
McMonagle	Pat	Waterloo Street	14	159
McMonagle	Sarah	Blucher Street	9	124
McMonagle	William	Clarendon Street	stables	127
McMonigle	William	Limewood Street	1	144
McMorris	Archie	Princes Terrace	1	152
McMorris	James	Fountain Hill	41, waterman's house	171
McMorris	Mrs	Wesley Street	4	165
McMorris	Robert J.	Bond's Street	18	166

Surname	First Name	Street	House Number	Page Number
McMorris	Samuel	MalvernTerrace	15	169
McMorris	Samuel	Primrose Street	9	174
McMorris	Samuel	Violet Street Upper	6	176
McMoyle	Mrs A.	Marlborough Avenue	26	147
McMullan	H. & Co.	East Wall	5	131
McMullan	Herbert	Hinton Park	4	172
McMullan	Hugh	Bishop Street		122
McMullan	James	Hayesbank Terrace	63	167
McMullan	James	Clooney Terrace	30	168
McMullan	Joseph	Violet Street Lower	19	176
McMurray	Hugh	Argyle Street	68	119
McMurray	Mrs	Foyle Road	104	136
McMurray	Robert	Creggan		131
McNair	Mrs	Kildarra Terrace	8	141
McNally	John C.	Beechwood Avenue	74	121
McNally	Patrick	Bluebellhill Terrace	174	144
McNamee	Bridget	Alexandra Place	24	119
McNamee	David	Nailor's Row	7	148
McNamee	Joseph	Long Tower	49	145
McNamee	Mrs	Sugarhouse lane	16	158
McNaught	Mrs	Sloan's Terrace	37	155
McNaught	Mrs	Strabane Old Road	84	175
McNaught	Mrs	Strabane Old Road	102	175
McNaul	Robert	Fountain Hill	42	171
McNaul	Robert	Victoria Road	10	176
McNeary	Mark	Claremont Villas	38, North Lodge	150
McNeary	Matthew	De Burgh Terrace	17	130
McNeary & Wiley		Bishop Street	20, 21	122
McNee	John	Brooke Villas	43	165
McNee	Mrs	Barry Street	20	121
McNeill	Henry	Henry Street	17	141
McNeill	Mrs	Beechwood Avenue	36	121
McNeill	William	Florence Street	26	170
McNeill	William	Spencer Road	140	175
McNelis	Neil	Laburnum Terrace	20	142
McNicholl	Henry	Grafton Street	21	138
McNulty	Daniel	Fox's Lane	5	137
McNulty	Edward	Deanery Street	5	130
McNulty	Ellen	Long Tower	24	146
McNulty	Ernest	Alexandra Place	4	119
McNulty	George	Henrietta Street	1	141
McNulty	Henry	Foyle Road	66	136
McNulty	James	Fahan Street	98	133
McNulty	James	Linenhall Street Lower	12	145
McNulty	James	St. Columb's Wells	101	157
McNulty	John	Alexandra Place	15	119
McNulty	John	Fountain Street	65	134

Surname	First Name	Street	House Number	Page Number
McNulty	John	Fountain Hill	31	171
McNulty	John	Spencer Road	66	175
McNulty	Mrs	Alexandra Place	1	119
McNulty	Mrs	Foyleview Terrace	18	156
McNulty	Mrs	Duddy's Row	6	169
McNulty	Rose	Glendermott Road	32	171
McNulty	Thomas	Morrison's Close	2	133
McNulty	William	Donegal Place	15	131
McNulty	William	Cross Street	34	168
McNulty	William J.	Long Tower	74	146
McNutt	Alex	Pennyburn	2	151
McNutt	David	Lewis Street	12	164
McNutt	James	Foyle Road	63	136
McNutt	John	Elmwood Terrace	37	132
McNutt	Juden	Governor Road	28	138
McNutt	Michael	Nelson Street	43	149
McNutt	Miss	Culmore Road	Grian-Lagh	129
McNutt	R. J.	Hayesbank Terrace	Fountain Villa	167
McNutt	R. J. & Son	Ferryquay Street		134
McNutt	Samuel	Union Street	25	176
McNutt	William George	Union Street	18	176
McPherson	John	Glenbrook Terrace	11	137
McPherson	Joseph	Ebrington Street	1	170
McPherson	Miss	Glendermott Road	72	171
McPherson	Mrs	Clooney Terrace	17	167
McPherson	Samuel	Alfred Street	34	165
McPherson	T.	Bond's Street	32	166
McPhilemy	John	Bishop Street	203	122
McPhillips	Patrick J.	Deanery Place	1	130
McPoyle	Dominick	Bishop Street	120	123
McQuade	Charles	Elmwood Terrace	40	132
McQuade	Charles	Walker's Place	47	159
McQuade	Mrs	Bishop Street	258	124
McQuaid	John	Lecky Road	98	144
McQuaide	Richard	Henrietta Street	7	141
McQuigg	Daniel	Wellington Street	21	160
McQuigg	George	Carlisle Pass	1	125
McQuigg	J. J.	Foyle Street	101	135
McQuigg	John	Wellington Street	54	160
McQuilken	Hugh	Adair Street	2	118
McQuilkin	Hugh	Cooke Street	7	128
McRitchie	Mrs	Marlborough Villas	3	146
McShane	Daniel	Fountain Hill	65A	171
McShane	Francis	Dungiven Road	97	170
McShane	John	Barnewall Place	22	165
McShane	Patrick	Ann Street	6	119
McShane	Patrick	Dungiven Road	81	170
McShane	William	St. Columb's Wells	63	157
McShane	William J.	Spencer Road	45	174
McSherry	Thomas	Bridge Street	21	124

Surname	First Name	Street	House Number	Page Number
McSherry	Thomas	Bridge Street	25	124
McSorley	William	Elmwood Terrace	25	132
McSwine	Alex	Fahan Street	65	133
McSwine	Daniel	Bridge Street	16	124
McSwine	Daniel	Lecky Road	269	143
McTaggart	James	Creggan Terrace	11	129
McTiernan	James	Bishop Street	292	124
McVeigh	Andrew	Great James Street	51	139
McVeigh	Daniel	Walker's Place	7	159
McVeigh	J. & Co.	Strand Road	16	156
McVeigh	J. & Co.	Strand Road	18	156
McVeigh	James	Nelson Street	9	149
McVeigh	John	Beechwood Park	92	121
McVicker	John G.	Crawford Square	9	129
McVicker	R. & A.	Shipquay Street	25	154
McVicker	Rev Samuel	Crawford Square	17	129
McWilliams	Michael	Strabane Old Road	82	175
McWilliams	R.	De Burgh Square	7	130
McWilliams	Samuel	Mill Street		173
Meehan	Charles	Francis Street	9	137
Meehan	John	Brook Street Avenue	3	125
Meehan	Joseph	Malvern Terrace	9	169
Meehan	Mrs	Pump Street	17	152
Meehan	Patrick	Brandywell Road	21	124
Meehan	Timothy	Abbey Street	14	117
Meenan	Bernard	Messines Park	29	128
Meenan	Catherine	Lecky Road	9	143
Meenan	Daniel	Brandywell Road	3	124
Meenan	Elizabeth	Argyle Street	32	119
Meenan	Jeremiah	Wellington Street	65	160
Meenan	John	Mountjoy Street	8	148
Meenan	John	Tyrconnell Street	27	158
Meenan	Joseph	Glenbrook Terrace	1	137
Meenan	Patrick	Chamberlain Street	13	126
Meenan	William	Northland Terrace	7	150
Megan	James	Marlborough Avenue	24	147
Mehaffey	C. A. & Son	Foyle Street	13	135
Mehaffy	C. A.	Culmore Road	Ballynatrua	129
Melaugh	Charles	Lecky Road	291	143
Melaugh	John	Bishop Street	224	123
Melaugh	Thomas	St. Columb's Wells	17	157
Melaugh	William J.	St. Columb's Wells	26	157
Mellon	Francis	Ashfield Terrace	43	162
Mellon	Frank	Lecky Road	271	143
Mellon	James	Artillery Street	3½	120
Mellon	James	Bishop Street	139	122
Mellon	James	Hogg's Folly	10	141
Mellon	John	Governor Road	41	138
Mellon	Mary	Deanery Street	42	130
Mellon	Rodger	Bishop Street	120	123

Surname	First Name	Street	House Number	Page Number
Mellon	William	Orchard Lane	4	151
Melville	J.	Butcher Street	6	125
Melville	John	Hawkin Street	19	140
Mendall	Harry	Ernest Street	17	163
Menmuir	J. Leslie	Albert Place	8	119
Menmuir	Mrs	Hawkin Street	44	140
Mercer	Thomas	Nassau Street Upper	15	149
Mercy, The Sisters of		Culmore Road	Thornhill	129
Mernor	Edward	Pine Street	3	174
Merrick	John	St. Columb's Wells	86	157
Merricks	John	Chamberlain Street	5	126
Merrigan	John	Bishop Street	254	124
Mervyn	Mrs	Spencer Road	92	175
Meyer	Edward	King Street	41	172
Michael	Mrs	Nassau Street Lower	1	148
Millar	Alex	Bond's Hill	11	166
Millar	Frederick	Kennedy Street	21	142
Millar	John	Strand Road Lower	151	156
Millar	Joseph	Spencer Road	63	174
Millar	Thomas	Grove Place	1	139
Millar	William	Hamilton Street	40	140
Millar	William	Ivy Terrace	30	142
Millar	Mrs D. G.	Edenbank	56	150
Millar	William	Nassau Street Lower	37	148
Millar & Beatty		Magazine Street Upper	3	146
Millar & Beatty Ltd		Bishop Street	7, 9	122
Millen	Thomas	West-End Park	5	161
Miller	Andrew	De Burgh Square	12	130
Miller	Andrew	Ferguson Street	22	134
Miller	Captain J. E. T.	Limavady Road	18	173
Miller	David	Asylum Road	4	120
Miller	David	Linenhall Street Upper	15	145
Miller	David	Pine Street	18	174
Miller	Henry	Bishop Street	95	122
Miller	Herbert	Edenmore Street	33	131
Miller	Hessy J.	Lewis Street	3	164
Miller	Hugh	Bellevue Avenue	10	121
Miller	J. & F.	Linenhall Street Lower		145
Miller	J. & F.	Richmond Street	19	153
Miller	J. & F.	Strand Road	43	155
Miller	James	Argyle Street	51	119
Miller	James	Fountain Street	80	135
Miller	James	King Street	43	172
Miller	Jeannie	Fountain Street	73	134
Miller	John	Bridge Street	12	124

Surname	First Name	Street	House Number	Page Number
Miller	John	Henry Street	1	141
Miller	John	Windmill Terrace	21	162
Miller	John	Spencer Road	69	174
Miller	Joseph	Howard Street	14	141
Miller	Maria C.	Asylum Road	11	120
Miller	Mary A.	Benvarden Avenue	41	166
Miller	Miss	Great James Street	6	139
Miller	Mrs	Nicholson Square	1	149
Miller	Mrs	Fountain Hill	37	171
Miller	Mrs	Spencer Road	20	175
Miller	Mrs Susan	Malvern Terrace	11	169
Miller	Richard	Dunfield Terrace	17	169
Miller	Robert	Governor Road	20	138
Miller	Samuel J.	Termon Street	2	175
Miller	Sir F. H.	Shipquay Place	Guildhall (Town Clerk)	154
Miller	Thomas	Victoria Street	5	159
Miller	William	Windmill Terrace	6	162
Miller	William	Windmill Terrace	10	162
Miller	James	Carlisle Road	32	125
Miller & Babington		Shipquay Street	33	154
Milligan	Cecil D.	Fairman Place	25	133
Milligan	Charles	Mary Street	20	147
Milligan	Mrs	Dark Lane	17	130
Milligan	Mrs	Gordon Place	1	138
Milligan	Mrs	Mountjoy Street	25	148
Mills	A. & Co.	Clarendon Street		127
Mills	Alex	Orchard Row	6	150
Mills	David	Pine Street	15	174
Mills	Ernest	Hayesbank Terrace	51	167
Mills	J. J.	Fountain Hill	36	171
Mills	John	Northland Road	33	150
Mills	Lieutenant L. J.	Limavady Road	31	172
Mills	Mrs	Dark Lane	8	130
Mills	Mrs	Ivy Terrace	27	142
Mills	Ralph	Carlisle Road	49	125
Mills	Samuel	Chapel Road	6	167
Mills	Thomas	Edenmore Street	27	131
Mills	Thomas	Strabane Old Road	96	175
Milne	G. G.	Foyle Street	13	135
Milne	George G.	Rosemount Terrace	1	165
Ming	Frederick	Fountain Place	31	135
Ming	Henry	Collon Terrace	8	128
Mitchell	Alex	Society Street	13	155
Mitchell	Captain Joseph	Clooney Terrace	36	167
Mitchell	David	Wesley Street	23	165
Mitchell	George	Florence Street	32	170
Mitchell	J. C.	Brooke view	49, Beausite	165
Mitchell	James	Blee's Lane		124

Surname	First Name	Street	House Number	Page Number
Mitchell	James	Crawford Square	14	129
Mitchell	James	Garden City		129
Mitchell	James	Meadowbank Avenue	7	147
Mitchell	James	Nassau Street Lower	34	148
Mitchell	James	Bentley Street	5	165
Mitchell	James Ltd	Foyle Road	1	136
Mitchell	James Ltd	John Street	12	142
Mitchell	Jane C.	Clooney Terrace	25	167
Mitchell	John	Governor Road	24	138
Mitchell	John	Guildhall Street		139
Mitchell	John	Shipquay Place	6, Northern Bank	154
Mitchell	John	Alfred Street	4	165
Mitchell	John	Bond's Street	12	146
Mitchell	John	Florence Street	29	170
Mitchell	John	Glendermott Road	80	171
Mitchell	John	Herbert Street	15	172
Mitchell	Joseph	Abercorn Road	60	118
Mitchell	Joseph	Kennedy Street	9	142
Mitchell	Joseph	Nassau Street Lower	9	148
Mitchell	Miss	Argyle Street	11	119
Mitchell	Miss	Diamond	10	130
Mitchell	Mrs	Fairman Place	24	133
Mitchell	Mrs A.	Queen Street	1	153
Mitchell	Robert	Abercorn Place	11	118
Mitchell	Robert	Aubrey Street	30	120
Mitchell	Robert	Dark Lane	1	129
Mitchell	Robert	Dark Lane	15	130
Mitchell	Robert	Ferguson Street	41	133
Mitchell	Robert	Society Street	13	155
Mitchell	Robert	Primrose Street	29	174
Mitchell	Samuel	Aubrey Street	8	120
Mitchell	Stewart sen	Major's Row	4	146
Mitchell	W. G.	William Street	36	161
Mitchell	William	Dark Lane	9	130
Mitchell	William	Orchard Row	16	150
Mitchell	William	Benvarden Avenue	19	165
Mitchell	William	Meehan's Row	3	173
Mitchell	William	Strabane Old Road	3	175
Mitchell	William Ltd	Foyle Street	9	135
Mitchell	William S.	Garden City		129
Mitchell & Co.		Spencer Road	5	174
Mitchell Bros.		Sackville Street	15	154
Molloy	Bernard	Adam Street	1	118
Molloy	Con	Lundy's Lane	1	145
Molloy	Con	Waterloo Street	31	159
Molloy	Hugh	Glasgow Street	4	138
Molloy	James	Aubrey Street	24	120
Molloy	John	Bellevue Avenue	5	121
Molloy	Joseph J.	London Street	11	145

Surname	First Name	Street	House Number	Page Number
Molloy	Michael	Townsend Street	2	158
Molloy	Miss	Bennett Street Upper	15	122
Molloy	Mrs	Albert Street	6	118
Molloy	Mrs	Foyleview Terrace	14	156
Molloy	Neil	New Street	6	128
Molloy	Robert	Glen Terrace	4	131
Molloy	William	Bellevue Avenue	37	121
Monaghan	Hugh	Barnewall Place	28	165
Montague	John	Lecky Road	104	144
Montague Burton & Co.		Ferryquay Street	34	134
Monteith	Miss	Princes Terrace	7	152
Monteith	Mrs	Dungiven Road	32	170
Monteith	Mrs	Spencer Road	90	175
Montgomery	A. Ltd	Duke Street	3	169
Montgomery	Alex	Clarendon Street	16	127
Montgomery	Alex. Ltd	Strand Road	74	157
Montgomery	Alexander	Cedar Street	3	126
Montgomery	J. R.	Orchard Lane	8, 9	151
Montgomery	J. R. Ltd	Foyle Street	46	136
Montgomery	J. R. Ltd	Foyle Road	43	136
Montgomery	John	Creggan Terrace	5	129
Montgomery	Miss	Palace Street	4	151
Montgomery	Miss	Shipquay Street	24	154
Montgomery	Mrs	Major's Row	9	146
Montgomery	Robert	Garden City		129
Montgomery	Robert	Limavady Road	9, St. Claire Villa	172
Moody	Miss	Governor Road	38	138
Moon	Henry	Marlborough Street	25	146
Mooney	D. A. & Co.	Foyle Street	69	135
Mooney	James	Orchard Row	26	150
Mooney	James	Donegal Street	17	163
Mooney	John	Chamberlain Street	7	126
Mooney	John	Harvey Street	1	140
Mooney	Mrs	Little James Street	11	145
Mooney	Mrs	Violet Street Lower	12	176
Mooney	Patrick	Nassau Street Lower	33	148
Mooney	Patrick	Osborne Street	18	164
Mooney	The Misses	Great James Street	18	139
Mooney	W. C.	Meadowbank Avenue	26	147
Mooney	William C. & Co.	Strand Road	32	156
Mooney	William H. S.	Dacre Terrace	2	126
Mooney	William J.	Barrack Street	7	120
Moore	Alex	St. Columb's Wells	35	157
Moore	Alexander	Dungiven Road	61	170
Moore	Ambrose	Carrigans Lane	25	126
Moore	Andrew	North Edward Street	5	149
Moore	Austin	Clarendon Street	51	127

Surname	First Name	Street	House Number	Page Number
Moore	B.	Bishop Street	2	123
Moore	Ben	West-End Terrace	10	161
Moore	Catherine	Thomas Street	24	158
Moore	Daniel	Long Tower	47	145
Moore	Daniel	Nailor's Row	27	148
Moore	David	Hawthorn Terrace	12	140
Moore	David	Marlborough Street	30	147
Moore	David	Spencer Road	9	174
Moore	Edward	Clarence Place	5	127
Moore	Ellen	Dark Lane	6	130
Moore	George	Long Tower	15	145
Moore	Hannah	Union Street	3	175
Moore	J & Co.	Ferryquay Street	18	134
Moore	James	Bishop Street	105	122
Moore	James	Nassau Street Lower	19	148
Moore	James	Hayesbank Terrace	Fountain Hill House	167
Moore	James	Violet Street Upper	9	176
Moore	James	Nassau Street Upper	39	149
Moore	John	Ewing Street	30	133
Moore	John	Fountain Street	29	134
Moore	John	Francis Street	57	137
Moore	John	High Street	15	141
Moore	John	Long Tower	17	145
Moore	John	Lower Road	10	146
Moore	John	Orchard Street	1	151
Moore	John	Emerson Street	12	170
Moore	John	Strabane Old Road	31	175
Moore	Joseph	Great James Street	4, Bazaar Buildings	139
Moore	Joseph	North Edward Street	6	149
Moore	Joseph	Pine Street	20	174
Moore	Leslie	Derry View Terrace	5	168
Moore	Maggie	St. Columb's Wells	2	157
Moore	Miss	Culmore Road	Kilroide, Shantallow	129
Moore	Miss	Spencer Road	7	174
Moore	Miss R. H.	Meadowbank Avenue	1	147
Moore	Mrs	Blee's Lane		124
Moore	Mrs	Miller Street	16	147
Moore	Mrs	Nelson Street	37	149
Moore	Mrs	Creggan Road	141	162
Moore	Mrs	Donegal Street	3	163
Moore	Patrick	Stanley's Walk	4	155
Moore	Rebecca	Pitt Street	5	151
Moore	Richard	William Street	55	161
Moore	Robert	Mount Street	8	164
Moore	Samuel	Fairman Place	7	133
Moore	Samuel	Irish Street		172
Moore	Thomas	De Burgh Terrace	15	130

Surname	First Name	Street	House Number	Page Number
Moore	Thomas	Bond's Hill	32	166
Moore	Thomas	Glendermott Road	5	171
Moore	William	Mount Street	7	164
Moore & Anderson		Bishop Street	66	123
Moorehead	John	Dungiven Road	25	169
Moorehead	Mrs	Limavady Road	16	173
Moore's Ltd		Bishop Street	10	123
Moorhead	Joseph	Bond's Street	19	166
Moraghan	Thomas	Lecky Road	209	143
Morahan	John J.	St. Columb's Wells	6	157
Moran	James	Nassau Street Lower	6	148
Moran	James	Mill Street	37	173
Moran	John	Edenmore Street	5	131
Moran	John	Hamilton Street	13	139
Moran	Joseph	Brandywell Road	12	124
Moran	Michael	Limewood Street	26	144
Moran	Mrs	Lower Road	25	146
Moran	Mrs	Strand Road	81, gate lodge	156
Moran	Mrs	Carlin Street	11	167
Moran	Robert	Bluebellhill Terrace	144	144
Moran	William	Eglinton Terrace	7	132
Morgan	James	Laburnum Terrace	8	142
Morgan	James	Lecky Road		144
Morrell	James T.	Duncreggan Road	6, Fairlie	131
Morrin	John	Beechwood Avenue	32	121
Morris	Matilda	Governor Road	29	138
Morris	John	Rossville Street	35	153
Morris	Mrs	Clarendon Street Lower		127
Morris	Mrs	Strand Road	44	156
Morrison	Albert	Windmill Terrace	11	162
Morrison	Andrew	Lewis Street	25	164
Morrison	Charles	Marlborough Terrace	11	147
Morrison	Charles	Creggan Road	79	162
Morrison	David	Fountain Street	56	134
Morrison	Florence	Northland Villas	1	120
Morrison	Henry	Fountain Street	41	134
Morrison	Hugh	Bishop Street	46	123
Morrison	James	Dacre Terrace	1	126
Morrison	James	Foyle Street	97	135
Morrison	James	Hawthorn Terrace	6	140
Morrison	James	Duke Street	39, 41	169
Morrison	John	New Row	4	156
Morrison	John J.	Epworth Street	9	163
Morrison	Lily	Creggan Road	117	162
Morrison	Matthew	Deanery Street	50	130
Morrison	Matthew	Hawthorn Terrace	13	140
Morrison	Mrs	Bridge Street	58	125
Morrison	Mrs	Victoria Park		176

Surname	First Name	Street	House Number	Page Number
Morrison	Patrick	Hollywell Row	65	143
Morrison	Robert	Carlisle Road	11	125
Morrison	Robert	Strabane Old Road	27	175
Morrison	S.	Quay Princes	coal yard	152
Morrison	S. & Co.	Quay Abercorn	coal yard	152
Morrison	S. & Co.	Quay Queen's	coal depot	152
Morrison	Samuel	Lewis Street	19	164
Morrison	Samuel & Co.	Quay Princes	office and coal yard	152
Morrison	Samuel & Co.	Strand Road	50	156
Morrison	Samuel & Co.	Duke Street	19	169
Morrison	Samuel & Co.	Duke Street	35	169
Morrison	Thomas	Little Diamond	11	145
Morrison	Thomas A.	Mountjoy Terrace	7	118
Morrison	William	Fountain Street	61	134
Morrison	William	Cross Street	37	168
Morrow	Alexander	Hayesbank Terrace	65	167
Morrow	James	Clooney Terrace	52	167
Morrow	John	Rossville Street	55	153
Morrow	Sergeant J.	Strand Road Lower	171, R.U.C. Barracks	156
Morrow	Sergeant John	Fairman Place	2	133
Morrow & Co.		Fountain Street	85	134
Mortimer	John & Co.	Foyle Street	38	136
Mortimer	Miss M.	Marlborough Street	1	146
Mortimer John & Co.		Water Street		160
Mortland	William	Bond's Street	30	166
Morton	John	Dunfield Terrace	15	169
Moss	Ellen	Elmwood Terrace	22	132
Moss	Mrs	Nailor's Row	28	148
Moss	Mrs	Nassau Street Lower	38	148
Mott	Mrs	West-End Park	17	161
Mount	William	Edenballymore	5	131
Mowbray	John	Fountain Place	16	135
Mowbray	Robert	Hawthorn Terrace	3	140
Mowbray	William	Glasgow Street	5	138
Mowbray	William	Glendermott Road	14	171
Moyne	M.	Magazine Street	22	146
Moyne	Mrs	Brook Street Avenue	11	125
Moyne	Robert	Messines Park	5	128
Muir	Alex C.	Carlisle Road	10	125
Mulberry	S. J.	Glendermott Road	6	171
Mulcahy	Daniel O'D.	Marlborough Street	20	147
Muldoon	John	Irish Street	19	172
Muldoon	Pat	Mill Street	32	173
Muldoon	Peter	Epworth Street	10	163
Muldoon	William	Irish Street	3	172
Mulhearn	Matthew	Union Street	33	176
Mulherin	Felix	Great James Street	1	139

Surname	First Name	Street	House Number	Page Number
Mulhern	Ellen	Miller Street	14	147
Mulhern	Felix	Strand Road	27	155
Mulhern	Felix	Strand Road	35	155
Mulhern	John	Cross Street	22	168
Mulhern	Margaret	Bishop Street	228, 230	123
Mulhern	Matthew	Glendermott Road	50	171
Mulhern	Miss E.	Emerson Street	3	170
Mulhern	Mrs	Spencer Road	89	174
Mulholland	George	Baronet Street	4	120
Mulholland	John	Nicholson Square	8	149
Mulholland	Mrs	Wapping Lane	19	159
Mulholland	Rosetta	Simpson's Brae	19	174
Mulholland	Thomas	Stanley's Walk	49	155
Mulholland	Miss R.	Brandywell Avenue	19	124
Mulholland & Co.		Bishop Street	4, 6, 8	123
Mullally	Alexander H.	Fairman Place	1	133
Mullan	Agnes	Fountain Hill	69	171
Mullan	Alexander	Bishop Street	142	123
Mullan	Bernard	Bishop Street	31	122
Mullan	Bernard	Long Tower		145
Mullan	Charles	Frederick Street	14	137
Mullan	Dr. Joseph E.	Carlisle Road	41	125
Mullan	George	Dark Lane	19	130
Mullan	George	Robert Street	20	174
Mullan	Hugh	Wesley Street	21	165
Mullan	James	Fahan Street	47	133
Mullan	James	Fahan Street	114	133
Mullan	James	Strabane Old Road	70	175
Mullan	John	Argyle Terrace	31	120
Mullan	John	Argyle Terrace	16	120
Mullan	John	Brook Street Avenue	7	125
Mullan	John	Donegal Place	stables	131
Mullan	John	Laburnum Terrace	6	142
Mullan	John	Tyrconnell Street	17	158
Mullan	John	Pine Street	33	174
Mullan	John E.	Richmond Street	12	153
Mullan	John F.	Strand Road	79	156
Mullan	Michael	Bishop Street	222	123
Mullan	Miss M.	Wellington Street	51	160
Mullan	Mrs	Wesley Street	19	165
Mullan	William	Fountain Hill	64	171
Mullen	Miss	East Wall	North-Western Hotel	131
Mulligan	William B.	Elmwood Terrace	38	132
Mullin	Charles	Union Street	14	176
Mullin	Daniel	Dungiven Road	7	169
Mullin	Frank J.	St. Columb's Wells	49	157
Mullin	James	Derry View	1A	168
Mullin	John	Donegal Place	23	131

Surname	First Name	Street	House Number	Page Number
Mullin	John	Donegal Place	18	131
Mullin	John	Meehan's Row	5	173
Mullin	Patrick	Rossville Street	78, 80	153
Mullin	Philip	St. Columb's Wells	56	157
Mulloy	Conn	Foyleview Terrace	8	156
Mulrine	Patrick	Cross Street	5	168
Mulrine	Patrick	Mill Street		173
Munn	A. M.	Bishop Street	The Courthouse	123
Munn	A. M.	Culmore Road	Lisleen	129
Munn	Alfred Moore	Bishop Street	The Courthouse	123
Munn	Michael	Chapel Road	8	167
Munn	William	Bishop Street	61	122
Munro	George & Co.	Castle Street	5	126
Murdock	Ross	Hawkin Street	20	140
Murphy	Daniel	Messines Park	46	128
Murphy	E.	Bishop Street	26	123
Murphy	Edward	Alfred Street	26	165
Murphy	Elizabeth	Morrison's Close	4	133
Murphy	James	Argyle Terrace	10	120
Murphy	James	Sloan's Terrace	23	155
Murphy	Michael	Argyle Terrace	24	120
Murphy	Mrs	Lecky Road	108	144
Murphy	Patrick	Glenview Avenue	23	137
Murphy	Patrick	Westland Villas	4	161
Murphy	Samuel	Union Street	17	176
Murphy	Sarah	Ernest Street	3	163
Murphy	Trevor H.	Bishop Street	85	122
Murray	Alex	Nassau Street Lower	36	148
Murray	Annie	Bishop Street	38	123
Murray	Bernard	Fountain Hill	104	171
Murray	Charles	Brandywell Road		124
Murray	Charles	Bluebellhill Terrace	208	144
Murray	D.	Marlborough Street	69, Dun-Shee	146
Murray	David	Simpson's Brae	9	174
Murray	Henry	Barry Street	39	121
Murray	Henry	William Street	53	161
Murray	Hugh	Bishop Street	89	122
Murray	Hugh	Philips Street	40	151
Murray	Hugh	Rossville Street	28	153
Murray	Hugh	Union Street	3	158
Murray	Hugh	Chapel Road	11	167
Murray	James	Abbey Street	55	117
Murray	James	Brandywell Avenue	12	124
Murray	James	Nassau Street Upper	37	149
Murray	John	Hollywell Street	8	141
Murray	John	Wellington Street	1	160
Murray	John	Cuthbert Street	1	168
Murray	John	Strabane Old Road	38	175

Surname	First Name	Street	House Number	Page Number
Murray	John	Strabane Old Road	92	175
Murray	Margaret	Grove Place	11	139
Murray	Margaret	Dungiven Road	89	170
Murray	Mary	Bishop Street	65	122
Murray	Mary	Hogg's Folly	6	141
Murray	Mary	Mill Street	33	173
Murray	Miss	William Street	64	162
Murray	Miss	Violet Street Lower	31	176
Murray	Miss A.	Butcher Street	13	125
Murray	Mrs	Alexandra Place	6	119
Murray	Mrs	Bishop Street	53	122
Murray	Mrs	Fahan Street	7	133
Murray	Mrs	Windsor Terrace	10	162
Murray	Mrs	Alfred Street	2	165
Murray	Neal	Bridge Street	45	124
Murray	Owen	Meave's Row	197	143
Murray	Patrick	Market Street	5	147
Murray	Rebecca	Deanery Street	9	130
Murray	Robert	Henrietta Street	14	141
Murray	Thomas	Abercorn Road	7	117
Murray	Thomas	Blee's Lane		124
Murray	Thomas	Deanery Street	37	130
Murray	William	Argyle Street	38	119
Murray	William	Sackville Street	4	154
Murray	William	Fountain Hill	39	171
Murray	William	Messines Park	15	128
Murrin	James L.	Bond's Hill	22	166
Musselwaite	George	Wapping Lane	5	159
Myles	James	Foyle Street	56	136
Nash	James	Nelson Street	14	149
Nash	John	Gallagher's Square	8	137
Nash	Laurence	Argyle Terrace	2	120
Nash	Laurence	Union Street	24	159
Nash	Lawrence	Northland Terrace	6	150
Nash	Mary Ann	Fahan Street	53	133
Nash	Mrs	Bishop Street	144	123
Nash	Patrick	Eglinton Place	14	132
Nash	Patrick	Gallagher's Square	10	137
Nash	Patrick	Glenbrook Terrace	5	137
Nash	Patrick	Creggan Road	1	162
Naylor	Mrs	Bennett Street Lower	47	122
Neely	Adam	Mountjoy Street	3	148
Neely	Adam F.	Strand Road	127	156
Neely	Head Constable A.	Spencer Road	158	175
Neely	Head Constable Alexander	Victoria Road	9, Police Barracks	176
Neely	James	Bishop Street	205	122
Neely	John	Bishop Street	213	123
Neely	Joseph	Distillery Brae Upper	3	168

Surname	First Name	Street	House Number	Page Number
Neely	Michael	Walker's Street	5	176
Neely	Mrs	Dacre Terrace	3	126
Neely	Mrs	London Street	5	145
Neely	R. & Co.	Magazine Street	12, 13	146
Neely	Robert	Clarendon Street	9	127
Neely	Robert	Cooke Street	10	128
Neely	Robert	Stewart's Terrace	13	155
Neely	Robert	Bond's Street	6	166
Neely	Robert	Glendermott Road	18	171
Neely	Robert	Iona Terrace	15	172
Neely	Robert	Irish Street	1	172
Neely	S. M.	Aberfoyle Terrace	13	156
Neely	Samuel	Wesley Street	5	165
Neely	Samuel J.	Bridge Street	34	124
Neely	Samuel J.	Carlisle Road	Methodist Church	125
Neely	W. J.	Strand Road	133	156
Neely & Wilkinson		Strand Road	72	157
Neill	Robert	Clarendon Street	41	127
Neill	Robert	Shipquay Street	11	154
Nelis	Andrew	Kennedy Street	6	142
Nelis	Catherine	Elmwood Street	3	132
Nelis	Ernest	Harding Street	31	140
Nelis	Francis	Foster's Terrace	175	143
Nelis	Mary	Mountjoy Street	9	148
Nelis	Mrs	Benvarden Avenue	55	166
Nelis	Patrick	Foster's Terrace	153	143
Nelis	Thomas	Nassau Street Lower	48	148
Nelis	William	Brandywell Avenue	23	124
Nelis	William	Lecky Road	126	144
Nelis John & Co.		Ferryquay Street	26	134
Nelson	John J.	Westland Terrace	11	161
Nelson	Thomas	Glasgow Terrace	35	138
Nelson	Thomas E.	Strand Road	104	157
Nelson	William	Great James Street	59	139
Nelson	William	Emerson Street	26	170
Nesbitt	Hannah	Harding Street	13	140
Nevin	Jane	Clooney Terrace	56	167
Nevin	Miss M. A.	Eden Terrace	5	131
Nevin	Robert	Kennedy Place	8	142
Newell	Robert B.	Aberfoyle Terrace	11	156
Newton	Robert	Edenmore Street	15	131
Nicell	John	Nassau Street Lower	40	148
Nicell	Michael	Governor Road	21	138
Nicell	Patrick	Creggan Road	38, 40	163
Nicell	Thomas	Park Avenue	10	151
Nicholl	Allan	Waterloo Street	23	159
Nicholl	Andrew	Foyle Road	35	136

Surname	First Name	Street	House Number	Page Number
Nicholl	George	Bluebellhill Terrace	206	144
Nicholl	John	London Street	8	145
Nicholl	Joseph	Nelson Street	63	149
Nicholl	Mrs	Bennett Street Upper	13	122
Nicholl	Mrs	Ewing Street	11	132
Nicholl	Patrick	Margaret Street	1	173
Nicholl	Robert	Fountain Hill	54	171
Nicholl	Robert	Union Street	20	176
Nicholl	Walter	Clarendon Street	1A	127
Nicholl	William	Fountain Hill	25	171
Nicholl	Mrs	Richmond Street	1	153
Nicholls	George	MalvernTerrace	13	169
Nicholls	Mitchell	Northland Terrace	2	150
Nicholson	William	Alfred Street	28	165
Nicholson	William	Bond's Hill	3	166
Nimmo	W. S. & Co.	Clarendon Street		127
Nimmon	Robert	Glen Cottages	Glenbank	131
Nimmons	R. & Co.	Clarendon Street		127
Nixon	Frank	Quarry Street	7	152
Nixon	George	Garden City		129
Nixon	George	Mount Street	5	164
Nixon	James	Windmill Terrace	14	162
Nixon	John	Florence Street	21	170
Nixon	Matthew	Ernest Street	1	163
Nixon	Robert	Charlotte Street	1	127
Nixon	Robert	Ferguson Street	61	134
Noble	Alex	Templemore Park	4	158
Noble	Alex	Alfred Street	16	165
Noble	John	Carlisle Road	3	125
Noble	John	Carlisle Road	31	125
Noble	John	Chamberlain Street	19, 21	126
Noble	John	Grafton Street	9	138
Noble	Thomas	Chamberlain Street	30	126
Nolan	Dr.	Myrtle Terrace	72	150
Norman	Constable F. W.	Dungiven Road	53	170
Norrby	Mrs	Creggan Road	101	162
Norrie	David	Great James Street	33	139
Norrie	Mrs	Kerr's Terrace	23	162
Norris	James	Grafton Street	13	138
Norris	James	Orchard Row	41	150
Norris	John	Beechwood Park	88	121
Norris	John	Corbett Street (Pilot's Row)	5	128
Norris	Mary	York Street	17	176
Norris	Mrs	Glendermott Road	68	171
Norris	Oliver	West-End Terrace	8	161
Norris	Robert	Bond's Place	1	166
Norris	Robert D.	Kennedy Place	6	142
Norris	W	Abercorn Road	33½	118
Norris	William	Bellevue Avenue	21	121

Surname	First Name	Street	House Number	Page Number
Nutt	Andrew	Fountain Street	36	134
Nutter	Samuel	Fountain Street	25	134
Nutter	Thomas	Fountain Street	37	134
Nutter	William	Messines Park	24	128
Nutter	William J.	Limewood Street	18	144
O'Brien	Herbert C.	King Street	18	172
O'Brien	James	Great James Street	66	139
O'Brien	James	Florence Street	9	170
O'Brien	John	Iona Terrace	27	172
O'Brien	Joseph	Marlborough Street	10	147
O'Brien	Mrs J.	Ann Street	21	144
O'Bryan	George	Mrs C. F. Alexander's Memorial Cottages	3	126
O'Bryan	James	George Street	workshop	138
O'Bryan	James	Henry Street	6	141
O'Bryan	John	Barrack Street	2	120
O'Bryan	John	Grove Place	20	139
O'Bryan	John	Nailor's Row	5	148
O'Bryan	Minnie	Gordon Terrace	6	138
O'Callaghan	Francis	Beechwood Park	102	121
O'Callaghan	John	Butcher Street	2A	125
O'Callaghan	Patrick	Dunfield Terrace	21	169
O'Carroll	William H.	Beechwood Street	4	121
O'Connell	Daniel	Howard Street	13	141
O'Connell	Daniel	William Street	35	161
O'Connell	James	Fulton Place	16	137
O'Connell	John	Gallagher's Square	4	137
O'Connell	John	Rossville Street	18	153
O'Connell	Mrs	Herbert Street	3	171
O'Connell	Rebecca	Elmwood Terrace	9	132
O'Connor	Bernard	Fountain Hill	116	171
O'Connor	John	Rossville Street	58	153
O'Connor	Miss	Ferryquay Street	27	134
O'Connor	Mrs	Charlotte Street	14	127
O'Connor	Mrs	Creggan Street	3	129
O'Connor	Mrs	Creggan Road	14	163
O'Connor	Rose	Fulton Place	22	137
O'Connor	S. & Co.	Foyle Street	13	135
O'Connor	Thomas	Osborne Street	12	164
O'Dogherty	Miss	Marlborough Park	53	162
O'Doherty	Andrew	Bishop Street	91	122
O'Doherty	Con	Waterloo Street	22	159
O'Doherty	Dr W. G.	Clarendon Street	11	127
O'Doherty	Edward H.	Magazine Street Upper	2	146
O'Doherty	H. C. & Son	Castle Street	10	126
O'Doherty	J.	New Market Street	6	149
O'Doherty	James	Eglinton Place	15	132
O'Doherty	James	Fahan Street	45	133
O'Doherty	James	Westland Avenue	22	160

Surname	First Name	Street	House Number	Page Number
O'Doherty	James E. & Co.	East Wall	4	131
O'Doherty	John	Fountain Hill	92	171
O'Doherty	Joseph	Sunbeam Terrace	9	122
O'Doherty	Miss	Clooney Terrace	9½	167
O'Doherty	Miss	Dungiven Road	30	170
O'Doherty	Mrs B.	Richmond Street	11	153
O'Doherty	Patrick	Spencer Road	170	175
O'Doherty	Rev. John	Creggan Street		129
O'Doherty	Thomas	Glendermott Road	8	171
O'Doherty	W. G. & Co.	Bishop Street	15	122
O'Doherty	W. G. & Co.	Society Street	1, 3	155
O'Doherty	William	Creggan Street	5	129
O'Doherty	William	Chapel Road	62	167
O'Doherty	William P.	Ewing Street	33	132
O'Donnell	Bridget	Fahan Street	106	133
O'Donnell	Captain C.	Strand Road	104	157
O'Donnell	Catherine	Pennyburn Terrace	4	151
O'Donnell	Charles	Glasgow Terrace	7	138
O'Donnell	Daniel	Nelson Street	30	149
O'Donnell	Daniel	Park Avenue	12	151
O'Donnell	Daniel	Rossville Street	2	153
O'Donnell	Daniel	Tyrconnell Street	14	158
O'Donnell	Daniel	Walker's Place	46	159
O'Donnell	David	St. Patrick Street	13	158
O'Donnell	Edward	Glendermott Road	100	171
O'Donnell	George	Sloan's Terrace	39	155
O'Donnell	Hugh	St. Columb's Wells	70	157
O'Donnell	Hugh	Creggan Road	52	163
O'Donnell	J.	Sackville Street	1	153
O'Donnell	J.	Strand Road	75	156
O'Donnell	J. F.	Beechwood Avenue	86	121
O'Donnell	J. F.	William Street	33	161
O'Donnell	J. J.	Strand Road	15, National Bank	155
O'Donnell	J. J.	Fountain Hill	80	171
O'Donnell	James	Elmwood Street	2	132
O'Donnell	James	Fahan Street	12	133
O'Donnell	James	Hamilton Street	21	139
O'Donnell	James	Hollywell Street	3	141
O'Donnell	James	Nailor's Row	8	148
O'Donnell	James	Wellington Street	44	160
O'Donnell	James	Benvarden Avenue	24	166
O'Donnell	James E. & Co.	East Wall	4	131
O'Donnell	John	Argyle Street	64	119
O'Donnell	John	Creggan Terrace	20	129
O'Donnell	John	Fahan Street	137	133
O'Donnell	John	Francis Street	61	137
O'Donnell	John	Marlborough Terrace	21	147
O'Donnell	John	St. Patrick Street	9	158
O'Donnell	John	William Street	125	161

Surname	First Name	Street	House Number	Page Number
O'Donnell	John	Strabane Old Road	14	175
O'Donnell	Joseph	Beechwood Street	22	121
O'Donnell	Joseph	Demesne Terrace	12	130
O'Donnell	Joseph	Elmwood Terrace	8	132
O'Donnell	Joseph	Gresham's Row	5	140
O'Donnell	Joseph	Linenhall Street Lower	35-40	145
O'Donnell	Joseph	St. Columb's Street	9	157
O'Donnell	Joseph	William Street	72	162
O'Donnell	Joseph jun.	Magazine Street	6	146
O'Donnell	Mary	Adam Street	8	118
O'Donnell	Mary	Tyrconnell Street	8	158
O'Donnell	Miss	Cottage Row	6	123
O'Donnell	Mrs	Strabane Old Road	62	175
O'Donnell	Neal	Fahan Street	40	133
O'Donnell	Neal	Hamilton Street	16	140
O'Donnell	Patrick	Bishop Street	148	123
O'Donnell	Patrick	Waterloo Street	4	159
O'Donnell	Patrick	Fountain Hill	110	171
O'Donnell	Patrick	Strabane Old Road	4	175
O'Donnell	Sarah	Sunbeam Terrace	17	122
O'Donnell	William	Creggan Road	30	163
O'Donnell	William	Creggan Road	34	163
O'Donnell	William	Strabane Old Road	86	175
O'Donohoe	Mrs	Waterloo Street	16	159
Offord	Alfred	York Street	7	176
O'Flynn	Mrs	Westland Terrace	19	161
O'Gara	Thomas	Artisan Street	14	162
O'Hagan	Bernard	Foyle Street	45, 47	135
O'Hagan	Charles	Donegal Street	16	163
O'Hagan	Daniel	Duke Street	63	169
O'Hagan	Denis	Ferguson Street	46	134
O'Hagan	George	New Street	1	164
O'Hagan	John	Gallagher's Square	5	137
O'Hagan	John	Wellington Street	35	160
O'Hagan	Miss	Creggan Road	151	163
O'Hagan	Mrs	Argyle Street	67	119
O'Hagan	Patrick	Collon Terrace	17	128
O'Hagan	Patrick J.	Ann Street	17	144
O'Hagan	Thomas	Bridge Street	38	125
O'Hagan	William	Glasgow Street	4	138
O'Hanlon	Edward	Fahan Street	136	133
O'Hanlon	Fred	Elmwood Terrace	1	132
O'Hanlon	Fred	Rossville Street	13	153
O'Hanlon	Frederick	Eden Place	2	132
O'Hanlon	Frederick	Westland Avenue	19	160
O'Hara	Charles	Limewood Street	29	144
O'Hara	Michael	Hamilton Street	44	140
O'Hara	Thomas	West-End Terrace	6	161
O'Hare	Michael	Creggan Street	37	129

Surname	First Name	Street	House Number	Page Number
O'Hare	Michael	Creggan Street	45, 57	129
O'Haron	Catherine	Lecky Road	128	144
O'Hea	John	Alfred Street	27	165
O'Hea	Miss L.	Bishop Street	249	123
O'Kane	Bernard	Bishop Street	207	122
O'Kane	Bernard	Bridge Street	36	124
O'Kane	Charles	King Street	12	172
O'Kane	Daniel	Walker's Place	5	159
O'Kane	Edward	Benvarden Avenue	16	166
O'Kane	Francis	Argyle Terrace	13	120
O'Kane	Frank	Meave's Row	201	143
O'Kane	Harold	St. Columb's Wells	92	157
O'Kane	J. G.	Florence Terrace	12	150
O'Kane	James	Frederick Street	9	137
O'Kane	James	Glasgow Street	5	138
O'Kane	James	High Street	2	141
O'Kane	James	Limewood Street	6	144
O'Kane	James	Osborne Street	16	164
O'Kane	Jane	Elmwood Terrace	3	132
O'Kane	John	Hamilton Street	2	140
O'Kane	John	Waterloo Street	10	159
O'Kane	Joseph G.	Foyle Street	7	135
O'Kane	Mary	Foster's Terrace	157	143
O'Kane	Mary	Spencer Road	131	175
O'Kane	Mary J.	Wellington Street	56	160
O'Kane	Michael	Argyle Terrace	41	120
O'Kane	Michael	Cedar Street	4	126
O'Kane	Michael	Hogg's Folly	1	141
O'Kane	Michael	Violet Street Lower	38	176
O'Kane	Most Rev. Dr.	Creggan Street		129
O'Kane	Mrs	Foyle Street	53	135
O'Kane	Mrs	Fulton Place	23	137
O'Kane	Mrs	Harvey Street	11	140
O'Kane	Mrs F.	North Edward Street	1	149
O'Kane	P. & Co.	Foyle Street	81	135
O'Kane	P. & Co.	Lewis Street	2	164
O'Kane	Patrick	Foster's Terrace	161	143
O'Kane	Patrick	Long Tower	70	146
O'Kane	Patrick	Dungiven Road	109	170
O'Kane	Patrick	King Street	37	172
O'Kane	Thomas	Osborne Street	1	164
Olphert	George	Ebrington Terrace	3	170
Olphert	James	Edenmore Street	35	131
Olphert	Matilda	Fountain Hill	44	171
Olphert	Thomas	Ashcroft Place	6	165
O'Mahoney	John	Edenballymore		131
O'Neill	Charles	Fahan Street	46	133
O'Neill	Charles	Ashfield Terrace	39	162
O'Neill	Cornelius	Grafton Terrace	6	139
O'Neill	Francis	Fahan Street	6	133

Surname	First Name	Street	House Number	Page Number
O'Neill	Hugh	Hogg's Folly	2	141
O'Neill	Hugh	Marlborough Terrace	20	147
O'Neill	James	Eden Place	5	132
O'Neill	James	Cross Street	4	163
O'Neill	James	Chapel Road	25	167
O'Neill	John	Eglinton Place	27	132
O'Neill	John	Limewood Street	40	144
O'Neill	John	Florence Street	20	170
O'Neill	Louise	Fountain Hill	25	171
O'Neill	Martha	Cochrane's Row	8	169
O'Neill	Miss	Northland Road	4, Ard-Owen	149
O'Neill	Miss	St. Columb's Street	5	157
O'Neill	Mrs	Fairman Place	17	133
O'Neill	Mrs	Donegal Street	29	163
O'Neill	Patrick	Stanley's Walk	17	155
O'Neill	Patrick	Chapel Road	7	167
O'Neill	Patrick J.	Sydney Terrace	4	139
O'Neill	James	Edenballymore	4	131
O'Neill & McHenry		Custom House Street		129
O'Neill & McHenry		Foyle Street	22	136
O'Neill & McHenry		Guildhall Street		139
O'Reilly	Alfred J.	Laburnum Terrace	7	142
O'Reilly	Bridget	Fahan Street	55	133
O'Reilly	Denis	Mitchelburne Terrace	84	136
O'Reilly	Mary	Westland Avenue	29	160
O'Reilly	Mary E.	Blucher Street	16	124
O'Reilly	Miss	Chapel Road	70	167
O'Reilly	Mrs M.	Elmwood Terrace	12	132
O'Reilly	Patrick	Marlborough Terrace	12	147
O'Reilly	Peter	Bishop Street	76	123
O'Reilly	Thomas	Ashfield Terrace	37	162
Organ	James	Walker's Place	19	159
O'Rorke	Elizabeth	William Street		161
O'Rourke	Hycinth	Chamberlain Street	2	126
O'Rourke	Hycreith	William Street	26	161
Orr	Andrew	Fountain Street	89	134
Orr	Bertie	Aubrey Street	17	120
Orr	Frank	Foyle Street	33A	135
Orr	George	Mountjoy Street	14	148
Orr	George	Spencer Road	123, shop	174
Orr	George	York Street	16	176
Orr	Henry	Charlotte Street	6	127
Orr	J. C.	Clarence Avenue	11	127
Orr	James	Pitt Street	7	151
Orr	James	Primrose Street	13	174
Orr	John	Governor Road	30	138
Orr	John	North Street	29	164

Surname	First Name	Street	House Number	Page Number
Orr	Johnston	Carlisle Road	12	125
Orr	Joseph	Great James Street	58	139
Orr	Joseph	Harding Street	7	140
Orr	Joseph	Duke Street	13	169
Orr	Joseph	Pine Street	10	174
Orr	Mrs	Bond's Street	37	166
Orr	Mrs P.	Duke Street	57	169
Orr	Mrs Sarah	Montrose Villas	22	150
Orr	Oswald	Ewing Street	17	132
Orr	Patrick	Epworth Street	7	163
Orr	Patrick	King Street	26	172
Orr	Robert	Messines Park	37	128
Orr	Robert	Fountain Street	88	135
Orr	Robert	Ashfield Terrace	35	162
Orr	Robinson	Mountjoy Street	28	148
Orr	Samuel	Albert Place	16	119
Orr	Samuel	Bond's Hill	11	166
Orr	Samuel	Clooney Terrace	1A	167
Orr	Samuel	Clooney Terrace	1B, workshop	167
Orr	Samuel	Pine Street	2	174
Orr	Samuel Kyle	Great James Street	52	139
Orr	Thomas	Epworth Street	6	163
Orr	Thomas	Cottage Row	44	164
Orr	William	Strand Road	139	156
Orr	William	Alfred Street	40	165
Orr	William A.	Albert Street	10	118
Osborne	D. C.	Clooney Park East	3, St. Moiras	172
Osborne	Harry	Argyle Terrace	19	120
Osborne	John	Foyle Street	51A	135
Osborne	Miss	Iona Terrace	3	172
Osborne	Miss	Clooney Park West	3, Ashlea	172
Osborne	William	Glendermott Road	84	171
Osborne & Patton		Bank Place	store	120
Osborne & Patton Ltd		Shipquay Street	27	154
Osmen	William	Myrtle Terrace	74	150
O'Sullivan	A. & Co.	Strand Road	19	155
O'Sullivan	Florence	Diamond	16	130
Owens	Edward	Harvey Street	3	140
Owens	George	The Rock	115	156
Owens	George	Foyleview Terrace	12	156
Owens	Henry	Lecky Road	72	144
Owens	Lizzie	Foster's Terrace	181	143
Owens	Lizzie	St. Columb's Wells	114	157
Owens	Margaret	Stanley's Walk	7	155
Owens	Mrs	Mill Street	31	173
Owens	William	Carlisle Road	35	125
Oxford	Christopher	Northland Avenue	3	150
Oxford	Edward James	Ferguson Street	45	134

Surname	First Name	Street	House Number	Page Number
Page	James	Lower Road	39	146
Page	Samuel	Messines Park	11	128
Page	William	Quarry Street	11	153
Palmer	Mrs	High Street	17	141
Palmer	Mrs	Mary Street	16	147
Park	George	King Street	49	172
Parke	Alex	John Street	23	142
Parke	Hugh	King Street	51	172
Parke	John	Dungiven Road	49	169
Parke	Miss	Abercorn Road	23	118
Parke	Mrs	Cross Street	27	168
Parke	R. H.	Great James Street	35	139
Parke	Thomas	Brooke Villas	45	165
Parke	Thomas	Meehan's Row	6	173
Parker	Mrs S. A.	Clarendon Street	65	127
Parkhill	Thomas	Ferguson Street	46A	134
Parkhill	Mrs E.	Ferguson Street	44A	134
Parkhill & Co.		Ewing Street		132
Parkinson	Mrs	Barry Street	7	120
Parks	Matthew	Carlisle Road	67	125
Parvin	Mrs	Collon Terrace	11	128
Patrick	Ellen Jane	Grove Place	6	139
Patterson	Cecilia	Gallagher's Square	3	137
Patterson	George	Meehan's Row	1	173
Patterson	J. & Son	Bishop Street	103	122
Patterson	J. & Son	Little James Street	13	145
Patterson	James	Florence Street	3	170
Patterson	Joseph	Lawrence Hill	2	143
Patterson	Minnie	Fountain Street	101	134
Patterson	Mrs	Marlborough Avenue	6	147
Patterson	Mrs	Queen Street	7	153
Patterson	Robert	Hempton's Close		134
Patterson	William	Great James Street	16	139
Patterson	William	Kennedy Street	22	142
Patterson Bros.		John Street	29	142
Patton	Arthur	Lecky Road	118	144
Patton	David	Glasgow Street	6	138
Patton	Lexie	Garden City		129
Patton	Thomas	Park Terrace	1	138
Payne	Henry	Florence Street	41	170
Payne	Joe	Epworth Street	12	163
Payne	William	Duke Street	9	169
Peacocke	The Right Rev. Joseph I.	Bishop Street	The Palace	122
Pentland	Thomas	Ewing Street	28	133
Pentland	William	Moat Street	4	148
Peoples	George	Gordon Place	2	138
Peoples	John	Spencer Road	34	175
Peoples	William	Moore Street	26	173
Peoples	William J.	Argyle Street	33	119

Surname	First Name	Street	House Number	Page Number
Percival	J. C.	Castle Street	2	126
Perry	A. W.	Bond's Hill	Old Manse	166
Perry	David	Beechwood Avenue	78	121
Perry	David E.	Great James Street	4	139
Perry	James W.	Fairman Place	14	133
Perry	Miss	Linenhall Street Lower	31	145
Perry	Mrs	Fountain Place	24	135
Perry	Mrs	Linenhall Street Lower	stables	145
Perry	Mrs W. L.	Limavady Road	1, Sunnymede	172
Perry	The Misses	Bond's Hill	18	166
Pettipice	Miss	Carlisle Road	46	126
Phelan	John	Abbey Street	35	117
Phillips	Arthur	Victoria Park	2	176
Phillips	H. B.	Shipquay Street	30, Beethoven House	154
Phillips	Mrs	Florence Street	8	170
Phillips	Mrs	Strabane Old Road	90	175
Phillips	Mrs K. C.	Limavady Road	8, Lanowlee Hall	172
Phillips	Nurse	Richmond Street	1	153
Phillips	W. L.	May Street	7	173
Phillips	William	Ferryquay Street	36	134
Philson	John	Fountain Hill	78	171
Philson	Mrs	Fountain Hill	72	171
Philson	Robert	Hayesbank Terrace	59	167
Piggot	J.	Beechwood Avenue	1, Ferenize cottage	121
Piggot	J. Anderson	Claremont Street	3	127
Piggott	John	Beechwood Avenue	17, Gleniffer	121
Pindall	Frank	King Street	53	172
Pine	Hugh	Rossville Street	64, 66	153
Pinkerton	Mrs	Grafton Street	11	138
Pinkerton & Co.		Quay Queen's		152
Pitts	E. A.	Foyle Street	13	135
Platt	Alex.	Dixon's Close	1	146
Platt	Mrs	Albert Street	40	119
Platt	Mrs	Queen Street	10	153
Platt	Mrs	West-End Park	15	161
Platt	W. H.	Foyle Street	48	136
Platt	William	Stewart's Terrace	5	155
Platt	William H.	Barry Street	5	120
Plews	Fred	Moore Street	31	173
Plews	Miss	Culmore Road	Shantallow	129
Plews	Nan	Florence Street	2B	170
Plews	Robert	Mitchelburne Terrace	87	136
Plews	William	Alfred Street	36	165
Plews	William	Meehan's Row	9	173
Plews	William	Pine Street	29	174

Surname	First Name	Street	House Number	Page Number
Plews	William G.	Mill Street	gasworks	173
Plummer	James	Bridge Street	15	124
Plummer	Miss	Columba Terrace	3	168
Plummer	Thomas	Adair Street	4	118
Pollock	George	Eden Terrace	4	131
Pollock	George	Windmill Terrace	29	162
Pollock	J. H.	Foyle Street	13	135
Pollock	J. H.	Deanfield	4, Ard-na-Hone	168
Pollock	John A.	Fountain Street		134
Pollock	John A. & Co.	Carlisle Road	8	125
Pollock	Miss	Abercorn Road	17	118
Pollock	Miss	Fountain Street	91	134
Pollock	Miss	Creggan Road	36	163
Pollock	Miss	Rosemount Terrace	13	165
Pollock	Miss A. S.	William Street	93	161
Pollock	William	Bennett Street Upper	12	122
Pollock	William	Bennett Street Lower	26	122
Pollock	William	Creggan		131
Pollock	J. A. & Co.	Strand Road	9	155
Pollock & Given		Sackville Street	13	154
Pomeroy	J. A.	George Street	10	138
Pomeroy	Mrs	Margaret Street	5	173
Pomeroy	Thomas	King Street	11	172
Pooley	H. & Son	Foyle Street	34	136
Porter	Alexander	Robert Street	13	174
Porter	Benjamin	York Street	13	176
Porter	C. & Co.	Foyle Street	16	135
Porter	David	Dungiven Road	22	170
Porter	Denis	Patrick Street	10	151
Porter	George	Carlin Street	2	167
Porter	Hugh	West-End Park	3	161
Porter	James	Fountain Street	4	134
Porter	James	Pennyburn	7	151
Porter	John	George Street	5	138
Porter	Mrs	Bennett Street Lower	32	122
Porter	Mrs	Nicholson Square	9	149
Porter	Mrs A.	Caw	Caw Villa	167
Porter	Mrs T.	Marlborough Street	44	147
Porter	Rebecca	Governor Road	9	138
Porter	Robert	Foyle Road	53	136
Porter	Robert	Foyle Road	58	136
Porter	Robert	Lawrence Hill	24	143
Porter	Robert	Nelson Street	39	149
Porter	Robert	Benvarden Avenue	9	165
Porter	Robert	Bond's Hill	33	166
Porter	Samuel	Wapping Lane	11	159
Porter	Sarah	Fountain Hill	35	171
Porter	Sergeant W.	McLaughlin's Close	4	134
Porter	Thomas	Cottage Row	1	123

Surname	First Name	Street	House Number	Page Number
Porter	Thomas	Glasgow Terrace	20	138
Porter	Thomas	Princes Street	1	152
Porter	Thomas	Wapping Lane	13	159
Porter	Thomas	Strabane Old Road	114	175
Porter	William	Bluebellhill Terrace	226	144
Porter	William	Alma Place	6	119
Porter	David	Clarence Avenue	14	127
Porter	Eliza	Creggan Street	29	129
Porter	James	Deanery Place	5	130
Porter	Patrick	Alma Place	5	119
Porter	Robert	Glen Terrace	6	131
Porter & Co.		Victoria Chambers		125
Porter & Porter		Ferryquay Gate	4, 6	134
Porter & Porter		Orchard Street	4	151
Porter & Roulston		William Street	4, 6	161
Porter Bros.		Park Avenue	5	151
Porter Bros.		Sackville Street	3	154
Porter Bros.		Strand Road	22	156
Porter Brothers		Abercorn Road	31	118
Pottinger	John H.	Dervock Place	10	168
Pounds	Frederick	Sloan's Terrace	33	155
Power	William	Fahan Street	10	133
Power	Winifred	Fountain Street	63	134
Powers	Shirt factory	North Edward Street		149
Powers	William	Gallagher's Square	6	137
Poyntz	George	Argyle Street	15	119
Poyntz	Marion	Northland Villas	3	120
Pratt	W. L.	Epworth Street	22	163
Price	A.	Shipquay Street	23	154
Price	Albert	Deanfield	8, Lesbury	168
Price	H. & Co.	Shipquay Place	2	154
Price	James	The Rock	101	156
Price	Miss	Beechwood Avenue	5, Sunnybank	121
Prior	Thomas	Primrose Street	11	174
Prior & Co.		Ferryquay Street	7	134
Purcell	James	Strabane Old Road	12	175
Purcell	Patrick	Irish Street	20	172
Purdie	Thomas	Bridge Street	62	125
Quigg	John	King Street	42	172
Quigg	Mary Ann	Abbey Street	59	117
Quigg	Miss E.	Emerson Street	9	170
Quigg	Mrs	Spencer Road	44	175
Quigg	Robert	Emerson Street	1	170
Quigley	A.	Northland Road	23 (gate lodge)	150
Quigley	Andrew	St. Columb's Wells	66	157
Quigley	Bernard	Creggan Street	23	129
Quigley	Bernard	Sloan's Terrace	12	155
Quigley	Francis	Carlin Street	15	167
Quigley	Henry	Long Tower	54	146

Surname	First Name	Street	House Number	Page Number
Quigley	Hugh	Messines Park	22	128
Quigley	Hugh	Howard Street	20	141
Quigley	Hugh	Northland Terrace	3	150
Quigley	Hugh	Creggan Road	95	162
Quigley	Hugh	Epworth Street	25	163
Quigley	Hugh	Carlin Street	13	167
Quigley	Hugh	Margaret Street	2	173
Quigley	James	Alma Place	8	119
Quigley	James	Bishop Street	62	123
Quigley	James	Messines Park	18	128
Quigley	James	Mitchelburne Terrace	99	136
Quigley	James	Magazine Street Upper	4	146
Quigley	James	Nelson Street	22	149
Quigley	James	William Street	58	162
Quigley	John	Brandywell Road	8	124
Quigley	John	Brandywell Avenue	16	124
Quigley	John	Edenmore Street	11	131
Quigley	John	Tyrconnell Street	5	158
Quigley	John	Donegal Street	26	163
Quigley	Joseph	Cooke Street	3	128
Quigley	Joseph	Ewing Street	13	132
Quigley	Matilda	Spencer Road	24	175
Quigley	Michael	St. Columb's Wells	96	157
Quigley	Miss E.	Albert Place	4	119
Quigley	Miss R.	Bishop Street	77	122
Quigley	Mrs	Bishop Street	135	122
Quigley	Mrs	St. Columb's Wells	78	157
Quigley	Mrs	Westland Terrace	17	161
Quigley	Mrs	Creggan Road	54	163
Quigley	Mrs	Ernest Street	20	163
Quigley	Mrs	Spencer Road	160	175
Quigley	Mrs Annie	Iona Terrace	29	172
Quigley	Patrick	Elmwood Terrace	11	132
Quigley	Sarah	Duke Street	71	169
Quigley	Sarah J.	Rossville Street	31	153
Quigley	Thomas	Ferguson Street	18	134
Quigley	William	Dark Lane	11	130
Quigley	William	William Street	99	161
Quigley	William	Creggan Road	5	162
Quigley	William	Creggan Road	129	162
Quigley	William	Glendermott Road	34	171
Quigley	William J.	Cottage Row	40	164
Quigley	William J.	Bond's Street	53	166
Quinlan	Mrs	Ebrington Street	17	170
Quinn	Francis	Westland Avenue	1	160
Quinn	James	Mountjoy Street	10	148
Quinn	James	St. Joseph's Avenue	4	158
Quinn	James	William Street	28	161
Quinn	James	Riverview Terrace	9	174

Surname	First Name	Street	House Number	Page Number
Quinn	John	East Wall		131
Quinn	John	Market Street	1	147
Quinn	John	Rossville Street	30	153
Quinn	John	Sugarhouse lane	17	158
Quinn	Joseph	Long Tower	32	146
Quinn	Mary	St. Mary's Terrace	37	167
Quinn	Michael	London Street	7	145
Quinn	Michael	Walker's Place	22	159
Quinn	Mrs Isabella	Union Street	9	176
Quinn	Patrick	Sloan's Terrace	35	155
Quinn	Richard	Creggan Street	11	129
Quinn	Sarah	York Street	30	176
Quinn	Susan	Wellington Street	42	160
Quinn	William	Bishop Street	233	123
Quinn & Co.		Foyle Street	20	136
Quinton	Alexander	Fountain Hill	102	171
Rabbitt	William	Maybrook Terrace	4	128
Radcliffe	John	Hamilton Street	27	140
Rafferty	F.	Water Street	3	160
Rafferty	Frank	Messines Park	45	128
Rafferty	John	Violet Street Lower	47	176
Rafferty	Thomas	Clarence Place	8	127
Ramsay	Charles	Marlborough Terrace	3	147
Ramsay	Ellen	St. Patrick Street	3	158
Ramsay	J.	Marlborough Terrace	1	147
Ramsay	James	Marlborough Terrace	6	147
Ramsay	James	Clyde Street	2	153
Ramsay	James	Artisan Street	7	162
Ramsay	John	Rosemount Avenue	17	164
Ramsay	John J.	Primrose Street	1	174
Ramsay	Margaret	Fountain Place	5	135
Ramsay	Michael	Long Tower	66	146
Ramsay	Miss M. J.	Violet Street Lower	2	176
Ramsay	Mrs	Long Tower	22	146
Ramsay	Sam	Walker's Place	26	159
Ramsay	Samuel	Long Tower	14	145
Ramsay	Samuel	Walker's Place	13	159
Ramsay	William	Long Tower	65	145
Ramsay	William	Walker's Place	30	159
Ramsey	Bernard	Aberfoyle Terrace	15	156
Ramsey	Charles	Rossville Street	store	153
Ramsey	David	Rossville Street	19	153
Ramsey	Edward	Marlborough Terrace	9	147
Ramsey	Samuel	Limewood Street	3	144
Ramsey	William	Primrose Street	3	174
Rank	Joseph Ltd	Foyle Street	30	136
Rankin	Andrew	Nassau Street Lower	29	148
Rankin	James	Edenmore Street	12	131
Rankin	John	Foyle Road	54	136
Rankin	John	Francis Street	39	137

Surname	First Name	Street	House Number	Page Number
Rankin	John	Rosemount Avenue	11	164
Rankin	Miss	Bentley Street	1	165
Rankin	Mrs	Albert Place	19	119
Rankin	Mrs	Edenmore Street	3	131
Rankin	Rev. L.	Limavady Road	13, Duniris Manse	172
Rankin	Robert	Bishop Street	155	122
Rankin	William	Cross Street	1	168
Reaney	Constable J.	Stewart's Terrace	18	155
Redden	William	Deanery Street	36	130
Reddy	Miss Sarah	Foyle Street	23, Criterion Hotel	135
Ree	Robert J.	Marlborough Street	27	146
Reed	Mrs	Northland Road	25, Red Roof	150
Reeves	Joseph	Fountain Street	64, 66	134
Reeves	William	Dark Lane	5	129
Reid	A. H.	Shipquay Street	Provincial Bank	154
Reid	Albert	Bond's Street	27	166
Reid	Andrew	Grafton Street	19	138
Reid	Andrew	Spencer Road	84	175
Reid	Annie	Benvarden Avenue	14	166
Reid	Benjamin	Deanfield	1	168
Reid	James	Hinton Park	2	172
Reid	John	Caroline Place	5	126
Reid	Joseph	Brandywell Road		124
Reid	Mary J.	Bond's Place	13	166
Reid	Michael	Bond's Street	4	166
Reid	Miss	Pump Street	23	152
Reid	Miss	Spencer Road	42, Nurses' Home	175
Reid	Mrs	Governor Road	4	138
Reid	Mrs	Princes Street	11	152
Reid	Mrs	Princes Street	15	152
Reid	Robert	King Street	44	172
Reid	Robert	Violet Street Upper	8	176
Reid	Sergeant J. E.	The Rock	103	156
Reid	Thomas	Albert Street	3	118
Reid	Vincent	Nassau Street Lower	2	148
Reid	Robert	Fountain Street	38	134
Reid & Co.	workshop	Bridge Street	10	124
Reid & Co.		Carlisle Road	1A	125
Reid & Co.		Victoria Chambers		125
Reilly	Edward	Bridge Street	56	125
Reilly	Hannah	Foster's Terrace	177	143
Reilly	James	Alexandra Place	7	119
Reilly	Jane	Ferguson Street	63	134
Reilly	John	New Street	1	126
Reilly	Mrs	Hawkin Street	1	140
Reilly	Mrs	Spencer Road	78	175

Surname	First Name	Street	House Number	Page Number
Reilly	Nurse	Princes Street	10	152
Reilly	Robert	Bond's Street	43	166
Reilly	Thomas E.	Orchard Row	33	150
Reinchs Nephew & Co.		Foyle Street	45, 47	135
Reuben	B.	Hawkin Street	14	140
Reynolds	James	Shipquay Street	40	154
Reynolds	Major D.	Limavady Road	23	172
Reynolds	Miss N.	Bishop Street	70	123
Reynolds	Mrs	Bond's Hill	11	166
Reynolds	S. G.	Creggan		131
Reynolds	William	Francis Street	51	137
Reynolds	William G.	Browning Drive	25	166
Reynolds	William	Market Street	Bastion House	147
Reynolds & Deane		Magazine Street	11	146
Rice	Miss	Edenmore Street	21	131
Richards	Evan	Mountroyal	5	150
Richards	Evan & Co.	William Street	73	161
Richards	G. E.	Clarence Avenue	20	127
Richmond	John	Messines Park	61	128
Richmond	Robert	Pine Street	1	174
Riddell	C. C.	Spencer Road	12	175
Riddle	Adam	Argyle Terrace	26	120
Riddles	Thomas	Charlotte Street	16	127
Riordan	Michael	Chapel Road	34	167
Risk	Samuel	Spencer Road	115	174
Risley	Miss H.	Epworth Street	16	163
Ritchie	Thomas	Bond's Place	7	166
Roache	James	Bishop Street	194	123
Robb	Andrew	Demesne Terrace	6, Ellerslie	130
Robb	Andrew	East Wall	9	131
Robb	James	Bishop Street	94	123
Robb	Samuel	Fountain Hill	41	171
Robb	Samuel	Spencer Road	39	174
Robb	John	Cuthbert Street	12	168
Roberts	Hugh	Florence Terrace	14	150
Roberts	Sergeant J.	Spencer Road	36	175
Roberts	Thomas	Rosemount Avenue	27	164
Roberts	William	Duddy's Row	4	169
Roberts & Sons		Foyle Street	51B	135
Roberts & Sons		Foyle Street	59	135
Roberts & Sons		Foyle Street	42	136
Robertson	A.	Park Avenue	27, Daisyville	151
Robertson	Alexander	Marlborough Street	40	147
Robertson	William	Argyle Street	58	119
Robinson	Andrew T.	Violet Street Upper	15	176
Robinson	Ann Jane	Chapel Road	17	167
Robinson	Catherine	Donegal Place	19	131
Robinson	Fisher	York Street	22	176

Surname	First Name	Street	House Number	Page Number
Robinson	Fred R.	Foyle Street	45, 47	135
Robinson	Frederick	Abercorn Place	8	118
Robinson	Henry	Albert Place	10	119
Robinson	Henry S.	Limavady Road	41, Eshcol	172
Robinson	Isabella	Chapel Road	56	167
Robinson	J. M.	Strand Road	6	156
Robinson	James	Fairman Place	12	133
Robinson	James	Gordon Terrace	7	138
Robinson	James	Lorne Street	4	145
Robinson	James	Rossville Street	2	153
Robinson	James	Windmill Terrace	4	162
Robinson	James	Dervock Street	5	168
Robinson	James	Dungiven Road	39	169
Robinson	James	Limavady Road	12	173
Robinson	James	Victoria Road	6	176
Robinson	James W.	Butcher Street	9A	125
Robinson	John	Asylum Road	2	120
Robinson	Joseph	Gordon Terrace	11	138
Robinson	Joseph	Primrose Street	23	174
Robinson	Mary	Edenmore Street	10	131
Robinson	Mary	Barnewall Place	14	165
Robinson	Miss M.	Dungiven Road	9	169
Robinson	Mrs	Argyle Terrace	37	120
Robinson	Mrs	Crawford Square	4	128
Robinson	Mrs	Francis Street	36	137
Robinson	Mrs	Northland Road	64, Holly lodge	150
Robinson	Mrs	Orchard Street	12	151
Robinson	Mrs	Park Avenue	6	151
Robinson	Mrs M.	Barnewall Place	3	165
Robinson	Samuel	Wapping Lane	47	159
Robinson	Sarah	Clooney Terrace	49	167
Robinson	Stewart	Bentley Street	11	165
Robinson	William	Howard Street	23	141
Robinson	William	Lecky Road	112	144
Robinson	William	Dungiven Road	19	169
Robinson & Davidson		Richmond Street	3	153
Roche	J. J. & M.	Foyle Street	119	135
Roche	J. J. & M.	John Street	5, 7	142
Rochfort	Miss	Great James Street	61	139
Rochfort	Miss M.	Strand Road	38	156
Rock	Dr Patrick	Bayview Terrace	1	120
Rodden	Bridget	Bridge Street	44	125
Rodden	Elizabeth	Wesley Street	10	165
Rodden	Mary	Rossville Street	77	153
Roddy	Daniel	Rossville Street	40	153
Roddy	Daniel	Wellington Street	57	160
Roddy	Daniel	William Street	57	161
Roddy	Edward	Strabane Old Road	80	175
Roddy	Henry J.	Stanley's Walk	40	155

Surname	First Name	Street	House Number	Page Number
Roddy	James	Union Street	6	158
Roddy	Mary A.	Glasgow Street	3	138
Roddy	Matilda	Wellington Street	55	160
Roddy	Michael	Mountjoy Street	6	148
Roddy	Peter	Great James Street	60	139
Roddy	Rose	Eglinton Terrace	5	132
Roddy	Rose	Long Tower	10	145
Roddy	Thomas	Fountain Hill	82	171
Roddy	William	Strabane Old Road	74	175
Roden	James A.	Carlisle Terrace	3	126
Rodgers	Anthony	Nelson Street	19	149
Rodgers	James	Ferguson Street	53	134
Rodgers	John	Messines Park	31	128
Rodgers	Margaret	Hogg's Folly	9	141
Rodgers	Sarah	Marlborough Avenue	29	147
Rodgers	William	Fahan Street	107	133
Rodgers	William	Marlborough Avenue	27	147
Rogers	Catherine	St. Columb's Wells	79	157
Rollo	John	Fountain Place	23	135
Rooks	John	Victoria Street	11	159
Rooks	W. J.	Magazine Street	2, Masonic Hall	146
Rooney	Edward	Chamberlain Street	25	126
Rooney	Hugh	Elmwood Road	1	132
Rooney	James	Waterloo Place	7	160
Rooney	James	Duke Street	65	169
Rooney	John	Brandywell Road	9	124
Rooney	Martha	Patrick Street	9	151
Rooney	Martin	Ferryquay Street	38	134
Rooney	Michael	Brook Street	4	125
Rooney	Miss	Patrick Street	13	151
Rooney	Patrick senior	Patrick Street	12	151
Rooney	Rose	Rossville Street	67	153
Rosborough	Robert	Dungiven Road	45	169
Rosborough & Co.		Ferryquay Street	6	134
Ross	Catherine	Florence Street	3	163
Ross	David	Strabane Old Road	52	175
Ross	James	Fahan Street	59	133
Ross	James	Pump Street	15	152
Ross	Mrs	Glendermott Road	54	171
Ross	Stuart C.	Bishop Street	16	123
Ross	Thomas	New Street	8	164
Ross	William	Blee's Lane		124
Ross	William	Browning Drive	2	166
Roulston	Albert	Bond's Hill	24	166
Roulston	Christopher	Miller Street	20	148
Roulston	James	Sir E. Reid's Market	2	154
Roulston	Mark & MacLaughlin	Foyle Street	72, 74	136

Surname	First Name	Street	House Number	Page Number
Roulston	Miss	New Market Street		149
Roulston	R.	Park Avenue	25, Laurel Villa	151
Roulston	S. J.	Beechwood Avenue	64	121
Roulston	William	Northland Road	78 (Dun Creich)	150
Roulston	William	Queen Street	5	153
Roulston	Mrs	Windmill Terrace	24	162
Roulston & Smyth		Strand Road	25	155
Roulston & Smyth		William Street	47	161
Roulstone	J. & R.	Foyle Street	34	136
Roulstone	William	Charlotte Place	1	127
Routledge	Benjamin	Abercorn Road	44	118
Routledge & co.		Carlisle Road	48-50	126
Rowan	Alex	Grove Place	2	139
Ruddock	Miss A. H.	Shipquay Street	16	154
Ruddock	Mrs	Bishop Street	54	123
Rundle	Harris Ltd.	Shipquay Street	38	154
Rush	Mary	Strabane Old Road	16	175
Russell	James	Clarendon Street	31	127
Russell	James	Robert Street	7	174
Russell	Joseph	Bishop Street	40	123
Russell	Joseph	Clooney Terrace		167
Russell	Mrs	Orchard Row	29	150
Russell	Mrs	Limavady Road	6, Glenard	172
Russell	R. H.	Magazine Street	11	146
Russell	Robert	Miller Street	11	147
Russell	Samuel	Windsor Terrace	1	162
Rutherford	Robert	Alexandra Place	3	119
Rutherford	Robert	Aubrey Street	1	120
Rutherford	Samuel	Alexandra Place	11	119
Rutledge	William	Duke Street	82	169
Ryan	George	Foyle Road	51	136
Ryan	James	Gortfoyle Place	13	171
Ryan	Mrs	North Street	37	164
Ryan	Patrick	Nassau Street Upper	6	149
Ryans	Edward	Rossville Street	56	153
Sabary	James	Brandywell Avenue	21	124
Sally	Michael	Ivy Terrace	33	142
Salvo	Elizabeth	Duke Street	17	169
Samuels	John	Clarendon Street	23	127
Samuels	John	Shipquay Street	8	154
Sanders	Daniel	St. Columb's Wells	68	157
Saville	R. W.	Melrose Terrace	20	173
Sawyers	Andrew	Fountain Hill	52	171
Sawyers	Sergeant T.	Laburnum Terrace	5	142
Scarlett	John	Argyle Street	5	119
Scarlett	William	Florence Street	14	164
Schlindwein	Mrs	Beechwood Avenue	58	121

Surname	First Name	Street	House Number	Page Number
Scott	Andrew	Deanfield	gate lodge	168
Scott	Archibald	Fountain Hill	66	171
Scott	Edward R.	St. Mary's Terrace	33, Ballintrae	167
Scott	Francis	Violet Street Lower	48	176
Scott	G. D.	Foyle Street	3	135
Scott	Harry E.	Beechwood Park	104	121
Scott	James	Abercorn Road	30	118
Scott	James	Fountain Place	28	135
Scott	John	Mitchelburne Terrace	93	136
Scott	John James	Clooney Terrace	8A	167
Scott	Joseph	Windmill Terrace	9	162
Scott	M & M	Diamond		130
Scott	M. & M.	Bishop Street	1	122
Scott	Matthew	Spencer Road	54	175
Scott	Mrs	Philips Street	37	151
Scott	Robert	Bishop Street	71	122
Scott	Robert	Foyle Road	115	136
Scott	Samuel	Duke Street	52	169
Scott	Samuel	Union Street	4	176
Scott	William	Nassau Street Lower	25	148
Scott	William	Brooke Villas	35	164
Scott Motor Company		Foyle Road	9, 10	136
Scott Motor Company		John Street		142
Seaton	Albert	Marlborough Road	2	147
Selfridge	Alex	Bond's Hill	12	166
Selfridge	Alexander	Duke Street	90	169
Selfridge	Mrs	Ebrington Terrace	10	170
Selfridge	Robert	Ebrington Terrace	11	170
Selfridge	William	Epworth Street	8	163
Selfridge	William	New Street	2	164
Semple	Charles	Harding Street	2	140
Semple	J. J.	Castle Street	6	126
Semple	Mrs	Carlisle Road	43	125
Semple	Professor R. J.	College Avenue	1	150
Semple	Samuel	Clooney Terrace	33	167
Semple	William	Creggan		131
Semple	William & Co.	Pump Street	1	152
Shanagher	Mrs	Myrtle Terrace	76	150
Shannon	J. & Co.	New Market Street	3	149
Shannon	Margaret	Bond's Hill	5	166
Shannon	Mrs	Grove Place	7	139
Shannon	Ruth	Melrose Terrace	15	173
Shannon	William	Asylum Road	12	120
Shannon	William	Nelson Street	47	149
Shannon & Rutledge		Fountain Street	85	134
Shannon Shirt Finishing		Magazine Street	8	146

Surname	First Name	Street	House Number	Page Number
Sharkey	Henry	St. Columb's Wells	111	157
Sharkey	James	Beechwood Street	3	121
Sharkey	Joseph	Cedar Street	9	126
Sharkey	Mary	Fahan Street	3	133
Sharkey	Mrs	Rossville Street	27	153
Sharkey	Patrick	Bluebellhill Terrace	194	144
Sharkey	William	Limewood Street	39	144
Shaw	Desmond	George Street	8	138
Shearin	William	New Street	2	128
Sheath	Joseph	Orchard Row	13	150
Sheehan	Edward	Howard Street	9	141
Sheehan	Edward	Howard Place	10	141
Sheerin	Andrew	Orchard street	St. Columb's Hall	151
Sheerin	Bernard	Union Street	29	158
Sheerin	John	Elmwood Street	24	132
Sheerin	John	Ann Street	11	143
Sheerin	Mary	Quarry Street	8	153
Sheerin	Michael	Rosemount Terrace	2	165
Sheil	Mrs	Foyle Street	115, 117 Metropole Hotel	135
Sheilds	Frank	Governor Road	22	138
Sheilds	Ross	Carrigans Lane	30	126
Sheils	Andrew	Osborne Street	10	164
Sheils	Bernard	Nailor's Row	17	148
Sheils	Dominick	Great James Street	76	139
Sheils	Hugh	Nelson Street	16	149
Sheils	John	Fox's Lane	4	137
Sheils	John	Fulton Place	10	137
Sheils	John	Strand Road	100	157
Sheils	Joseph	Eden Place	6	132
Sheils	Mrs	Thomas Street	1	158
Sheils	Mrs	Wapping Lane	25	159
Sheils	Mrs	Benvarden Avenue	31	166
Sheils	Mrs	Chapel Road	5	167
Sheils	Ross	Moat Street	6	148
Sheils	Sarah	Strand Road	106	157
Sheils	William	Union Street	23	176
Shellcote	George	Lecky Road	273	143
Shelvey	Edward	Bond's Place	9	166
Shepherd	William	Albert Street	28	118
Sheppard	Harold	Sackville Street	Victoria Club	154
Sheppard	Mrs	Albert Street	15	118
Sheppard	Mrs M. A.	Park Villas	59	165
Sheppard	W. J.	Diamond	10	130
Sheppard	W. J.	Little James Street	13	145
Sheridan	Peter	Nicholson Square	15	149
Sheridan	Robert	Patrick Street	14	151
Sherlock	Patrick	Marlborough Avenue	16	147

Surname	First Name	Street	House Number	Page Number
Sherrard	Edward	Pine Street	11	174
Sherrard	Hugh	Elmwood Terrace	32	132
Sherrard	Joseph	Great James Street	15	139
Sherrard	Samuel	William Street	85, 87	161
Sherrard	Samuel	Glendermott Road	88	171
Sherrard	William	Dungiven Road	111	170
Sherrard	William J.	Fahan Street	103	133
Sherry	P. A.	New Market Street	4	149
Shields	Francis	Wapping Lane	33	159
Shields	Herbert	Glenview Avenue	13	137
Shields	James	Wesley Street	24	165
Shields	John	Creggan		131
Shields	Miss	Governor Road	23	138
Shields	Mrs	Abercorn Road	15	118
Shields	Mrs	Nicholson Terrace	16	149
Shields	Robert	Henry Street	10	141
Shields	William	Glenbrook Terrace	24	137
Shiels	Bridget	Philips Street	21	151
Shiels	Frank	St. Columb's Wells	52	157
Shiels	Helena	Wellington Street	27	160
Shiels	John	Argyle Street	29	119
Shiels	Patrick	Florence Street	12	164
Shiels	Peter	Union Street	24	176
Shirkey	William	Cross Street	28	168
Sidebottom	George	Carlisle Road	15	125
Sidebottom Bros.		Carlisle Road	17	125
Simmons	A. E.	Richmond Street	9	153
Simmons	Fred J.	Claremont Villas	36, Cul Edan	150
Simmons	R. P. & Co.	Carlisle Road	30	125
Simms	Bernard	Primrose Street	33	174
Simms	John	Foyle View	6	137
Simms	Lucy	Brook Street Avenue	5	125
Simms	Margaret	Major's Row	3	146
Simms	Mrs	Albert Street	22	118
Simms	William	Linenhall Street Lower	10	145
Simpson	Alexander	London Street	5	145
Simpson	Charles	Ferguson Street	36	134
Simpson	David	Clooney Terrace	54	167
Simpson	Elizabeth	Dungiven Road	71	170
Simpson	Gerald	St. Columb's Court	6	157
Simpson	Gerald	New Street	14	164
Simpson	James	Baronet Street	1	120
Simpson	James	Ashcroft Place	2	165
Simpson	Joseph	Fountain Hill	120	171
Simpson	Mary J.	Bond's Street	53	166
Simpson	Miss	Deanery Street	40	130
Simpson	Mrs	East Avenue	2	170
Simpson	Mrs	King Street	9	172

Surname	First Name	Street	House Number	Page Number
Simpson	Nurse	Sackville Street	8	154
Simpson	Robert	Strand Road	34	156
Simpson	Robert	Florence Street	14	170
Simpson	Robert	King Street	45	172
Simpson	Robert A.	Cuthbert Street	16	168
Simpson	Sam	Cross Street	38	168
Simpson	Thomas	Termon Street	1	175
Simpson	W. A.	Kennedy Place	5	142
Simpson	William	King Street	15	172
Simpson	William J.	Iona Terrace	9	172
Simpson	William S.	Dunfield Terrace	31	169
Sinclair	Miss	Strand Road	10	156
Sinclair	Richard	Hawthorn Terrace	7	140
Skeat	Mrs	Duke Street	69	168
Skerry's College		Bayview Terrace	4	120
Skinner	R. J.	West-End Park	1	161
Skinner	R. J. & Co.	Foyle Road	9, 10	136
Slevin	Edward	New Street	3	128
Slevin	Edward	Fahan Street	4	133
Slevin	Francis	Donegal Place	20	131
Slevin	Robert	Bishop Street	238	124
Sloan	David	Northland Avenue	6	150
Sloan	David	Florence Street	15	163
Sloan	James	Great James Street	46	139
Sloyne	John	Hawkin Street	35	140
Small	Edward	Beechwood Avenue	12	121
Small	Miss M.	Carlisle Road	16	125
Smalls	John	Wellington Street	13	160
Smallwoods	John	Dungiven Road	15	169
Smallwoods	Joseph	Ivy Terrace	20	142
Smallwoods	Joseph	Dungiven Road	31	169
Smallwoods	Joseph	Florence Street	40	170
Smallwoods	Mrs	Gordon Place	9	138
Smallwoods	Robert	Miller Street	4	147
Smallwoods	Samuel	Dungiven Road	17	169
Smallwoods	Thomas	Dungiven Road	37	169
Smallwoods	William	St. Columb's Road		172
Smallwoods	William	Dungiven Road	27	169
Smedley	Herbert	Barrack Street	8	120
Smiley	T. & J.	Strand Road	3	155
Smith	Andrew	Lecky Road	29	143
Smith	Arthur	Marlborough Avenue	20	147
Smith	Bridget	Emerson Street	6	170
Smith	Charles	Nelson Street	10	149
Smith	David	Dunfield Terrace	11	169
Smith	Edward	Nelson Street	24	149
Smith	Edward	Artisan Street	18	162
Smith	Ernest	Alfred Street	17	165
Smith	Francis	Strabane Old Road	100	175
Smith	G. H.	Demesne Terrace	14	130

Surname	First Name	Street	House Number	Page Number
Smith	Herbert	Northland Road	13	150
Smith	Hugh	Beechwood Avenue	34	121
Smith	Hugh	Tyrconnell Street	25	158
Smith	Ivan R.	Hinton Park	7	172
Smith	J. W. T.	Lawrence Hill	11, Breezemount	143
Smith	James	Dark Lane	2	130
Smith	James	Emerson Street	32	170
Smith	James	Fahan Street	18	133
Smith	Jane	Charlotte Place	4	127
Smith	John	Brook Street	1	125
Smith	John	Fountain Street	98	135
Smith	John	Wellington Street	60	160
Smith	John	Benvarden Avenue	3	165
Smith	Joseph	Bishop Street	122	123
Smith	Mary A.	Clarke Terrace	238	144
Smith	Miss S.	Albert Place	4	119
Smith	Mrs	Castle Street	3	126
Smith	Mrs	Harvey Street	10	140
Smith	Mrs	Lawrence Hill	1	143
Smith	Mrs	Orchard Street	15	151
Smith	Mrs	Creggan Road	22	163
Smith	Mrs	Carlin Street	19	167
Smith	Mrs H.	Hawkin Street	22	140
Smith	Patrick	Chapel Road	38	167
Smith	Philip	Laburnum Terrace	21	142
Smith	R.	Limavady Road	35	172
Smith	R. A.	Marlborough Street	75, Silverbirch	146
Smith	Rev. B.	Chapel Road	Parochial House	167
Smith	Richard	Charlotte Street	22	127
Smith	Robert	Aubrey Street	7	120
Smith	Robert	Fountain Street	31	134
Smith	Robert	Barnewall Place	21	165
Smith	Samuel	Glendermott Road	46	171
Smith	Samuel	Glendermott Road	86	171
Smith	Samuel	Violet Street Lower	27	176
Smith	Thomas	Chapel Road	50	167
Smith	William	Bellevue Avenue	8	121
Smith	William	Little James Street	14	145
Smith	William	Northland Avenue	2	150
Smith	William	Tyrconnell Street	22	158
Smith	William	Cuthbert Street	5	168
Smith	William	Deanfield	16, Colleen	168
Smith	Mrs	Society Street	7	155
Smith & Co.		Shipquay Street	10	154
Smy	William	Ewing Street	7	132
Smyth	A. L.	Shipquay Street	6	154
Smyth	Charles	Chapel Road	3	167
Smyth	G. H. & Co.	William Street	111	161

Surname	First Name	Street	House Number	Page Number
Smyth	George	Donegal Street	12	163
Smyth	H. T.	Aberfoyle Crescent	1	118
Smyth	H. T.	Strand Road	41	155
Smyth	Isabella	Northland Avenue	5	150
Smyth	James	Bishop Street	35	122
Smyth	James	Fairman Place	15	133
Smyth	James	Glasgow Terrace	40	138
Smyth	James	Long Tower	store	145
Smyth	James	Florence Street	7	170
Smyth	James	Strabane Old Road	124	175
Smyth	John	Northland Avenue	18	150
Smyth	John	Mount Street	17	164
Smyth	John	Dunfield Terrace	9	169
Smyth	John C.	Robert Street	10	174
Smyth	Joseph	William Street	89	161
Smyth	L. A. & Co.	Great James Street	2A	139
Smyth	Leslie	Ferguson Street	3	133
Smyth	M.	Brooke View	47, Craigmore	165
Smyth	Margaret	St. Columb's Wells	37	157
Smyth	Matthew	Florence Street	38	170
Smyth	Miss	Rockmount Villas	26	150
Smyth	Mrs	Bishop Street	58	123
Smyth	Mrs	Governor Road	16	138
Smyth	Mrs	Ivy Terrace	5	142
Smyth	Mrs	Ivy Terrace	14	142
Smyth	Mrs M. A.	Clarence Avenue	15	127
Smyth	R. & Co.	Foyle Street	44	136
Smyth	Rev. Michael	Victoria Place	Parochial House	159
Smyth	Robert	Beechwood Avenue	24, Fairbank	121
Smyth	Robert	Corporation Street	17	128
Smyth	Robert & Son	Quay Princes	office and stores	152
Smyth	Samuel	Argyle Terrace	4	120
Smyth	Samuel	Robert Street	9	174
Smyth	Thomas	Foyle Street	70	136
Smyth	William	Fountain Place	12	135
Smyth	William	Glasgow Terrace	27	138
Smyth	William	Hogg's Folly	19	141
Smythe	Alexander	Harding Street	11	140
Snodgrass	Thomas	Spencer Road	21	174
Spain	D.	Bishop Street	12, 14	123
Spain	David	Abercorn Road	58	118
Speers	Miss	Abercorn Road	55	118
Speers	Mrs	Fountain Street	44	134
Speers	Mrs	Lewis Street	21	164
Spence	H. A.	Foyle Street	7	135
Spence	J. A.	Kennedy Place	7	142
Spence	John A.	Beechwood Avenue	84	121
Spence	Miss	Park Villas	55	165

Surname	First Name	Street	House Number	Page Number
Spence	Mrs	Queen Street	4	153
Spence	Oliver	Emerson Street	4	170
Spence	Samuel	Duke Street	104	169
Spence	Stewart	Florence Street	9	163
Spiller	E. F.	Shipquay Street	39, Belfast Bank	154
Spiller & Bakers Ltd		Quay Princes	stores	152
Spillers & Bakers		Foyle Street	35	135
Spinks	Mrs Annie	Dunfield Terrace	27	169
Spratt	Edward	Clooney Terrace	21	167
Sproule	Robert	Ernest Street	11	163
Sproule	Thomas	Laburnum Terrace	19	142
Stafford	Charles A.	Kennedy Place	10	142
Starrett	David	Kennedy Street	8	142
Starrett	Edward	Sloan's Terrace	34	155
Starrett	Patrick	Violet Street Lower	35	176
Starrett	Robert	Sloan's Terrace	30	155
Starrett	Samuel	Dungiven Road	107	170
Starrett	William	Creggan Road	77	162
Starrett	William	Cottage Row	16	164
Starrett	William	York Street	12	176
Starritt	Alex	Princes Street	27	152
Starritt	Miss	St. Columb's Court	3	157
Starritt	Samuel	Duke Street	86	169
Starrs	Mary	Moore Street	4	148
Starrs	Patrick	Hamilton Street	39	140
Steadman	James H.	Crawford Square	13	129
Steele	Andrew	Academy Terrace	2	118
Steele	Andrew	Foyle Street	44	136
Steele	Catherine	Osborne Street	5	164
Steele	Daniel	Wellington Street	63	160
Steele	John	Charlotte Street	8	127
Steele	John	Eglinton Terrace	1	132
Steele	John	Ferguson Street	32	134
Steele	Miss	Ivy Terrace	29	142
Steele	Mrs	Ivy Terrace	4	142
Steele	Norman J.	Columba Terrace	4	168
Steele	Sarah	Ferguson Street	26	134
Steen	James	Strand Road	34	156
Stephenson	Andrew	Artisan Street	20	162
Sterriett	W. S.	Shipquay Street	14	154
Sterritt	A. A.	Abercorn Road	20	118
Sterritt	Mrs	Foyle Street	99	135
Sterritt	Mrs	Marlborough Terrace	13	147
Sterritt	Robert	Dervock Place	9	168
Stevenson	Doctor	Bond's Hill	Bond's hill	166
Stevenson	Ellen	St. Columb's Road		172
Stevenson	H & Co.	Strand Road	1	155

Surname	First Name	Street	House Number	Page Number
Stevenson	H. & Co.	William Street	95	161
Stevenson	Hugh & Co.	Duke Street	36	169
Stevenson	John	Marlborough Terrace	27	147
Stevenson	John	Orchard Row	20	150
Stevenson	John	May Street	11	173
Stevenson	Mrs D.	Crawford Square	16	129
Stevenson	R. J.	Magazine Street	9, office	146
Stevenson	Robert	Sydney Terrace	2	139
Stevenson	Robert T.	Marlborough Road	4	147
Stevenson	Samuel	Bishop Street	250	124
Stevenson	William	Messines Park	14	128
Stewart	A. L.	Rosemount Avenue	19	164
Stewart	Constable Robert G.	Corporation Street	25	128
Stewart	David	Barry Street	29	121
Stewart	Edward	Lecky Road	80	144
Stewart	G. E.	Castle Street	4	126
Stewart	George E.	Demesne Terrace	8, Sunnymede	130
Stewart	Gerald	Donaghy's Row	1	140
Stewart	Isaac	Fairman Place	16	133
Stewart	James	Messines Park	23	128
Stewart	James	Garden City		129
Stewart	James	Glenview Avenue	5	137
Stewart	James	Nassau Street Lower	11	148
Stewart	James	Sackville Street	21	154
Stewart	James	MalvernTerrace	3	168
Stewart	John	Beechwood Park	94	121
Stewart	John	Blucher Street	30	124
Stewart	John	Governor Road	31	138
Stewart	John	Lower Road	11	146
Stewart	John	Clooney Terrace	20	167
Stewart	Joseph	Blucher Street	32	124
Stewart	Joseph	Edenmore Street	36	132
Stewart	Matt	Shipquay Street	2	154
Stewart	Matthew	Abercorn Place	10	118
Stewart	Matthew	Diamond		130
Stewart	Michael	St. Columb's Terrace	95	143
Stewart	Miss	Diamond	12	130
Stewart	Miss	Francis Street	37	137
Stewart	Moses	London Street	22	145
Stewart	Moses	Florence Street	13	163
Stewart	Mrs	Albert Street	21	118
Stewart	Mrs	Culmore Road	Sorrento	129
Stewart	Mrs	Ivy Terrace	13	142
Stewart	Mrs	Benvarden Avenue	29	165
Stewart	Mrs	Benvarden Avenue	20	166
Stewart	Mrs	Duke Street	29	169
Stewart	Mrs	Duke Street	76	169
Stewart	R.	Strand Road	8	156
Stewart	Richard	Albert Place	9	119

Surname	First Name	Street	House Number	Page Number
Stewart	Richard	Duncreggan Road	13	131
Stewart	Robert	Bellevue Avenue	18	121
Stewart	Robert	Duncreggan Road	10	131
Stewart	Robert	Nicholson Square	4	149
Stewart	Samuel & Co.	Foyle Street	22	136
Stewart	Sarah	Governor Road	33	138
Stewart	T. A.	Fairman Place	4	133
Stewart	Thomas	Glendermott Road	96	171
Stewart	William	Bennett Street Upper	1	121
Stewart	William	Blee's Lane		124
Stewart	William	Fountain Street	83	134
Stewart	William	Kennedy Street	16	142
Stewart	William	Nassau Street Lower	41	148
Stewart	William	Nelson Street	61	149
Stewart	William	Nelson Street	64	149
Stewart	William	Princes Terrace	4	152
Stewart	William	Lewis Street	7	164
Stewart	William	Clooney Terrace	29	167
Stewart	William J.	Olive Terrace	1	173
Stewart & Co.		Carlisle Road	44	126
Stinson	James	Distillery Brae Upper	2	168
Stirling	Mrs	Marlborough Street	8	147
Stitt	Edward	Westland Terrace	8	161
Stitt	Robert	Beechwood Street	12	121
Stone	A. H.	John Street	45	142
Stone	Harry	Bentley Street	12	165
Stone	James	Bishop Street	278	124
Stone	James	New Street	11	126
Stone	Sergeant R.	Barry Street	24	121
Storey	Mrs	Foyle Road	109	136
Strahan	Mrs C. E.	Riverview Terrace	14	174
Strain	Andrew	Princes Street	25	152
Strain	Elizabeth	Walker's Place	23	159
Strain	Mrs	Hawthorn Terrace	32	140
Strange	A.	Strand Road	40	156
Strange	Andrew	Bishop Street	102A	123
Strange	Andrew	Kennedy Place	2	142
Strange	John	Bishop Street	102A	123
Strawbridge	David	Herbert Street	8	172
Strawbridge	Hugh	Violet Street Lower	20	176
Strawbridge	James	Ashfield Terrace	45	162
Strawbridge	John	Iona Terrace	5	172
Strawbridge	Mrs	Margaret Street	17	173
Strawbridge	Patrick	Bluebellhill Terrace	198	144
Streams	Edward	Albert Street	34	119
Strickland	Frank	York Street	5	176
Stringer	Thomas	De Burgh Terrace	8	130
Stringer	Thomas	Shipquay Place	Guildhall (Accountant)	154
Strunks	Joseph	Princes Street	2	152

Surname	First Name	Street	House Number	Page Number
Strunks	Vincent	Limewood Street	4	144
Struthers	Alexander	Messines Park	42	128
Struthers	James	Victoria Terrace	12	120
Struthers	James	Messines Park	48	128
Struthers	William	Collon Terrace	2	128
Stuart	Mrs T. A.	Deanfield	10	168
Stuart	R. & J.	Spencer Road	23	174
Stuart	Robert	Simpson's Brae	10	174
Summerville	Alex	Ernest Street	16	163
Swan	Robert junior	Glendermott Road	42	171
Swan	Robert senior	Glendermott Road	38	171
Swann	James Aitkin	Lone Moor		145
Swann	W. J.	Beechwood Avenue	28	121
Swann	W. J. & Co.	Waterloo Street	42	160
Sweeney	(chemist)	North Edward Street	4	149
Sweeney	Daniel	Nailor's Row	9	148
Sweeney	David	Hogg's Folly	21	141
Sweeney	Edward	Creggan Road	153	163
Sweeney	Francis	Florence Street	25	170
Sweeney	Frank	Thomas Street	14	158
Sweeney	George	Fitters Row	261	123
Sweeney	Hugh	Howard Street	27	141
Sweeney	James	Foyle Road	64	136
Sweeney	James	Lecky Road	57	143
Sweeney	James	Strand Road	23	155
Sweeney	James & Co.	Foyle Street	35	135
Sweeney	John	Sunbeam Terrace	2	122
Sweeney	John	Clarendon Street Lower	1	127
Sweeney	John	Thomas Street	2	158
Sweeney	John	Cross Street	33	168
Sweeney	Margaret	Waterloo Street	61	159
Sweeney	Mary A.	Orchard Lane	7	151
Sweeney	Michael	New Street	9	128
Sweeney	Michael Ltd	Strand Road	70	157
Sweeney	Miss	Cottage Row	10	164
Sweeney	Miss Sarah	Herbert Street	2	172
Sweeney	Mrs	Dark Lane	7	130
Sweeney	Mrs	Mountroyal	1	150
Sweeney	Mrs	Simpson's Brae	17	174
Sweeney	Mrs M.	Howard Street	7	141
Sweeney	Myles	Bluebellhill Terrace	162	144
Sweeney	Patrick	Ann Street	21	119
Sweeney	Patrick	Foyle Street	49	135
Sweeney	Patrick	King Street	46	172
Sweeney	Rose	St. Columb's Wells	112	157
Sweeney	Rose A.	St. Columb's Wells	107	157
Sweeney	Samuel	Nailor's Row	34	148
Sweeney	Sarah	Nailor's Row	34	148
Sweeney	Susan	Tyrconnell Street	12	158

Surname	First Name	Street	House Number	Page Number
Sweeney	Thomas	Patrick Street	8B	151
Sweeney	William	Barry Street	15	121
Sweeney	William	Limewood Street	34	144
Sweeney	William	Mountjoy Street	15	148
Sweeney & Co.		East Wall		131
Sweenie	Mrs	Florence Terrace	18	150
Sweeny	H.	Strand Road	57	155
Sweeny	Mrs	Clarendon Street	10	127
Sweet	A. H.	Shipquay Place	1	154
Tachley	John	Long Tower	41	145
Tagart	Mrs	Mountain Street	18	173
Taggart	Charles	Long Tower	69	145
Taggart	James	Brandywell Road	16	124
Taggart	John	Strand Road	123	156
Taggart	Margaret	Nassau Street Upper	8	149
Taggart	Margaret	Spencer Road	100	175
Taggart	Mrs	Albert Street	23	118
Taggart	Mrs	Nassau Street Upper	29	149
Taggart	Richard	Grafton Street	27	139
Taggart	Samuel	Clarendon Street	43	127
Taggart	Samuel	Foyle Road	9, 10	136
Taggart	Samuel	John Street	54	142
Tait	William	Princes Street	7	152
Taite	Mrs	Fountain Place	22	135
Tate	Maggie	Bridge Street		124
Tate	Stewart	Emerson Street	31	170
Taylor	Alex	Ashcroft Place	4	165
Taylor	Andrew	Fountain Hill	55	171
Taylor	Catherine	Gallagher's Square	1	137
Taylor	Constable J.	Sloan's Terrace	28	155
Taylor	Constable S.	Mountjoy Street	19	148
Taylor	Edward	Collon Terrace	10	128
Taylor	James	Barry Street	26	121
Taylor	John	Fountain Street	111	134
Taylor	John	Great James Street	54	139
Taylor	Joseph	Fountain Hill	53	171
Taylor	Joseph	Herbert Street	4	172
Taylor	M. & L.	Spencer Road	18	175
Taylor	Mary	Alma Terrace	41	136
Taylor	Miss	Barnewall Place	26	165
Taylor	Mrs	Fountain Hill	70	171
Taylor	Robert	Lecky Road	255	143
Taylor	Samuel	Herbert Street	14	172
Taylor	Thomas	New Street	5	128
Taylor	Thomas	Fountain Street	106½	135
Taylor	William	New Street	7	128
Taylor	William	Glenbrook Terrace	18	137
Taylor	William	Shipquay Street	18	154
Taylor	William	West-End Park	9	161
Taylor	William	Spencer Road	107	174

Surname	First Name	Street	House Number	Page Number
Teagan	Joseph	Riverview Terrace	5	174
Teasdel	Arthur	Aberfoyle Crescent	9	118
Teasey	William	Bond's Place	8	166
Tedley	John	Barnewall Place	8	165
Tees	James	Aberfoyle Terrace	33	156
Temple	John	George Street	3	138
Temple	Mrs	Victoria Street	6	159
Temple	William	George Street	1	138
Templeton	Edward	Asylum Road	9	120
Templeton	James	Moat Street	3	148
Tennett	Captain	Limavady Road	33	172
Thomas	Hugh	Nassau Street Upper	21	149
Thomas	Leonard	Barnewall Place	16	165
Thomas	Mrs	William Street	39, City Dispensary	161
Thomas	Thomas	Glasgow Street	3	138
Thomas	William	Bennett Street Lower	57	122
Thomas	Andrew	Argyle Street	52	119
Thompson	Adam	Garden City		129
Thompson	Alexander & Co.	Duke Street	74	169
Thompson	Andrew	Charlotte Street	2	127
Thompson	Andrew	Columba Terrace	1	168
Thompson	Archibald	Clarendon Street	30	127
Thompson	Daniel	Aubrey Street	32	120
Thompson	Daniel	Gordon Place	4	138
Thompson	David	Glasgow Street	6	138
Thompson	Dealtry P.	Duncreggan Road	11	131
Thompson	George	Northland Avenue	21	150
Thompson	George A.	Albert Street	16	118
Thompson	George B.	Strabane Old Road	29	175
Thompson	Henry	Ferryquay Street	11, 13	134
Thompson	J. H.	College Terrace	12	128
Thompson	James	Argyle Street	46	119
Thompson	James	Argyle Street	50	119
Thompson	James	George Street	12	138
Thompson	James	Meadowbank Avenue	20	147
Thompson	James F.	Marlborough Street	38	147
Thompson	John	Abercorn Road	26	118
Thompson	John	Bellevue Avenue	39	121
Thompson	John	Bishop Street	136	123
Thompson	John	Bridge Street	19	124
Thompson	John	Mitchelburne Terrace	88	136
Thompson	John	Queen Street	11	153
Thompson	M. A. & G.	Ferryquay Street	17	134
Thompson	Malcolm	Ebrington Terrace	4	170
Thompson	Miss Jennie	Francis Street	47	137
Thompson	Mrs	Victoria Terrace	10	120

Surname	First Name	Street	House Number	Page Number
Thompson	Mrs	Meadowbank Avenue	Foyle Temperance Hotel	147
Thompson	Mrs	Meadowbank Avenue	13	147
Thompson	Mrs	Nassau Street Upper	5	148
Thompson	Mrs	Creggan Road	105	162
Thompson	Mrs R.	Strand Road Lower	143	156
Thompson	Mrs S.	Melrose Terrace	9, Olivet	173
Thompson	Mrs W.	Abercorn Road	41	118
Thompson	N. R.	Carlisle Road	18, 20	125
Thompson	Philip	Tyrconnell Street	3	158
Thompson	Right Rev. James	Crawford Square	21	129
Thompson	Robert	Duncreggan Road	1	131
Thompson	Robert	Nassau Street Upper	9	149
Thompson	Robert M.	Marlborough Street	36	147
Thompson	Samuel	Alma Place	9	119
Thompson	Samuel S.	Marlborough Street	79, Morston	147
Thompson	T. G.	Dungiven Road	105	170
Thompson	Thomas	Wesley Street	12	165
Thompson	W.	Shipquay Street	18	154
Thompson	W. R.	Spencer Road	77	174
Thompson	William	Kennedy Street	7	142
Thompson	William	Duke Street	23, 25	169
Thompson	William & Co.	Prince Arthur Street	stores	152
Thompson	William & Co.	Shipquay Street	27	154
Thompson	William & Co. Ltd	Quay Queen's		152
Thompson	William & Co. Ltd.	Linenhall Street Lower		145
Thompson-Edwards Motor Co		Strand Road	78	157
Thornley	F. E.	Bayview Terrace	2	120
Thornley	F. E.	Custom House Street	Income Tax Office	129
Thornton	Patrick	Orchard Row	3	150
Thornton	Sergeant F.	Creggan Road	18, R.U.C. Barracks	163
Thorpe	William	Glendermott Road	19	171
Tiernan	Charles	Westland Avenue	31	160
Tierney	James	Demesne		130
Tierney	Joseph	Fahan Street	38	133
Tierney	Mrs	Fahan Street	42	133
Tierney	Patrick	Nailor's Row	40	148
Tierney & Kelly		Foyle Street	45, 47	135
Tighe	Mrs	Mitchelburne Terrace	86	136
Tillie & Henderson		Abercorn Road		117
Tillie, McDermott & Munn		Shipquay Street	40	154
Timoney	Edward	Bluebellhill Terrace	178	144

Surname	First Name	Street	House Number	Page Number
Timoney	William	Ivy Terrace	34	142
Tinney	Annie	Patrick Street	1	151
Tinney	Edward	Hawthorn Terrace	30	140
Tinney	Edward	Strand Road	110	157
Tinney	Robert	Blucher Street	11	124
Tipping	George W.	Eden Terrace	7	131
Todd	Constable	Edenballymore		131
Todd	Finlay L.	Beechwood Park	96	121
Todd & Mark		Shipquay Street	6	154
Toland	Bartley	Collon Terrace	18	128
Toland	Ellen	Adam Street	4	118
Toland	George	Violet Street Lower	40	176
Toland	Henry	Artisan Street	6	162
Toland	James	Donegal Place	11	131
Toland	James	Fahan Street	63	133
Toland	James	Artisan Street	4	162
Toland	James	Cross Street	11	168
Toland	John	Rossville Street	60	153
Toland	Michael	Beechwood Street	1	121
Toland	Michael	Donegal Place	13	131
Toland	Michael	Lecky Road	14	144
Toland	Mrs	Sloan's Terrace	32	155
Toland	William	Eglinton Place	12	132
Tombe	Hugh	Mountjoy Terrace	8	118
Toms	Stanley	Hinton Park	15	172
Toner	James	Nelson Street	48	149
Toner	John	Sugarhouse lane	20	158
Toner	Mrs K	Fulton Place	15	137
Toner	William	Rossville Street	51	153
Torney Bros, Ltd		Linenhall Street Lower		145
Torrans	Mrs E.	Hawthorn Terrace	16	140
Torrens	Abraham	Aberfoyle Terrace	31	156
Torrens	James	Violet Street Lower	26	176
Torrens	John	Wapping Lane	45	159
Torrens	Mrs	Little James Street	12	145
Torrens	Samuel	Harding Street	29	140
Torrens	Samuel	Violet Street Lower	52	176
Torrens	Thomas	Little James Street	12	145
Tosh	Mrs	Corporation Street	3	128
Tosh	Robert	Violet Street Lower	37	176
Towers	F. C.	Northland Road	17, Alt-an-Aros	150
Towers	Mrs	Crawford Square	6	128
Townley	David	Brooke Villas	31	164
Townsend	W. F.	William Street	8	161
Toye	E. J.	Foyle Street	3	135
Toye	Edward	Glasgow Street	2	138
Toye	James	St. Columb's Wells	45	157
Toye	James	Waterloo Street	15	159
Toye	Patrick	Stanley's Walk	36	155

Surname	First Name	Street	House Number	Page Number
Toye	Robert	William Street	45	161
Toye	Sarah	Glasgow Street	2	138
Tracey	John	Meehan's Row	10	173
Tracey	Michael	Waterloo Street	67	159
Tracey	Michael	William Street	2	161
Tracey	Patrick	John Street	51, 53	142
Tracey	Thomas	Bridge Street	72, 74	125
Tracey	Thomas	John Street	1	142
Tracey	William	MalvernTerrace	1	168
Tracy	Annie	Dungiven Road	12	170
Tracy	John	Custom House Street		129
Tracy	Patrick	Dervock Place	1	168
Tracy	Patrick	Union Street	6	176
Tracy	Robert	Dervock Place	7	168
Tracy	William	Margaret Street	8	173
Trainor	Catherine	North Street	9	164
Trainor	Patrick	New Street	8	128
Trainor	Thomas	Alfred Street	22	165
Trainor	William	Florence Street	22	170
Travers	Bernard	Fahan Street	93	133
Travers	Bernard	Nailor's Row	34	148
Travers	James	Nelson Street	36	149
Travers	James	Nelson Street	46	149
Traynor	Margaret	Elmwood Street	18	132
Trimble	James	Hawkin Street		140
Trimby	G. E.	Pump Street	1	152
Trotter	Alex	Kennedy Street	14	142
Trotter	Mrs	Albert Street	12	118
Tuck	Solomon	Abercorn Place	7	118
Turner	Constable G.	York Street	14	176
Turner	John	Henry Street	9	141
Turner	John	Simpson's Brae	5	174
Turner	Mrs	Gortfoyle Place	5	171
Turner	R. S.	Beechwood Avenue	13, Burnside	121
Turner	Robert	Florence Street	8	164
Tyler	John & Sons	Ferryquay Street	9	134
Tyler	John & Sons	Foyle Street	4	135
Tyre	Mary Ann	Nelson Street	40	149
Underwood	William A.	Glenbrook Terrace	17	137
Ussher	Alex	King Street	4	172
Ussher	John	Grove Place	12	139
Ussher	Mrs	King Street	2	172
Ussher	Samuel	Barrack Street	14	120
Vaccaro	John	Lecky Road	25	143
Vance	Moses A.	Park Villas	61	165
Vaughan	Albert E.	Alfred Street	31	165
Vaughan	Alfred	Hawkin Street	10	140
Vaughan	Stanley	Strand Road	62	157
Venerable	Charles	Alfred Street	56	165
Verner	W. & Sons	Foyle Street	45, 47	135

Surname	First Name	Street	House Number	Page Number
Verscheur	William	Spencer Road	28	175
Villa	Denis	Creggan Terrace	9	129
Villa	Laurence	Fulton Place	5	137
Villa	Patrick	Elmwood Terrace	19	132
Vint	Constable William	Barry Street	8	121
Virtue	Miss D.	Grove Place	16	139
Wade	Daniel	Blucher Street	12	124
Wade	James	Nassau Street Upper	7	149
Wade	John	Glasgow Street	1	138
Wafer	Lloyd S.	Glendermott Road	1	171
Walden	Miss M.	Great James Street	62	139
Walker	Andrew	De Moleyn Park	1	130
Walker	Andrew	Florence Street	15	170
Walker	Andrew	Glendermott Road	15	171
Walker	David	Glasgow Terrace	13	138
Walker	Edward	Messines Park	21	128
Walker	George	Beechwood Avenue	27, Dunard	121
Walker	George	Strabane Old Road	7	175
Walker	Henry	Alfred Street	9	165
Walker	James	Sunbeam Terrace	19	122
Walker	James	Ewing Street	9	132
Walker	James H.	Nicholson Square	17	149
Walker	John	Ewing Street	15	132
Walker	John	Nassau Street Upper	1	149
Walker	John	Windmill Terrace	12	162
Walker	John	Violet Street Lower	8	176
Walker	Lavinia	Strabane Old Road	9	175
Walker	Major T.	Browning Drive	1	166
Walker	Miss	Great James Street	10	139
Walker	Miss Kathleen	Orchard Row	11	150
Walker	Miss M.	Grove Place	15	139
Walker	Mrs E.	Fairman Place	22	133
Walker	Mrs W.	De Burgh Square	1	130
Walker	Patrick	Blucher Street	13	124
Walker	Robert	Bellevue Avenue	16	121
Walker	Robert	Charlotte Place	2	127
Walker	Robert	Union Street	27	158
Walker	Robert	Glendermott Road	4	171
Walker	Robert	York Street	10	176
Walker	Samuel	Bond's Street	28	166
Walker	Susan	Barnewall Place	7	165
Walker	T.	Victoria Park	1, gate lodge	176
Walker	Thomas	Wesley Street	9	165
Walker	William	Fountain Street	51	134
Walker	William	St. Columb's Court	2	157
Walker	William	Alfred Street	5	165
Walker	William H.	Glendermott Road	9	171
Wallace	Albert	Alfred Street	3	165
Wallace	Alexander	Foyle Road	33	136

Surname	First Name	Street	House Number	Page Number
Wallace	David	Spencer Road	144	175
Wallace	Elizabeth J.	Edenmore Street	2	131
Wallace	Hugh	Violet Street Lower	24	176
Wallace	J. W.	Hawkin Street	32	140
Wallace	James	Philips Street	41	151
Wallace	James	Society Street	13	155
Wallace	Miss	Clarendon Street	34	127
Wallace	Miss	Diamond	12	130
Wallace	Miss	Magazine Street Upper	3	146
Wallace	Miss	Meadowbank Avenue	11	147
Wallace	Mrs	Edenmore Street	8	131
Wallace	Robert	Albert Street	11	118
Wallace	Robert	Duke Street	29	169
Wallace	Robert	Spencer Road	128	175
Wallace	Thomas	Strand Road	10	156
Wallace	Thomas G. junior	Browning Drive	27	166
Wallace	Thomas senior	Browning Drive	15	166
Wallace	William J.	Hawkin Street	33	140
Waller	H. E.	Culmore Road	Troy	129
Waller	H. E. & Co.	Castle Street	9	126
Walls	James	William Street	25	161
Walls	Robert	Orchard Row	19	150
Walmsley	George	Lecky Road	Gaslight Co.	144
Walmsley	George	Bluebellhill Cottage		155
Walsh	Annie	Nelson Street	31	149
Walsh	Bernard	Alexandra Place	10	119
Walsh	James	Primrose Street	25	174
Walsh	John	Hogg's Folly	15	141
Walsh	John	Northland Avenue	20	150
Walsh	Mrs	Clarendon Street	8	127
Walsh	Mrs	Union Street	14	158
Walsh	Patrick	Howard Place	2	141
Walsh	John	Stanley's Walk	8	155
Walshe	J. J.	Shipquay Street	9, Munster & Leinster Bank	154
Wands	James	Ebrington Gardens		166
Ward	John	Governor Road	26	138
Ward	John	Violet Street Lower	39	176
Ward	Joshua	Nicholson Terrace	8	149
Ward	Miss M.	Westland Avenue	9	160
Ward	Mrs	Waterloo Street	20	159
Ward	Patrick	Bishop Street	151	122
Ward	Patrick	William Street	101	161
Ward	Thomas	Stanley's Walk	21	155
Ward	V. & Son	John Street	6, 8, 10	142
Ward	V. S.	Abercorn Road	8	118
Ward	Vincent & Son	Foyle Road	1	136
Ward	William	Bishop Street	257	123

Surname	First Name	Street	House Number	Page Number
Ward	William	Fahan Street	113	133
Ward	William	John Street	4	142
Ward	John	Dark Lane	23	130
Warden	James	Corporation Street	13	128
Warke	John	Abercorn Road	52	118
Warke	John	Emerson Street	7	170
Warke	Joseph	Emerson Street	34	170
Warke	Letitia Jane	Moore Street	35	173
Warke	Matthew	Windmill Terrace	27	162
Warke	Miss	Alexandra Terrace	48	150
Warnock	Thomas	Melrose Terrace	19	173
Warr	Frank	Bennett Street Lower	33	122
Warren	Miss Mary J.	Cottage Row	4	123
Wasson	John	Miller Street	5	147
Wasson	John	Park Avenue	21	151
Wasson	Joseph	Grafton Street	31	139
Wasson	Joseph	Creggan Road	97	162
Wasson	Joseph	Lewis Street	9	164
Wasson	Mrs	Moore Street	9	173
Wasson	William	Rosemount Terrace	10	165
Watchman	L.	Carlisle Road	44A	126
Waterstone	Arthur	Fountain Place	33	135
Waterstone	William	Bond's Street	31	166
Watkins	Miss	Union Street	8	176
Watkins	Robert	Benvarden Avenue	57	166
Watson	A.	De Burgh Terrace	5	130
Watson	Andrew	Eden Place	13	132
Watson	Dr. J.	Northland Road	6	149
Watson	Henry W.	Bishop Street		122
Watson	James	Carrigans Lane	3	126
Watson	James	Governor Road	2	138
Watson	James	Columba Terrace	7	168
Watson	John James	Bridge Street	5	124
Watson	John James	Orchard Street		151
Watson	Marcus	Foyle Road	47	136
Watson	Mary A.	Ann Street	18	119
Watson	Miss	Ferguson Street	65	134
Watson	Miss	Clooney Terrace	32	168
Watson	Miss Kathleen	Clarendon Street	73	127
Watson	Mrs	McLaughlin's Close	3	134
Watson	Mrs	Tamneymore		175
Watson	Mrs E.	Harvey Street	14	140
Watson	Mrs M.	Robert Street	8	174
Watson	R.	Dungiven Road		170
Watson	R. M.	Demesne Terrace	11	130
Watson	R. M. & Co.	William Street	41	161
Watson	Sophia	Orchard Row	14	150
Watson	Thomas	Clarence Avenue	13	127
Watson	Thomas	Clooney Park West	5, St. Kilda	172
Watson	William	St. Columb's Street	11	157

Surname	First Name	Street	House Number	Page Number
Watt	A. A. & Co. Ltd.	Linenhall Street Lower		145
Watt	A. A. Ltd	Shipquay Street	33	154
Watt	D. & Co.	Clarendon Street Lower	5	127
Watt	D. & Co.	Fahan Street	133, 135	133
Watt	D. & Co. Ltd	Spencer Road	111, stores	174
Watt	David & Co.	Abbey Street		117
Watt	David & Co.	Abbey Street		117
Watt	David & Co.	Frederick Street		137
Watt	David & Co.	Quay Queen's	stores	152
Watt	David & Co. Ltd	William Street		162
Watt	David & Co. Ltd	Bond's Hill		166
Watt	David & Co. Ltd	Simpson's Brae	distillery	174
Watt	G.	Shipquay Street	33	154
Watt	Gerald A.	Culmore Road	Drumleary	129
Watt	James	Creggan Road	91	162
Watt	Mrs	Northland Road	8, Edenmore House	149
Watt	David & Co. Ltd	Duke Street		169
Watters	S. B.	Strand Road	4	156
Waugh	Rev. R. M. L.	Dacre Terrace	4	126
Webb	George	Foster's Terrace	163	143
Webb	John	Thomas Street	19	158
Webb	Thomas	Eden Place	9	132
Weekes	William	Spencer Road	132	175
Weigold	E. W.	Spencer Road	7	174
Weir	Dr A. L.	Bayview Terrace	5	120
Weir	Matthew	Fahan Street	123	133
Weir	W. H.	Bayview Terrace	5	120
Welch	J. H.	Culmore Road	Dunruadh	129
Welch, Margetson & Co.		Carlisle Road		125
Welch, Margetson & Co.		Fountain Street	laundry	134
Welsh	Mrs S. H.	Simpson's Brae	15	174
Welsh	Philip	Ewing Street	10	132
West	William	Beechwood Avenue	20	121
Whan & Co.		Sackville Street	21	154
White	Andrew	Gordon Place	5	138
White	David	The Rock	115	156
White	George	Messines Park	39	128
White	George	Fulton Place	17	137
White	Gerald	Dunfield Terrace	39	169
White	John	Academy Terrace	3	118

Surname	First Name	Street	House Number	Page Number
White	John	Chamberlain Street	8	126
White	John	Strand Road	46	156
White	John	St. Columb's Wells	40	157
White	Joseph	Glendermott Road	27	171
White	Miss	Orchard Row	37	150
White	Mrs Thomas	Clarence Avenue	22	127
White	T. & Co.	Castle Street	3	126
White	Thomas	Castle Street	1	126
White	William	Albert Street	26	118
White	William	Fountain Street	45	134
White	Mrs	Ivy Terrace	39	142
White	Thomas	St. Columb's Terrace	103	143
Whiteside	Alex	Henrietta Street	5	141
Whiteside	George	Benvarden Avenue	6	166
Whiteside	John C.	Princes Street	3	152
Whiteside	Robert	Lower Road	5	146
Whiteside	William	Miller Street	15	147
Whittington	David	Westland Avenue	15	160
Whittington	John	Florence Street	18	164
Whittington	Miss C.	Bellevue Avenue	9	121
Whittle	Percy W.	Carlisle Road	Opera House	125
Whittle	Percy W.	Horace Street	1	141
Whoriskey	Hugh	Philips Street	25	151
Whoriskey	Miss	Union Street	12	158
Whorriskey	Florence	St. Columb's Wells	118	157
Whyte	Fred	Moore Street	1	173
Whyte	Jacob	Clarendon Street	18	127
Whyte	James	Garden City		129
Whyte	Jane	Glendermott Road	12	171
Wightman	A.	Shipquay Street	10	154
Wightman	Alexander	Lawrence Hill	16	143
Wightman	William	Richmond Street	3	153
Wiley	Rebecca	Nicholson Terrace	3	149
Wilkin	Thomas	Park Villas	57	165
Wilkinson	J. N.	Lorne Street	5	145
Wilkinson	John N.	Lorne Street	1	145
Wilkinson	John N.	Queen Street	2	153
Wilkinson	Miss	Bellevue Avenue	41	121
Wilkinson	Mrs	Hayesbank Terrace		167
Wilkinson	Samuel	Glenbrook Terrace	13	137
Wilkinson	William	Bluebellhill Terrace	186	144
Wilkinson & Co.		Magazine Street	4	146
Williams	John	Bishop Street	37	122
Williams	John	Pump Street	20	152
Williams	Mrs	Brandywell Road	19	124
Williams	Thomas	Abercorn Road	33	118
Williams	Harold P.	Alexandra Terrace	50	150
Williams	J. A.	Northland Road	80, The Willows	150

Surname	First Name	Street	House Number	Page Number
Williams	James	Lower Road	35A	146
Williams	Leo	Clarke Terrace	234	144
Williams	Mrs	Marlborough Avenue	22	147
Williams	Richard	Kennedy Street	4	142
Williams	William	Marlborough Avenue	8	147
Williams	John	William Street	18	161
Williamson	Edward	Great James Street	41	139
Williamson	James	Horace Street	2	141
Williamson	James	Richmond Street	14	153
Williamson	Joseph	Mountjoy Terrace	10	118
Williamson	Joseph C.	College Terrace	4	127
Williamson	M. & Co.	Shipquay Street	7	154
Williamson	Mrs	Charlotte Street	13	127
Williamson	Samuel	Princes Street	21	152
Williamson	Alex	Kerr's Terrace	11	162
Williamson	David	Lewis Street	5	164
Williamson	James	Kerr's Terrace	13	162
Williamson	John	Bond's Street	22	166
Williamson	John	Pine Street	8	174
Williamson	Mrs	Creggan Road	137	162
Williamson	Mrs	Florence Street	34	170
Williamson	Rosena	Union Street	1	158
Williamson Bros.		Strand Road	94	157
Willis	Fred	Bishop Street	100	123
Willis	Mrs	Quarry Street	18	153
Willmann	Romain	Strand Road	8	156
Willmann	Romain	West-End Park	13	161
Willoughby	John C.	Iona Terrace	11	172
Wilson	A. & Co.	Lorne Street	7	145
Wilson	A. & Co.	Quay Abercorn	stores	152
Wilson	Alexander	Spencer Road	10	175
Wilson	Alexander	Spencer Road	72	175
Wilson	Charlotte	Lewis Street	22	164
Wilson	David	Violet Street Lower	59	176
Wilson	Edward	Limavady Road	53	172
Wilson	Henry	George Street	4	138
Wilson	I. H.	Waterloo Place	3, 4, Ulster Bank	160
Wilson	J. Howard	Crawford Square	10	129
Wilson	James	May Street	1	173
Wilson	John	Barry Street	13	121
Wilson	John	Bishop Street	145	122
Wilson	John	Charlotte Street	10	127
Wilson	John	Northland Road	8, lodge	150
Wilson	John	Emerson Street	23	170
Wilson	John	Fountain Hill	30	171
Wilson	John H. & Co.	Castle Street	8	126
Wilson	Joseph	Bridge Street	17	124
Wilson	Joseph	North Street	25	164

Surname	First Name	Street	House Number	Page Number
Wilson	Joseph	York Street	26	176
Wilson	Martha	Ebrington Street	13	170
Wilson	Michael	Hamilton Street	42	140
Wilson	Miss	Edenmore Street	30	132
Wilson	M. J.	Clarendon Street		127
Wilson	Mrs	Wapping Lane	43	159
Wilson	Mrs	Creggan Road	24	163
Wilson	Mrs	North Street	7	164
Wilson	Mrs Isabel	Bishop Street	34	123
Wilson	R. A.	Clooney Park West	1, Hinton	172
Wilson	Robert	Albert Street	2	118
Wilson	Robert	Barry Street	3	120
Wilson	Robert	Society Street	13	155
Wilson	Robert	Glendermott Road	104	171
Wilson	Robert	Moore Street	18	173
Wilson	S. & Co.	John Street	48	142
Wilson	Samuel	Cooke Street	6	128
Wilson	Samuel	Strand Road	132	157
Wilson	Samuel	Clooney Terrace	6	167
Wilson	Samuel	Violet Street Lower	57	176
Wilson	Thomas	Henry Street	7	141
Wilson	W. W.	Bishop Street	13	122
Wilson	William	Beechwood Avenue	11	121
Wilson	William	Fountain Street	79	134
Wilson	William	Fountain Place	13	135
Wilson	William	Gordon Place	11	138
Wilson	William	Grove Place	14	139
Wilson	William	Henry Street	5	141
Wilson	William	Marlborough Avenue	4	147
Wilson	William	Wellington Street	48	160
Wilson	William	Westland Avenue	21	160
Wilson	William	Clooney Terrace	48	167
Wilson	William	Glendermott Road	17	171
Wilson	William J.	Strand Road	48	156
Wilson & Gillespie		Shipquay Street	8	154
Wilton	Captain J. M.	Marlborough Avenue	21	147
Wilton	Mrs	Fountain Street	47	134
Wilton	R. M.	Eden Terrace	9	131
Wilton	Thomas	Lower Road	27	146
Winters	Miss	Lecky Road	115	143
Wiseman	Thomas	Westland Terrace	1	161
Wolfe	William A.	Abercorn Road	5	117
Wolseley	F.	Quay Queen's	coal merchant	152
Wolseley	Frederick	Aberfoyle Terrace	5	156
Woodburn	Matthew	Beechwood Avenue	76	121
Woodburn	Professor G.	College Avenue	2	150
Woods	Constable W.	Creggan Road	12	163
Woods	Constable W. J.	Nicholson Square	22	149
Woods	Frederick	Eden Terrace	14	131

Surname	First Name	Street	House Number	Page Number
Woods	John	Butcher Street	9A	125
Woods	John	Foyle Road	77	136
Woods	Margaret	Foyle Road	78	136
Woods	Matthew	Governor Road	25	138
Woods	Mrs	Bishop Street	60	123
Woods	Robert	Windmill Terrace	1	162
Woolsey	Garnett	De Moleyn Park	2	130
Woolworth	F. W.	Market Street	3	147
Woolworth	F. W. & Co.	Ferryquay Street	30, 32	134
Wordie & Co.		Alma Place		119
Wordie & Co.		Foyle Street	30	136
Wray	Alexander	Pine Street	19	174
Wray	David	Academy Terrace	9	118
Wray	David	Bishop Street	50	123
Wray	David	Marlborough Street	7	146
Wray	Henry	Albert Street	24	118
Wray	Henry	Fountain Hill	46	171
Wray	James	Foyle Road	61	136
Wray	James	Windmill Terrace	28	162
Wray	John	Alma Terrace	43	136
Wray	Miss	Castle Street	2	126
Wray	Mrs	Kennedy Place	11	142
Wray	Mrs	Dunfield Terrace	25	169
Wray	R. J.	Albert Place	3	119
Wray	Samuel	Wapping Lane	39	159
Wray	Thomas	Bond's Street	11	166
Wray	William	Nailor's Row	37	148
Wray	William	Wapping Lane	37	159
Wray	William H.	Bond's Street	25	166
Wren	William	Clarendon Street	1A	127
Wright	Albert	Victoria Street	7	159
Wright	Alex	Cuthbert Street	13	168
Wright	David	Clarendon Street	57	127
Wright	Frederick	Gordon Terrace	2	138
Wright	Jane	Mountjoy Terrace	11	118
Wright	John	London Street	13	145
Wright	John	Victoria Street	15	159
Wright	John	Barnewall Place	9	165
Wright	Joseph	Orchard Row	30	150
Wright	Miss	College Terrace	8	128
Wright	Richard	Fountain Hill	88	171
Wright	Robert	Creggan		131
Wright	Robert	Fountain Street	114	135
Wright	Samuel	Dark Lane	4	130
Wright	Thomas	Bishop Street	101½	123
Wright	Thomas	Ferguson Street	20	134
Wright	Thomas	New Market Street		149
Wright	Thomas B.	Fairman Place	9	133
Wylie	John	Adair Street	1	118

Surname	First Name	Street	House Number	Page Number
Wylie	John	Linenhall Street Upper	7	144
Wylie	Mrs	Mary Street	4	147
Wylie	Mrs	St. Columb's Court	4	157
Wylie	Mrs	West-End Park	4	161
Wylie	Richard	Philips Street	22	151
Wylie	T. C.	Castle Street	7	126
Wylie	Thomas	Aberfoyle Terrace	29	156
Wylie	Thomas	Strand Road	42	156
Yanarelli	A. & Co.	Clarendon Street		127
Yanarelli	A. & Co.	Strand Road	67-79	155
Young	Alexander	Barrack Street	6	120
Young	Alexander	Fountain Place	34	135
Young	Alfred A.	Spencer Road	121	174
Young	Archibald	Fountain Place	30	135
Young	Constable R. J. S.	Benvarden Avenue	38	166
Young	David	Hempton's Close		134
Young	Elizabeth	Mitchelburne Terrace	90	136
Young	Elizabeth	Donegal Street	24	163
Young	George	Bellevue Avenue	20	121
Young	Gilbert	Caw	Broomhill	167
Young	H. E.	Strand Road	24	156
Young	H. F.	Aberfoyle Terrace	17	156
Young	H. F.	Waterloo Place	10	160
Young	Henry	Bishop Street	198	123
Young	J. Ff.	St. Columb's Court		157
Young	James	Albert Place	12	119
Young	John	Marlborough Street	12	147
Young	John	Mountjoy Street	17	148
Young	John ff.	Bishop Street		123
Young	Joseph	Dungiven Road	85	170
Young	Mrs	Osborne Street	6	164
Young	Mrs M.	King Street	10	172
Young	Robert	Ivy Terrace	3	142
Young	Robert	Mary Street	24	147
Young	Samuel	Hayesbank Terrace	43	167
Young	Thomas	Fountain Street	103	134
Young	Thomas	Florence Street	18	170
Young	William	Moat Street	5	148
Young	William	Hayesbank Terrace	45	167
Young	William	King Street	1	172
Young	William	Spencer Road	22	175
Young & Moore		Water Street	4	160
Young & Rochester		Ebrington Gardens		166
Zammitt	George	Corbett Street (Pilot's Row)	10	128
Zammitt	Mrs	Artillery Street	3	120

www.ingramcontent.com/pod-product-compliance
Lightning Source LLC
Chambersburg PA
CBHW080550230426
43663CB00015B/2784